THE NATIONS
IN DEUTERO - ISAIAH
A Study on Composition and Structure

Andrew Wilson

Ancient Near Eastern Texts and Studies
Volume 1

The Edwin Mellen Press
Lewiston/Queenston

Library of Congress Cataloging-in-Publication Data

Wilson, Andrew
    The nations in Deutero-Isaiah.

    (Volume 1 in the series Ancient Near Eastern texts
& studies)
    Includes bibliographical references and index.
    1. Bible. O.T. Isaiah XL-LV--Criticism, interpretion,
etc. 2. Gentiles in the Old Testament. I. Title.
II. Series: Ancient Near Eastern texts and studies ;
v. 1.
BS1520.W55 1986   224'.106   86-21790
ISBN 0-88946-086-8

This is volume 1 in the continuing series
Ancient Near Eastern Texts and Studies
Volume 1 ISBN 0-88946-086-8
ANETS Series ISBN 0-88946-085-X

The Edwin Mellen Press   The Edwin Mellen Press
Box 450   Box 67
Lewiston, New York   Queenston, Ontario
USA 14092   CANADA L0S 1L0

Printed in the United States of America

To Reverend Sun Myung Moon

"Arrested and convicted, he was taken away,
And of his generation, who took notice?. . .
Although he had done no violence,
And there was no deceit in his mouth."

TABLE OF CONTENTS

LIST OF TABLES

*

Standard abbreviations for journals and reference works are set forth in
JBL 95 (1976) 331-46.

INTRODUCTION

1. Recent Discussion of Universalism and Nationalism

In recent years there has been some dispute over Deutero-Isaiah's attitude towards the nations. Earlier attempts to find a theology of mission in Deutero-Isaiah have been met by others who have pressed the case for the prophet as an extreme nationalist. The text appears to support both positions. In some passages the nations who fight against Israel will be defeated,[1] are expendable as a ransom for Israel's sake,[2] come before Israel in chains, lick the dust of Israel's feet, and even eat their own flesh,[3] while Yahweh addresses Israel in intimate terms. On the other hand Yahweh calls upon the nations to turn and be saved,[4] appoints the servant as "a light to the nations,"[5] and declares that his salvation will reach to all peoples who wait to receive his instruction and deliverance.[6] The nations will be amazed at the salvation which Yahweh has wrought for Israel,[7] and recogni-

---

[1] Isa 41:11-13; 49:25; 51:22-23; 54:15-17.

[2] Isa 43:3-4.

[3] Isa 45:14, 49:23, 49:26a; cf. 42:17; 45:16; 47:1-15; 51:22.

[4] Isa 45:22-23.

[5] Isa 42:6; 49:6.

[6] Isa 42:4,23; 49:6; 51:4-6.

[7] Isa 40:5; 41:5; 42:10-12; 45:6; 49:26b; 52:10.

zing Yahweh as God, they will run of their own accord
to serve Israel, God's witness people.[8]

Three basic stances have emerged regarding this
issue in recent scholarship, none of which has gained a
position of dominance. The traditional approach has
appreciated the profound universalism in Deutero-Isaiah
as the climax of missionary consciousness in the Hebrew
Bible. Thus H. H. Rowley has described Israel the servant in Deutero-Isaiah as a missionary leading the
world to "right religion."[9] For Blank, Deutero-Isaiah
ascribes to Israel the role of prophet to the nations,
"the prophetic role of speaking for God and of God."
Moreover, Israel's God offered the nations salvation:

> The Second Isaiah was without apology; the true
> missionary spirit was his: he was enthusiastic-
> ally evangelistic. He was convinced that
> Israel's God had something of value to offer--an
> abundant reward for such as acknowledge him.
> And this reward he called "salvation." With
> self-confident words the God of Second Isaiah
> invites the nations: "Turn to me and be saved,
> all you ends of the earth!"[10]

---

[8]Isa 55:4-5.

[9]H. H. Rowley, The Servant of the Lord (London: SCM,
1952) 88; Israel's Mission to the World (London: SCM,
1939) 15. Cf. H. W. Robinson, "The Hebrew Conception of
Corporate Personality," in Werden und Wesen des Alten
Testaments, ed. J. Hempel (Berlin, 1936) 49-62.

[10]Sheldon Blank, Prophetic Faith in Isaiah, (New
York: Harper & Bros., 1958) 148-158. Other exponents
of this view include P. Volz, Jesaja II, übersetzt und
erklärt, KAT IX/2 (Leipzig, 1932) 168-9; A. Lods, The
Prophets and the Rise of Judaism, tr. S. H. Hooke (London, 1937) 243f.; T. C. Vriezen, Die Erwählung Israels
nach dem Alten Testament (Zürich, 1953) 65ff.; P.
Auvray and J. Steinmann, Isaïe, BJ (Paris, 1957) 15;

Exegetes who have taken this view often explain away or minimize the significance of the nationalistic passages. For Torrey some are interpolations (i.e. **baz-ziqqîm** in 45:14) while others show the influence of older litera-ry traditions (i.e. 52:1).[11] For Begrich and Gelston they represent an inherited tradition which the prophet was largely unable to transcend or repudiate.[12] Simi-larly, for Westermann the most egregious language is a residue of older forms which the prophet utilized to express his message and does not "represent what inter-ested him personally."[13]

Davidson takes another tack: he sees the priority of Israel's glorification as the first step by which the nations would recognize Yahweh's blessing and then want the same for themselves. Hence "particularism and uni-versalism are not opposites, they are the tension points in the paradoxical Old Testament doctrine of mission."[14] Torrey, followed by Gottwald, also keeps these poles in tension by suggesting that the prospect of judgment of the nations is the prelude to the salva-tion of the righteous among them.[15]

Ulrich E. Simon, A Theology of Salvation: A Commentary on Isaiah 40-55 (London: SPCK, 1953) 137-39; G. Ernest Wright, The Book of Isaiah, Layman's Biblical Commenta-ry 11 (Richmond: John Knox, 1964) 88-89.

[11]C. C. Torrey, The Second Isaiah, a New Interpreta-tion (New York: Scribner's, 1928) 119-131.

[12]J. Begrich, Studien zu Deuterojesaja, (München: Kaiser, 1963) 85f. A. Gelston, "The Missionary Message of Second Isaiah," SJT 18 (1965) 316.

[13]Claus Westermann, Isaiah 40-66, OTL (London: SCM, 1966) 22.

[14]R. Davidson, "Universalism in Second Isaiah," SJT 16 (1963) 166-185.

[15]Torrey, 121-26. Norman Gottwald, All the Kingdoms of the Earth (New York: Harper & Row, 1964) 330ff.

A second interpretation understands Deutero-Isaiah
to be an intensely nationalistic prophet who sought to
preserve the faith and integrity of Israelites scattered amongst the nations and to encourage them with
the hope of Israel's restoration at the nations' ex-
pense. Norman Snaith has attacked those who attribute
a missionary theology to Deutero-Isaiah; in his view
the prophet was

> ...essentially nationalistic in attitude. He is
> actually responsible for the narrow and ex-
> clusive attitude of post-exilic days.... The
> whole prophecy is concerned with the restoration
> and exaltation of Jacob-Israel, the Servant of
> the Lord, the Righteous Remnant, and any place
> which the heathen have in the new order is
> entirely and debasingly subservient.[16]

The gentile nations may witness and marvel over
Israel's salvation, but they are not included in it.
     In a more qualified expression of this view, Martin-
Achard, echoing the position of Kaufmann, denies that
Second Isaiah actively sought the nations' conversion;

---

[16]N. H. Snaith, "The Servant of the Lord in Deutero-
Isaiah," in Studies in Old Testament Prophecy presented
to Professor Theodore H. Robinson (Edinburgh, 1950)
191. See also his "Isaiah 40-66: A Study of the Teach-
ing of Second Isaiah and its Consequences," in Studies
in the Second Part of the Book of Isaiah, VTSupp 14
(Leiden: Brill, 1967) 154-65. Cf. P. A. H. de Boer,
Second Isaiah's Message, OTS 11 (Leiden: Brill, 1956)
80-101; H. M. Orlinsky, "The So-called 'Servant of the
Lord' and 'Suffering Servant' in Second Isaiah," in
Studies in the Second Part of the Book of Isaiah,
VTSupp 14, 36-51; Fredrick Holmgren, With Wings as
Eagles: Isaiah 40/55, an Interpretation (Chappaqua, NY:
Biblical Scholars Press, 1973) 26-70; R. N. Whybray,
Isaiah 40-66, New Century Bible (London: Oliphants,
1975) 31-32, 111-12; idem. The Second Isaiah, Old Tes-
tament Guides (Sheffield, JSOT, 1983) 62-65.

nevertheless he believed the glorification of Israel
would be an object for the nations to contemplate and
wonder at:

> The Chosen People does not have to make propa-
> ganda in order to win mankind for its God.   It
> is enough that, by its very existence, it should
> testify to the greatness of Yahweh.   It is by
> granting life to His People that Yahweh makes it
> the light of the world.[17]

Such a theology would be universalistic in the sense
that Yahweh's purpose was indeed to be recognized and
honored among the nations, but it would not be the
active missionary theology proposed by Blank.   In the
encounter between Yahweh and the nations Israel would
have a passive role.

These exegetes reinterpret the so-called "missionary"
passages in line with what they see as the basically
nationalist message of the prophet.   For example, while
le-'ôr gôyīm (42:6; 49:6), is commonly translated "a
light to the nations," Snaith renders it "a light of
the gentiles," meaning a beacon for Israelites scattered throughout the nations to guide their way home,[18]
and de Boer, Orlinsky and Martin-Achard propose to
render it "a light 'respected by' or 'dazzling' the
nations."[19]   The parallel phrase berît ᶜām is similarly

---

[17]R. Martin-Achard, A Light to the Nations (Edinburgh: Oliver & Boyd, 1959) 31; cf. Yehezkel Kaufmann,
The Babylonian Captivity and Deutero-Isaiah, History of
the Religion of Israel IV,2, trans. C. W. Efroymson
(New York: Union of American Hebrew Congregations,
1970) 120, 136-39, 148-49.

[18]Snaith, "Teaching... Consequences," 155-6; cf.
Holmgren, 57-8.

[19]de Boer, 93; Martin-Achard, 28ff.; Orlinsky, 97-
117.

disputed. By its context parallel with **gôyīm** and with
cām in 42:5 meaning all humanity, it has been plausibly
taken to refer to a plurality of peoples. But given
that **cām** in the singular refers to Israel in 23 out of
25 instances (42:5 being a notable exception), these
interpreters read it as denoting the covenanting or
consolidation of the scattered people of God, a national covenant of Israel.[20] They similarly understand the
tôrâ and **mišpaṭ** which go out to the nations (42:4;
51:4) not as God's instruction in right religion, but
rather as God's judgment vindicating Israel in the
midst of the nations.[21] Hollenberg has essayed a more
radical reinterpretation of these passages by suggesting that the "nations" with whom the prophet disputes
over idolatry and to whom the prophet appeals at the
conclusion of the disputation in 45:22--"turn to me and
be saved, all the ends of the earth!"--are those Jews
living among the nations who have assimilated and for-
saken Yahwism in favor of the customs and religions of
the nations in which they lived.[22]

A third alternative has been to reconstruct a development in the oracles of Isa 40-55 from a nationalistic
to a more universalistic message. According to
Lindblom, Deutero-Isaiah changed his mind during the

---

[20]de Boer, 94; Snaith, 157-8; Orlinsky, 107-111,
Kaufmann, 152.

[21]de Boer, 92; Snaith, 164-5; Holmgren, 69. Concur-
ring is Westermann, 95f.; among those critical of this
position are John L. McKenzie, Second Isaiah, AB 20
(Garden City: Doubleday, 1968) 37f.; C. R. North, The
Second Isaiah: Introduction, Translation and Commentary
to Chapters XL-LV (Oxford: Clarendon, 1964) 108f.

[22] D. E. Hollenberg, "Nationalism and 'The Nations'
in Isaiah XL-LV," VT 19 (1969), 21-36. For our cri-
tique of his position, see below, pp. 101-103.

course of his ministry when, in the autobiographical second servant song, God revealed to him that his mission was to extend beyond Israel to the gentiles. This mission was a "new thing," a revelation born out of the anguish of the prophetic community when Cyrus failed to live up to expectations. At this late stage in the prophet's career, he also confronted a split in the community between those faithful exiles and those who had fallen away.[23] Stuhlmueller similarly identifies three stages in the prophet's career recorded in three strata of the text: chapters 41-48 were written before the fall of Babylon and stress the new exodus, the role of Cyrus and Yahweh's "new thing" in redeeming Israel; chapters 49-55 were written after the fall of Babylon and proclaim a new role for Zion while expressing an increasingly polemical tone towards the recalcitrant Israelites; and the latest stratum contains the servant songs. These songs glimpse for the first time salvation for the nations, even though such universalism may have been implicit and unconscious in the earlier stages of the prophet's thought.[24]

The apparent universalism of the servant songs in contrast to the narrower focus upon Israel in the remainder of chs. 40-55 has been one argument for the songs' separate authorship.[25] Thus Mowinckel identi-

---

[23]J. Lindblom, The Servant Songs in Deutero-Isaiah: A New Attempt to Solve an Old Problem Lunds Universitets Arsskrift, N.F. Avd. 1 Bd. 47 Nr. 5 (Lund, 1951) 26, 66ff.

[24]Carroll Stuhlmueller, "Deutero-Isaiah: Major Transitions in the Prophet's Theology and in Contemporary Scholarship," CBQ 42 (1980) 1-29.

[25]C. R. North, The Suffering Servant in Deutero-Isaiah: An Historical and Critical Study (London: Oxford, 1948) 184.

fied the author of the servant songs as a later disciple of Deutero-Isaiah who lived in Palestine and whose
theology was considerably more universalist than his
mentor in Babylon.[26] In this view Deutero-Isaiah was a
nationalist primarily concerned with the restoration of
Israel, but the outlook of the servant in the songs was
considerably broader: "his preaching will reach out to
all the peoples of the earth, who are longing for the
true religion (xlii.4) and be the means of their salvation.... "[27]

2. Universalism and Nationalism as Complementary Themes

A cause for confusion regarding the place of the
nations in Deutero-Isaiah is that the very categories
"universalism" and "nationalism" are modern abstrac-
tions external to the biblical material. The prophet's
message cannot neatly be fitted into the mold of modern
universalism in the sense that Protestant Christianity
is viewed as a universal religion not attached to any
particular state nor confined to the shape of any
nationalistic creed. Indeed, even in the modern
context of theological reflection on the Jewish or
Christian doctrines of election, this may be a false
dichotomy. The election of a particular people--be it
Israel or the Church--is understood in its best sense
as election to service. The election of a particular
people is inseparable from the universal mission to
which it is called.

---

[26]S. Mowinckel, He That Cometh (New York: Abingdon,
1954) 250-55.

[27]Mowinckel, 207.

The appropriate starting point for any biblical exegesis is with the writer's own purposes and cultural environment. Deutero-Isaiah prophesied to meet the situation in which he lived and drew from the inherited traditions of Israel. To begin with, we may identify the primary purpose underlying Deutero-Isaiah's ministry as to encourage the Israelite exiles to have faith in God's lordship. To that purpose, he brought older traditions universalistic in scope: (1) the prophetic tradition of Yahweh the universal sovereign who judges the nations and uses a foreign nation as his instrument to chastize Israel, (2) the royal cult's depiction of Yahweh as the divine warrior who creates order in the cosmos, brings fertility to the entire earth and defends his dwelling in Zion against all the nations who would fight against it, and (3) the related imperial Solomonic ideology which justified the imperial sway of the king as the anointed representative of Yahweh the universal ruler.[28] Yet Deutero-Isaiah did not utilize these traditions in order to make an argument for universalism or mission as such; they remained subservient to the prophet's purpose to encourage faith among his compatriots.

Nevertheless, the very context of Deutero-Isaiah's pronouncements spoken or written to an audience living in exile among gentiles would accentuate the universal-

---

[28]With this starting point, we cannot share the assumption of Orlinsky and Snaith that the religion of pre-exilic Israel was nationalistic, envisioning God as universal only in the naturalistic sense of creator. Cf. H. M. Orlinsky, "Nationalism-Universalism and Internationalism in Ancient Israel," in *Translating and Understanding the Old Testament, Essays in Honor of H. G. May*, ed. H. T. Frank and W. L. Reed (Nashville: Abingdon, 1970) 213; also "The So-called 'Servant'," 99; Snaith, "Teaching... Consequences," 154.

istic aspects of these traditions. In circumstances
where Israel appeared to be but a pawn at the mercy of
nations far larger than itself, the claim for Yahweh's
universal sovereignty became an important basis of hope
for the despairing exiles. Israel could have hope for
its own redemption because God moved in the affairs of
all nations. Whatever universalism may be found here,
even notices of the nations turning to Yahweh, complements and supports the prophet's purpose to encourage
his own people.

In the following chapters, the place of the nations
in Deutero-Isaiah will be discussed from four perspectives: Chapter 2 will study the trial scenes in which
Yahweh advocates his sovereignty as a claim before
Israel and the nations. Chapter 3 will examine polemics against idolatry denying the validity and efficacy
of the nations' religions. Chapter 4 will treat the
prophet's eschatology and particularly the motif of the
nations in procession bearing tribute to Zion.
Chapter 5 will discuss the international jurisdiction
of the servant of Yahweh.

3. The Problem of Formal and Literary Structure

In approaching the texts of Deutero-Isaiah significant for determining his view of the place of the
nations, the exegete is unavoidably faced with the
preliminary and perennial problem of determining the
formal and literary structure of Isa 40-55 in order to
delimit the individual units. Form critics have analyzed Deutero-Isaiah into a large number of short peri-

copes defined by spoken formal genres.[29] In this view, the prophet's spoken utterances were then collected and edited into the received text. On the other hand, critics sensitive to large-scale rhetorical structure have demarcated larger units. Neither of these two approaches has been able to win universal acceptance.

The assumption that Deutero-Isaiah communicated primarily by short, spoken oracles in the tradition of preexilic prophets is far from certain. Melugin concludes the form-critical part of his research by observing that Deutero-Isaiah has imitated and modified traditional prophetic genres and wrested them from their original setting to create stylized units in the service of his message,[30] what Gressmann called "the dissolution of the prophetic types."[31] The evident distance between Deutero-Isaiah and preexilic formal genres befits his exilic _Sitz_ _im_ _Leben_. He was not a prophet giving oracles to kings or speaking at the temple, for in exile there was no king and no formal community center. The institutional matrix of prophecy was altered by exile. Thus Ezekiel spoke to the community elders from his house (Ezek 8:1) and Jeremiah circulated letters. Hence even some form critics have

---

[29]Recent studies include Claus Westermann, _Sprache_ _und_ _Struktur_ _der_ _Prophetie_ _Deuterojesajas,_ Calwer Theologische Monographien 11 (Stuttgart: Calwer, 1981); Antoon Schoors, _I_ _am_ _God_ _your_ _Savior:_ _A_ _Form-critical_ _Study_ _of_ _the_ _Main_ _Genres_ _in_ _Is._ _XL-LV,_ VTSupp 24 (Leiden: Brill, 1973); Roy F. Melugin, _The_ _Formation_ _of_ _Isaiah_ _40-55,_ BZAW 141 (Berlin: de Gruyter, 1976).

[30]Melugin, _Formation,_ 21-22,24,25,44,63,69,71,77.

[31]Hugo Gressmann, "Die literarische Analyse Deuterojesajas," _ZAW_ 34 (1914) 295, as quoted in Muilenberg, "The Book of Isaiah, Chapters 40-66," _IB_ 5 (New York and Nashville: Abingdon, 1956) 385.

recognized Deutero-Isaiah to be a writer[32] and understand form criticism to be a tool to uncover the
prophet's message which was built upon antecedent oral
genres.

The difficulty with a strict methodological assumption of an identity between the spoken formal genre and
the units of Deutero-Isaiah springs from the text
itself. Claus Westermann, though a form critic, is
perceptive enough to recognize composite oracles in the
later chapters of Deutero-Isaiah which span several
genre units:

> What is less intelligible is the division into
> two different kinds of discourse. With few
> exceptions, chs. 40-45 are composed of short
> oracles, each belonging to one single literary
> category, but after ch. 45 the major place is
> taken by poems of considerable length which
> combine several literary categories. I myself
> am quite sure that the oracles were originally
> spoken, but the longer poems like 49.14-26 or
> 51.9-52.3 may have been literary productions
> from the beginning.[33]

Westermann also finds composite units in the earlier
chapters on the basis of rhetorical structure,[34] and he

---

[32]So H. Gunkel, "Die Propheten a/s Schriftsteller und
Dichter," in H. Schmidt, Die grossen Propheten, (Göttingen, 1915) xxxix; L. Köhler, Deuterojesaja Stilkritisch untersucht, BZAW 37 (Giessen: Töpelmann, 1923)
80; and others.

[33]Westermann, Isaiah 40-66, 28.

[34]Isa 40:12-31 is also identified as a single complex composition by Shoors, 258-9. Westermann also
sees compound units built of multiple formal genres in
Isa 43:1-4,5-7; 44:6-8,21-22; 44:24-45:7.

notes that certain adjacent oracles are loosely attached to one another.[35]

While form criticism has the advantage of a consistent methodological basis, recognition of larger rhetorical units in Isa 40-55 raises the question of how the individual forms are combined into larger units. Those who apply the method of redaction criticism take as their starting point the assumption that the units as defined by form criticism existed as independent oracles prior to their collection by either the prophet or a disciple. Mowinckel's view that the originally independent units were arranged by a loose association of catchwords[36] has been rejected by many in favor of some conscious principle of organization based upon content[37], an imitation of a legal proceedings or of a liturgy,[38] or a combination of features including

---

[35]Isa 42:18-25 and 43:1-7; Isa 43:22-28 and 44:1-5; See Westermann, 114, 134.

[36]S. Mowinckel, "Die Komposition des deuterojesajan-ischen Buches," ZAW 49 (1931) 87-112, 242-60. He is followed by Schoors, 297 n. 2.

[37]K. Elliger, Deuterojesaja in seinem Verhältnis zu Tritojesaja, BWANT 63 (Stuttgart: Kohlhammer, 1933) 232; McKenzie, 35; John Goldingay, "The Arrangement of Isaiah XLI-XLV," VT 29 (1979) 298f.

[38]Eva Hessler ("Gott der Schöpfer: Ein Beitrag zur Komposition und Theologie Deuterojesajas, diss. Greifs-wald, 1961) regards the book of consolation as the text of a continuous legal proceeding; see the summary in Melugin, 78-81. H. Ringgren ("Zur Komposition von Jesaja 49-55," in Beiträge zur alttestamentlichen Theo-logie, Festscrift für Walther Zimmerli zum 70. Geburts-tag, ed. H. Donner, R. Hanhart, R. Smend [Göttingen: Vandenhoeck & Ruprect, 1977] 371-76) sees the book's unity in a liturgy for the autumn festival.

theme, structure and rhetoric.[39] Melugin's study in particular carefully affirms both the integrity of formal units and their arrangement into larger redactional units by a secondary editing.[40]

No proposal for redactional arrangement to date has met with widespread approval,[41] and this approach may well be a false lead. If the rhetorical and structural features of the larger units are so dense as to influence the integrity and structure of their component formal units, then the hypothesis underlying the approach of redaction criticism, that the formal units preexisted their arrangement as independent utterances of the prophet, loses its cogency. In the course of our research into Deutero-Isaiah we have been impressed by this very density of structural and rhetorical features, and we must dissent from the assumption that the subsidiary formal units were ever independent except as prototypes in the mind of the prophet.[42] Rather, it

---

[39]Particularly noteworthy is the suggestion of Westermann (Sprache und Struktur, 81-84) followed by Tryggve N. D. Mettinger (A Farewell to the Servant Songs: A Critical Examination of an Exegetical Axiom, Regiae Societatis Humaniorum Litterarum Ludensis, Scripta Minora [Lund: C.W.K. Gleerup, 1983]) that the collection is structured by the strategic placement of hymns of praise. See our discussion on pp. 60-61, below. They also consider Isa 40:1-11 to be a prologue defining the message of the entire book.

[40]Melugin, 87-89. For a summary of other recent views, see Andreas Richter, "Hauptlinien der Deutero-jesaja-Forschung von 1964-1979," in Westermann, Sprache und Struktur, 116-22.

[41]Whybray, The Second Isaiah, 40-41; North, The Second Isaiah, 8-9,12.

[42]On the structuralist concern for formal patterns as partly "occupations of mind," see Rolf Knierim, "Old Testament Form Criticism Reconsidered," Int 27 (1973) 435-68.

appears that the formal units have been subsumed into
the stanzas of larger units at the primary level of
composition.

This brings us to rhetorical criticism,[43] the second
school of criticism applied to this prophet. Chiasm
and verbal repetition,[44] strophes or stanzas of many
lines with parallel structure and length,[45] and recurrent rhetorical themes or polarities[46] are some of the
devices by which Deutero-Isaiah constructs long compositions of multiple stanzas. These units may also be
defined by conformity to larger traditional and formal

[43]See James Muilenberg, "Form Criticism and Beyond,"
JBL 88 (1969) 1-18; "The Book of Isaiah, Chapters 40-
66," in IB 5 (New York and Nashville: Abingdon, 1956);
Richard Clifford, Fair Spoken and Persuading: An Inter-
pretation of Second Isaiah (New York: Paulist, 1984);
Torrey, The Second Isaiah; P.-E Bonnard, Le Second
Isaïe, son disciple et leurs editeurs (Paris: Gablada,
1972); H. C. Spykerboer, The Structure and Composition
of Deutero-Isaiah: With Special Reference to the Polemics Against Idolatry (Groningen, 1976); Menachem
Haran, "The Literary Structure and Chronological Framework of the Prophecies in Is. XL-XLVIII," VTSupp 9
(Leiden: E.J. Brill, 1963) 127-132; idem., Between
Ri'shonôt and Hadashôt: A Literary study into the group
of prophecies Isaiah XL-XLVIII (Jerusalem: Magnes,
1963); Kaufmann, 75-94. All these scholars are sensitive to larger rhetorical units, although not all would
necessarily call themselves rhetorical critics.

[44]Muilenberg, IB 5, 388-91; Kaufmann, 78-81.

[45]Muilenberg, 391-93; Clifford, 38-40. Prosodic
analysis into parallel strophes or stanzas has been of
value for the study of early Israelite poetry. See
David Noel Freedman, "Strophe and Meter in Exodus 15,"
in Pottery, Poetry and Prophecy: Studies in Early
Hebrew Poetry (Winona Lake, IN: Eisenbrauns, 1980) 187-
227; Michael David Coogan, "A Structural and Literary
Analysis of the Song of Deborah," CBQ 40 (1978) 143-
165. On the other hand, Torrey (175-78) is skeptical
of any analysis into strophes.

[46]Clifford, 41-58; Haran, "Literary Structure," 137.

complexes derived from prophecy and the cult.[47]
Precise delineation of these structural features is
necessary for delimiting the compositional unit. As a
writer, the prophet would have shared with others of
his day a lively interest in the written word and the
structural possibilities of poetry.[48] The contemporary
poems in Lamentations were written as acrostics, and
the vision cycle of Zech 1-6 and the long vision in
Ezek 40-48 were each structured in a large scale
chiasmus. Others regard the prophet to be an orator
whose basic unit was the sermon, again constructed out
of multiple genre units.[49] We can well agree with
Kaufmann, who argued that Deutero-Isaiah consciously
refashioned and combined older forms in an archaizing
style of poetry which imitated the detached oracles of
the preexilic prophets.[50]

However, attempts using rhetorical criticism to
delimit sermonic or literary units have been incon-
clusive and plagued by subjectivity; they have failed
to arrive at any consensus regarding the book's literary structure. Table 1 compares the short formal units
delimited by Westermann with various proposals by rhetorical critics and others who delimit longer units.

Our approach to the structure of Deutero-Isaiah is
an eclectic blend of rhetorical criticism and form
criticism which we term compositional analysis. This

---

[47]Bonnard, 33-36, sees the theology of covenant as
the key for delimiting 18 extended poems.

[48]Muilenberg, 386; Torrey, 92.

[49]Simon, 20-24; Clifford, 4-5, 38-41; Kaufmann,
94-95.

[50]Kaufmann, 79, 81-84. He regards the transitions
and breaks in style between the formal units as artificial and contrived.

TABLE 1: Rhetorical Units in Isa 40-55

Westermann	Muilenberg	Clifford	Torrey	Bonnard	Kaufmann	Melugin*
40:1-11	40:1-11	40:1-11	Chs. 34,35 40	40:1-11	Chs. 34,35 40	40:1-11
40:12-31 [19-20]	40:12-31	40:12-31	41	40:12-31	41:1-16	40:12-31
41:1-5 [6-7] 8-13 14-16 17-20 21-29	41:1-42:4	41:1-42:9		41:1-20	41:17-20 41:21-29 42:1-9	41:1-20
42:1-4 5-9 10-13 14-17 18-25			42:1-43:7	41:21-42:17		41:21-42:13
43:1-7 8-15 16-21 22-28	42:5-17 42:18-43:7 43:8-13 43:14-44:5	42:10-43:8 43:9-44:5	43:8-44:5	42:18-43:8 43:9-21 43:22-44:5	42:10-43:14 43:16-44:5	42:14-43:7 43:8-21 43:22-44:5
44:1-5 6-8 [9-20] 21-22 23	44:6-8, [9-20] 21-23	44:6-23	44:6-23	44:6-23	44:6-28	44:6-20 44:21-23
44:24-45:7 8 9-13	44:24-45:13	44:24-45:13	44:24-45:25	44:24-45:25	45:1-13	44:24-45:13

TABLE 1 (cont'd)

14,15,16-17 18-19 20-25	45:14-25			45:14-25	45:14-25
46:1-4 5-8 9-13	46	46	46	46	46
47	47	47	47	47	47
48:1-11 12-17 18-19 20-21	48	48	48	48:1-11 48:12-21	48
49:1-6 7-12 13 14-26	49	49	49	49:1-13 49:14-26	49:1-13 49:14-26
50:1-3 4-9 50:10-51:8 (emended)	50:1-51:8	50	50	50:1-2 4-9 10-11	50
51:9-52:3	51:9-52:12	51:1-16 51:17-52:12	51:1-52:12	51:1-52:12	51:1-8 51:9-52:12
52:4-6 7-10 11-12 52:13-53:12	52:13-53:12	52:13-53:12	52:13-53:12	52:13-53:12	52:13-53:12
54:1-10 11-17	54	54	54	54	54:1-55:13
55:1-5 6-11 12-13	55	55:1-56:8	55	55	

*Melugin's units are redactional.
H. C. Spykerboer and U. Simon regard Isa 40-55 as a single rhetorical unit.

term is not meant to announce a new method. It denotes
an approach to the basic units of Deutero-Isaiah as
literary or sermonic compositions rather than short
oracular utterances, yet it differs from rhetorical
criticism in being a full interpretive method that is
not limited to an ahistorical consideration of the
surface literary structure. It is fair to say that
most exegetes since Muilenberg who recognize larger
units in Deutero-Isaiah also employ an eclectic methodology that goes beyond rhetorical criticism as narrowly
defined.[51] Form criticism, rhetorical criticism and
examination of history of traditions are used together
to define and delineate the literary units of this
prophet, who is, after all, a transitional figure
coming at the end of the classical prophetic tradition
and at the beginning of the more scholastic writings of
Trito-Isaiah, Deutero-Zechariah and later apocalyptic
writers. The unique nature of Deutero-Isaiah necessi-
tates a comprehensive methodology that differs from
what is adequate for the preexilic prophets.

One important result of this method is the finding
that the larger units as delineated in part by rhetorical features exhibit their own formal integrity.
Traditions which lie behind certain of Deutero-Isaiah's
compositional units--such as the cultic songs of
Yahweh's victory over the nations who rage against Zion
or the prophetic covenant lawsuit--are themselves long
and complex forms with definite Sitze im Leben. These
lengthy forms at home in preexilic prophecy or the
cult, rather than the concise oral units posited by
most form critics, coincide quite well with the compositional units of Deutero-Isaiah as discerned by their

---

[51]E.g. Clifford, 35-37.

rhetorical features. Hence we find no inherent inconsistency between rhetorical criticism and form criticism understood in its broadest sense. The apparent
inconsistency has been due rather to a faulty appli-
cation of form-critical method in studies of this
prophet.

That error appears to have stemmed from an early and
uncritical derivation of the forms characteristic of
Deutero-Isaiah from a study of that prophet in near
isolation from other biblical or ancient Near Eastern
texts. As a result, there have been no methodological
controls for distinguishing between the prophet's use
of living forms and the peculiarities of his individual
literary style. This has resulted in a serious weakness in traditional form-critical studies: such hypothetical forms as the salvation oracle and the trial
speech which are deemed characteristic of Deutero-
Isaiah suffer from a lack of clear antecedent traditions.

Compositional analysis gives an alternative explanation for the origin of these so-called formal units in
Deutero-Isaiah. They are constituitive stanzas of
longer literary, prophetic or cultic forms with a clear
tradition history.[52] Therefore, although we may occa-
sionaly refer to stanzas of the prophet's compositional
units by conventional form-critical designations as
"trial speeches" or "salvation oracles," we do not mean
to endorse the view that these stanzas necessarily have
the status of distinct forms in Deutero-Isaiah or an
independent background in preexilic prophecy or the
cult. These terms, like the appellation "servant
song," serve only as conventional designations for
passages with certain common characteristics whose

---

[52]Cf. below, pp. 107-113, 319-323.

formal identity and integrity are in question.

Exegesis of passages in Deutero-Isaiah which discuss the place of the nations is naturally influenced
by the delimiting of large compositional units. A
traditional form-critical approach would isolate the
relevant passages--trial speeches, polemics against
idolatry, the few passages depicting the nations bearing gifts to Zion and the servant songs--and then
simply treat them together. However, because we have
found it necessary to discuss the prophet's writings as
compositions containing multiple subunits, there is no
simple correspondence between compositional units and
the themes of our study. Instead, Deutero-Isaiah's
writings may be likened to a string quartet, inter-
weaving these several themes throughout his compositions. For example, from the perspective of conventional form criticism Isa 41:1-20 contains a trial
speech, a polemic against idolatry, several salvation
oracles and a proclamation of salvation; and Isa 43:8-
44:5 joins a trial speech, a proclamation of salvation,
a second trial speech and a salvation oracle. Yet
within the two larger compositions, these "forms"
occupy the position of stanzas. Taking these larger
compositions as the primary units, adequate exegesis of
the specific passages relevant for our discussion of
the nations will require a discussion of their function
as stanzas within the larger compositional units. In
order to treat these passages in context, a considerably larger portion of the corpus of Deutero-Isaiah will
necessarily have to be studied than is customary in
most discussions of this issue. We will find that the
labor required for a thorough exegesis from this perspective may bear fruit, shedding light upon a number
of difficult questions of interpretation.

CHAPTER 1
THE TRIAL OF THE NATIONS AND THEIR GODS

The first perspective to be considered in this study
of the role of the nations in Deutero-Isaiah is found
in the trial speech (Gerichtsrede) where the nations
and their gods are arraigned before Yahweh's judgment.
While we dissent from calling the trial speech an
independent Gattung, this term is a useful descriptive
designation for texts which share common characteristics; these are Isa 41:1-5, 41:21-29, 43:8-13, 44:6-8,
and 45:20-25. This study will treat these speeches in
the context of their respective compositional units:
Isa 41:1-4 and 41:21-29 open each half of the double
unit 41:1-20,21-42:17; 43:8-13 opens the unit 43:8-
44:5; 44:6-8 introduces 44:6-23; and 45:20-25 concludes
the unit 45:14-25.

As will be shown, the setting and themes of the
trial speeches persist throughout the longer units.
These units are shaped in part by the ritual pattern of
the Jerusalem cult where Yahweh's universal rule was
depicted by successive images: victory over the nations
raging against Mount Zion, Israel's deliverance, the
enthronement of the victorious divine king and his
earthly counterpart, and the procession to the temple
accompanied by the fructification of nature. The forensic language of the trial scenes may be a secondary
modification by the prophet of what had been a tradition of the preexilic cult. There are further variations: Isa 43:8-44:5 also contains a second type of
trial speech directed against Israel (43:18-25) and
partakes of a second preexilic tradition--the prophetic

lawsuit. Isa 45:14-25 inverts the pattern: a victory
procession to Zion opens the unit and is followed by
the trial speech as its substantiation. The trial
speech Isa 44:6-8 is properly an introduction to a long
polemic against idolatry; hence its discussion will be
deferred to the following chapter.

After exegesis of these compositional units, we
shall turn to the specific function of the trial speech
against the gods of the nations for Deutero-Isaiah's
exilic ministry. Through the vehicle of the trial,
Yahweh's lordship becomes a universal claim set forth
before the nations.

1. Isa 41:1-42:17: A Diptych Affirming Yahweh's Lordship and Victory over the Nations and their Gods

a. Text and Structure

Isa 41:1-20 and 41:21-42:17 are complementary and
parallel halves of an extended diptych. Form critics
who assume Deutero-Isaiah to be a speaker of short,
disconnected oracles have distinguished several independent units in each half: opening trial speeches in
which the gods of the nations are judged to be futile
illusions, oracles of salvation proclaiming God's support for Israel His servant, and concluding salvation
oracles depicting the march of the divine warrior leading his people through the desert with the attending
transformation of nature. Our analysis regards these
"formal units" as stanzas of a single composition on
the basis of both rhetorical and formal criteria. We
note preliminarily that Isa 42:1-4,5-9, the so-called
first servant song and its appendix,[1] are not treated

---

[1]E.g. Westermann, Isaiah 40-66, 20, 101.

as strands separate from the body of Deutero-Isaiah's prophecy. The consensus since Duhm that the servant songs form a separable stratum rests on weak foundations and has been effectively critiqued of late by Mettinger.[2] Hence we will not assume an a priori disjunction unless supported by the text.

41:1-4   meter

Come before me in silence,[a] O coastlands,	7
and let the nations [ ][b] approach.	7
Let them consult together,	6
let us come together[c] for judgment.	6
	1:1::1:1

Who has stirred up vindication from the east,	7
summoned him to his ranks?[d]	7
Who gives up nations before him,	7
and causes him to subdue[e] kings?	7
	1:1::1:1

His sword makes them like dust,	7
and like driven stubble, his bow.[f]	6
He pursues them, he presses on unscathed,	7
upon a path his feet had not traveled.[g]	7
	1:1::1:1

Who has acted and done [this]?[h]	6
summoning generations[i] from the beginning?	6
I, Yahweh, am the first;	6
with the last, I am He.	7
	1:1::1:1

41:5-7

The coastlands have seen and are afraid,	8
the ends of the earth tremble,[j]	7
they have drawn near and come.[k]	7
	1:1:1

Each helps[l] his neighbor,	7
to his brother he says, "be strong."	7
The smith encourages the engraver,	7
he who beats the anvil,[m] he who pounds out with the mallet,	7
Saying of the riveting, "it is good;"	7
he fastens it with nails,	7
<he sets it up>[n] so it cannot be moved.	7
	1:1::1:1::1:1

---

[2]Tryggve N. D. Mettinger, *A Farewell to the Servant Songs: A Critical Examination of an Exegetical Axiom*, Scripta Minora, Regiae Societatis Humaniorum Litterarum Ludensis (Lund: CWK Gleerup, 1983).

41:8-10

```
But you, Israel, are my servant,                            8
    Jacob whom I have chosen,                               8
    offspring of Abraham, my friend.                        7
You whom I have grasped from the ends of the earth,         9
    from its far corners I summoned you;                    9
I say to you, "You are my servant,                          9
    I chose you, and I have not cast you aside."            9
                              1:1:1::1:1::1:1

Do not fear, for I am with you;                            3/6
    do not dread,P for I am your God.                      3/6
I will strengthen you and I will help you,                 4/5
    Yea, support you with my victorious right hand.        10
                          (b:b):(b:b)::(b:b):1
```

41:11-13

```
Surely they will be ashamed and humiliated,                 9
    all those who snortq at you;                            6
They will be reduced to nothing and will perish,            8
    the peopler who quarrel with you;                       5
                                      1:b::1:b

Though you seek after them you will not find them,S         9
    the people who struggle against you;                    6
They will be reduced to nothing and void,                   7
    the people who war against you.                         6
For I am Yahweh your God,                                   9
    who grasps your right hand,                             6
Who says to you, "Do not fear,                              8
    I will help you."                                       6
                          1:b::1:b::1:b::1:b
```

Isa 41:14-16

```
Do not fear, worm Jacob,                                    8
    . . . . . . Israel.t
I myself will help you,u says Yahweh,                       9
    your redeemer, the Holy One of Israel.                  9
                                      1:x::1:1

Now I will make you into a threshing sledge,                8
    keen, new, full of double-edged blades;                 8
You will thresh the mountains and pulverize them,           7
    the hills you will make like chaff.                     7
You will winnow them, the wind will carry them off,         7
    the storm wind will scatter them.                       7
                              1:1::1:1::1:1

And you will rejoice in Yahweh,                             8
    in the Holy One of Israel you shall exult.              9
                                          1:1
```

41:17-20

```
The poor [    ]ᵛ seek water, but there is none;            9
    their tongues are parched with thirst.                 9
I, Yahweh, <myself>ʷ will answer them,                    10
    the God of Israel will not forsake them.              10
                                                    1:1::1:1
```

```
I will open streams on the bare heights,                   9
    springs in the midst of the valleys,                   9
I will turn the desert into ponds,                         8
    parched land into water fountains;                     8
                                                    1:1::1:1
```

```
I will place cedars in the desert,                         6
    acacias, myrtles and olive trees;                      8
I will set cypresses in the wilderness,                    8
    plane trees and pine trees together;                   8
                                                    1:1::1:1
```

```
In order that people may see and acknowledge,             9
    both recognizeˣ and understand,                        9
That the hand of Yahweh has done this,                     8
    the Holy One of Israel has created it.                 8
                                                    1:1::1:1
```

Isa 41:21-24

```
Bring near your advocates,ʸ                                6
    says Yahweh                                            4
Bring forward your contenders,                             8
    says the King of Jacob.                                5
Let them approach,ᶻ let them tell us                       9
    what is to happen.ᵃᵃ                                   5
                                        1:b::1:b::1:b
```

```
The former things, what did they mean?                     7
    Did they foretellᵇᵇ them, that we may understand?ᶜᶜ   8
Or declare to us the things to come,ᵈᵈ                     8
    that we may know their outcome;ᵉᵉ                      7
Predict the things to come hereafter,                     10
    that we may know that you are gods.                    10
Yea, do good or do evil,                                   8
    that we may dread and fearᶠᶠ together.                 8
                                    1:1::1:1::1:1::1:1
```

```
Indeed, you are nothing,                                   5
    your work is nothing,ᵍᵍ                                5
an abomination is he who choosesʰʰ you.                    7
                                                     b:b:1
```

Isa 41:25-29

```
I have stirred up one from the north and he has comeⁱⁱ 9
    from the rising of the sun I called on hisʲʲ name.    9
He tramplesᵏᵏ rulers like clay,                            8
    like a potter treads the mire.                         8
                                                    1:1::1:1
```

Who foretold it from the outset that we might know; 9
  from beforehand, that we might say "he is right"? 9
But there is none who declares it, 4
  none who proclaims, 4
  none who hears your words. 7
                     1:1::b:b:1

. . . . . to Zion . . . . [11]
  to Jerusalem I gave a herald. 11

I look--and <behold>,[mm] there is no one; 7
  among these there is no counselor; 7
  I ask, but who[nn] will answer? 7
Behold, all of them are nothing,[oo] 4
  their works are nothing, 4
  their images are wind and emptiness.[pp] 7
                 1:1:1::b:b:1

Isa 42:1-4

Behold my servant, whom I uphold, 6
  my chosen one, in whom I delight, 8
I have put my spirit upon him; 7
  he shall bring forth justice[qq] to the nations. 7
                 1:1::1:1

He will not cry out, he will not shout, 7
  he will not make his voice heard in the street; 7
Though a bruised reed, he will not be broken, 8
  though a smoldering wick, he will not be quenched,[rr] 7
  but certainly he will bring forth justice. 7
                 1:1::1:1:1

He will not tire, he will not be crushed,[ss] 8
  until he establishes justice on the earth, 7
  the coastlands wait[tt] for his law. 9
                 1:1:1

Isa 42:5-9

Thus says the God Yahweh, rubric
Who creates the heavens and spreads them out, 9
  who spread out the earth and its spawn, 9
Who gives breath[uu] to humanity upon it, 8
  and life-spirit to those who walk about it: 8
                 1:1::1:1

I [ ][vv] called you in righteousness, 8
  and I take you by the hand; 7
I form you and I appoint you, 9
  a covenant to humanity, a light to the nations; 8
To open blind eyes, 8
  to bring out prisoners from the dungeon, 8
  from prison those who dwell in darkness. 8
                 1:1::1:1::1:1:1

I^{ww} am Yahweh, that is my name,   8
   my glory I will give to no other,   9
   nor my praise to idols.   9
The former things now have occurred,   8
   and I fortell new things;   8
   before they sprout, I announce them to you.   9
              1:1:1::1:1:1

Isa 42:10-13

Sing to Yahweh a new song,   8
   his praise to the ends of the earth.   8
Let the sea and what fills it ro[ar],^{xx}   7
   the coastlands and their inhabitants;   7
Let the desert and its towns lift up their voice,   7
   the villages where Kedar dwells;   7
Let the inhabitants of Sela sing for joy,   7
   let them shout from the mountaintops.   7
Let them ascribe glory to Yahweh,   8
   among the coastlands declare his praise.   10
       1:1::1:1::1:1::1:1::1:1

Yahweh goes forth like a warrior,   7
   like a man of war he bestirs himself,^{yy} 7
With passion he shouts, he utters a battle-cry,   7
   over his foes he prevails.   7
           1:1::1:1

Isa 42:14-17

For a long time I have kept silent,^{zz}   6
   I have been mute and restrained myself;   5
Now I cry out like a woman in labor;   6
   I will gasp and pant.   6
          b:b::b:b

I will dry up mountains and hills,   8
   I will make all their vegetation wither;*   5
I will turn rivers into shoreline,   8
   pools I will dry up;   5
          1:b::1:b

And I will lead the blind on a way they know not,   11
   on paths [ ]** I will lead their march;   7
I will turn the dark regions# before them into light,   9
   the rough places into level ground.   6
These are the things I will do for them,   9
   and I will not abandon them.   5
        1:b::1:b::1:b

But they will be turned back and thoroughly shamed,   9
   those who trust in idols;   6
Those who say to molten images,##   8
   "you are our gods."   6
        1:b::1:b

TEXTUAL NOTES

The method of prosodic analysis used here analyzes
meter by syllable count according to the well known
method developed by Cross and Freedman. More recently
Cross has insisted that the number of syllables is a
consistent measure of symmetry only between lines within a single bicolon or tricolon, hence for larger
patterns the general notation b(reve) and l(ongum) is
used.[3] Mechanical textual emendations to account for
the history of scribal transmission, including: drop-
ping prosaizing particles such as conjunctions, direct
object markers, relative particles and the definite
articles, replacing converted perfects with imperfects,
and positing long pronominal forms such as **hû'â** as found
in Qumran texts, are made in order to approximate the
original prosody and are not otherwise noted.

[a]Reading with MT and 1QIsa[a]. G ἐγκαινίζεσθε
< *hiḥḥādišû, a dālet/rēš confusion.

[b]See discussion.

[c]G ἀναγγειλάτωσαν appears to be a translation of
*yiqrā'û.

[d]The usual translation of MT **raglô** as Cyrus's feet
(read **raglâw** with 1QIsa[a] and G) "whom victory meets" is
insensitive to the holy war imagery begun in the first
colon (**mî hēᶜîr**), and requires emendation of the verb,
removing the **'ālep** and reading **yiqrēhû**. With

---

[3]See David Noel Freedman, "Strophe and Meter in
Exodus 15," in Pottery, Poetry, and Prophecy (Winona
Lake: Eisenbrauns, 1980), 187-227; and other studies in
that volume. For Cross's most recent views, see
"Studies in the Structure of Hebrew Verse: The Prosody
of Lamentations 1:1-22," in The Word of the Lord Shall
Go Forth, Essays in Honor of David Noel Freedman
(Winona Lake: Eisenbrauns, 1983) 129-155.

Clifford,[4] I take ṣedeq, "vindication," as the object
of hēᶜîr and a personification of Cyrus whom Yahweh has
called (cf. 43:3,4: 'eqrā' lĕkâ bi-šmekâ). See the
parallel Hab 3:5, where Dabr and Reshep march before
the divine warrior:

> lĕpānâw yēlek deber
> yēṣē' rešep lĕ-raglâw

Like Dabr and Reshep, Ṣedeq was a member of the heavenly hosts (Ps 89:15). This division of the bicolon is
supported by 1QIsa[a] which reads an initial **wāw** in
wyqr'hw, and it brings out parallelism lost in the
traditional rendering.

[e]1QIsa[a] reads **yôrîd** the hiphil of **yrd,** but given the
scroll's tendency to modernize that is probably not the
correct verb. MT is pointed as an apocapated hiphil of
rdy, which gives a short 5 syllable line. G is of no
help here. Based upon the parallel in Isa 45:1 pointed
as from the root **rdd,** many scholars have suggested that
the verb be repointed **yārōd,** "he subdues." But the
hiphil **yārēd** is more consistent with the sense of
Yahweh as the main actor in Cyrus's conquests.

[f]G reads plural suffixes, making "their swords" and
"their bows" objects of the verb. But the texts of MT
and 1QIsa[a] are superior: "dust" and "stubble" are used
in battle imagery and imagery of the divine warrior to
describe the fate of the vanquished enemy, not of their
weapons (cf. Ps 18:42, 2 Kgs 13:7, Zeph 1:17, Exod
15:7, Isa 5:24, 40:24). The sword and the bow belong
to Cyrus. Note the wordplay of **qaš** and **qaštô,** and the
parallel initial **yittēn** in this and the preceeding
bicolon.

---

[4]Clifford, "The Function of Idol Passages in Second
Isaiah," <u>CBQ</u> 42 (1980) 452.

[g]1QIsa[a] reads **ybynw**, which draws an interesting parallel to Ps 77:20, a description of the Exodus in which Yahweh as the divine warrior battles the primordial Sea: "your paths are not known." However, the figure of feet understanding is a mixed metaphor, and the reading in MT **yābô'** is consistent with several preceeding verbs of motion. The dual **raglâw** can take a singular verb. Note the chiasm and wordplay between **raglâw** here and in v. 2.

[h]G is paraphrastic here and adds ταῦτα.

[i]G < *qr'h mdrwt.

[j]We read **yeḥĕrādû** with MT. 1QIsa[a] reads **yaḥdâw** by haplography of a **rēš**. The same textual tradition underlies G, which paraphrastically transposes ἅμα to the end of the verse.

[k]1QIsa[a] **w'tywn** is due to a **waw/yōd** confusion from from MT **ye'ĕtāyûn** reinterpreted as a late Aramaizing form of the perfect. For consistency we also render MT **qārĕbû** as an imperfect **yiqrĕbû**, positing a haplography.

[l]Read the singular to agree with the subject and parallel verbs.

[m]1QIsa[a] **plṭš** is a dissimilation of a doubled consonant under Aramaic influence according to Kutscher,[5] though in Aramaic the dissimilated consonant is a nasal rather than a liquid.

[n]We adduce a haplography of **hĕkînô** metri causa and supported by G: καὶ θήσουσιν αὐτά. Since the Greek systematically has plurals, our reconstruction is a singular. Cf. Isa 40:20.

---

[5]E.Y. Kutscher, The Language and Linguistic Background of the Isaiah Scroll (1QIsa[a]) (Leiden: Brill, 1974), 515.

Ptiŝtā[c], the Qal of the root ŝt[c], now well established as a synonym for yr' from the Ugaritic cognate
tt[c] in CTA 5.2.7 and 6.6.30 and the Phoenician ŝt[c] in
the Karatepe inscription (KAI, 26A.II.4).

[q]We repoint as han-nōḥărîm, a Qal participle of nḥr,
"to snort," known from nominal forms (Job 39:20, 41:12;
Jer 8:16).[6] MT reads the niphal of ḥārâ, but it is
rare, and in none of its three occurrences (Isa 41:11;
45:24; Cant 1:o) does the verb have a medio-passive
meaning distinguishable from the Qal.

[r]1QIsa[a] and G precede with kol.

[s]This colon is missing from 1QIsa[a]; it comes at a
seam in the scroll.

[t]MT has mĕtê yiśrā'ēl; 1QIsa[a], Aq., Vulg. render the
consonantal MT as mêtê, "dying ones." G may be interpreting mĕtê in accordance with the expression mĕtê
mispār, "a people few in number," a reading which has
led some to emend mĕtê mĕ'āṭ (cf. Gen 34:30). Others
understand the text on the basis of Akkadian mutu,
"louse" or "maggot," or emend to rimmat, "worm" (cf.
Isa 14:11, Job 25:6).[7] However the colon is short (5
syllables), suggesting that a word is missing. Without
new manuscript evidence, the text cannot be recovered.

[u]With 1QIsa[a], we read masculine suffixes to give a
consistent meter.

[v]The colon as it stands is too long; we omit
wĕ-hā-'ebyônîm as an early expansion. We also render
the verb baqqĕŝû a Qal perfect; cf. G. The plural

---

[6]G.R. Driver, JTS 36 (1935), 398-9.

[7]For a discussion of these renderings, see
Schoors, 59-61; Driver, JTS 36 (1935) 399-400.

participle **mĕbaqqĕšîm** was generated by dittography of both the preceding and succeeding **mem** and by attraction to the immediately preceding substantives.

^W MT has a short colon; we read a second pronoun **'ānōkî** with G, which also has an expanded divine name.

^x 1QIsa^a reads **wybynw** with a correction to **wyśymw** written <u>supra lineam</u>. Note the wordplay on repeated **yāśîm** and **yaḥdāw**, which have very different meanings in vv. 19b and 20a.

^y See discussion.

^z Emendation to the intransitive Qal **yiggĕšû** is suggested by the Greek, ἐγγισάτωσαν; Targ. **ytqrbwn**. The shift to **yaggîšû** would result from attraction to nearby **haggîšû** and **yaggîdû**.

^aa We read **tiqrēnâ** with MT, G; 1QIsa^a reads **tqr'wn**, "what you have decreed."

^bb The clause **mâ hēnnâ** depends upon the following verb. MT has the imperative **haggîdû**, which should have the meaning "Foretell!" as throughout the trial speeches. But the argument rather turns on whether the former things had been foretold in the past--cf. v. 26 where gods are queried as to whether they had predicted (**higgîd**) the now evident rise of Cyrus. Hence, with Schoors, we read a perfect **higgîdu**. This is preferable to the view of Westermann, for whom the issue is whether the gods can now interpret past events and show their purported activity behind them.[8]

^cc We read **lēb** with G and omit the pronominal suffix of MT **libbānû** <u>metri causa</u>; it could have arisen by dittography.

---

[8]Schoors, 216-17; Westermann, 71-2.

dd The two cola are transposed following Schoors, BHS.

ee 1QIsaᵃ reads 'w 'ḥrwnwt. The second 'ô is a dittography and the noun 'aḥărônôt is a modernizing form, as Kutscher[9] has pointed out that 3 out of 4 instances of 'aḥărît in MT are written 'aḥărôn in 1QIsaᵃ. The scribe may also have been influenced by the preceeding rî'šônôt.

ff Reading wĕ-nîrā' with the ketîb, against G, 1QIsaᵃ and the qerē' which mistakenly render the verb nir'eh in parallel to ništāᶜâ misconstrued as the hithpael of šᶜh, "to gaze about." The latter verb is actually the Qal of štᶜ, "to fear" (see note #p on 41:10). The consonantal MT nštᶜh and 1QIsaᵃ wnr'h can be vocalized as cohortatives, but we prefer the short form of both verbs metri causa.

gg We read mē-'epes for MT mē-'āpaᶜ; G < *mē-ᶜāpār.

hh G reads a plural verb for MT yibḥar. Torrey, troubled by the lack of gender agreement, suggests emending to tôᶜeh hab-bōḥēr bākem, "He who chooses you goes astray." However, tôᶜēbâ is not the subject of yibḥar but a predicate nominative secondarily linked to yibḥar bākem. MT is also preferable on grounds of prosody. This tricolon, like v. 29 also at the end of a stanza, shows b:b:l meter.

ii MT way-ya't; 1QIsaᵃ reads the plural way-ya'tiyyû; G καὶ τὸν < *w't is the result of haplography.

jj For this crux, 'eqrā' bišmô is a standard emendation of MT yiqrā' bišmî.[10] MT makes Cyrus a believer

---

[9] Kutscher, 365.

[10] Cf. Westermann, 69; G. Fohrer, Das Buch Jesaja, Bd. 3 (Neukirchen-Vluyn: Neukirchener, 1970) 44; Schoors, 218-19; and BHK.

in Yahweh. G, reading MT as its <u>Vorlage</u>, deals with
the   problem   by   reading   the   passive   κληθήσονται.
Schoors   relies   upon G to render 1QIsa[a] **wyqr' bšmw** in
the   passive   voice   **way-yiqqārē' bišmô**.   But **'eqrā'**
bišmô, denoting God's active naming of Cyrus, is
preferable to both MT and the passive constructions
because it renders the prophet's image of Yahweh's
activity behind Cyrus and it respects the parallel
structure to the bicolon. Deutero-Isaiah consistently
speaks of Yahweh's election (of Israel in 43:1) or commission (of Cyrus in 45:3) as his calling a person by
name in the active voice.

[kk]With most commentators we emend MT **yābō'** "he
comes" (1QIsa[a] with G **yābō'û**) to **yābūs** "he tramples."
MT could be generated by haplography of **sāmek**, with the
'ālep appearing as a later correction.

[ll]This verse is corrupt, and no satisfactory reconstruction has yet been advanced. One might draw upon
the parallel phrases in 42:9 and 41:22b, but the verb
is lacking.   The Greek ἀρχὴν Σιων δώσω καὶ Ἰερουσαλημ
παρακαλέσω εἰς ὁδόν is of little help. G ὁδόν < *'rḥ
could conceivably be a metathesis from **'ḥr** or **'ḥrwn,**
but is more likely an error for **'r'h** from the following
verse.   The conventional emendation of **hinnām** to
higgadtîhâ has no textual support, and **higgîd**, a common
word in the trial speeches, would not likely suffer
such a corruption.[11]

_____

[11]For   a   survey of   interpretations,   cf. Antoon
Schoors, "Les choses antérieures et les choses nouvelles   dans les oracles deutéro-Isaïens," <u>ETL</u> 40
(1964), 28-30. A somewhat tortured interpretation
which seeks to preserve the text of MT has been proposed by Neil J. McEleney, "The Translation of Isaias
41:27," <u>CBQ</u> 19 (1957) 441-43.

mmMT has a 5-7-8 triplet, and its short first line, wĕ-'ēre' wĕ-'ēn 'îš, may have suffered corruption due to proximity to the preceding verse. To give balanced prosody we transpose hinnēh from the previous verse, an emendation suggested by the G, ἰδοὺ. Otherwise the G departs far from the MT in an attempt to make sense of the verse. ἀπὸ γὰρ τῶν ἐθνῶν possibly arose to complement ἀπὸ τῶν εἰδώλων αὐτῶν, which is in turn based upon *mē-'ĕlîlām or *mē-'ĕlōhîm, a corruption of mē-'ēlleh in the following colon of MT.

nnMT reads "I ask them and they answer," which makes little sense. This emendation to 'ĕš'āl û-mî yāšîb dābār assumes only a simple wāw/yōd confusion and a misdivision of the consonants. The plural yāšîbû arose after mî was confused with the third person plural pronominal suffix.

ooRead 'āyin with 1QIsaᵃ, Targ. 'yn; MT has 'āwen due to wāw/yōd confusion.

ppG reads a plural participle by interpreting the consonantal MT niskêhem as nōsĕkêhem; MT is the original reading. This triplet, like v. 24 at the conclusion of the preceding stanza, has b:b:l meter and is introduced by hēn.

qq1QIsaᵃ reads mišpāṭî by attraction to rûḥî. MT, which lacks the suffix, is the superior reading.

rrWe repoint MT yišbōr and yĕkabbennâ as passive verbs yiššābēr and yikbe[]h denoting the servant's humility, consistent with the image in v. 4. This emendation is supported by 1QIsaᵃ (ykbh) and G.

ssMT yārûṣ is repointed as yērōṣ, the niphal of rṣṣ; but see Eccl 12:6.

[tt]1QIsa[a] ynḥylw is reading a piel perfect yiḥḥêlû with secondary Aramaic nasalization of the geminate ḥet. The perfect indeed improves the meter.

[uu]We transpose nĕšāmâ and rûḥ metri causa

[vv]1QIsa[a] omits yhwh; it is an expansion in MT.

[ww]The long form of the pronoun 'ān<ōk>î improves the meter.

[xx]yir<ʿam> is a standard emendation for MT yôrĕdê; it is based upon parallels in Ps 96:11; 98:7; 1 Chr 16:32. We expect each bicolon to begin with a verb denoting singing and rejoicing. Another possible emendation is to 'addîrê yām, "the mighty sea", cf. Ps 93:4, Exod 15:10.

[yy]Freedman first suggested this transposition of qin'â to the following bicolon. On yāʿîr as an internal causative, see Pss 35:23; 73:20; Job 8:6.[11]

[zz]1QIsa[a] 'ḥšyty shows conflation of a perfect and an imperfect.

[*]This bicolon is absent from some G mss.

[**]Omit the second lō' yādāʿû of MT as a dittography; it violates the l:b meter. The scansion is also helped by reading the initial verbs as imperfects.

[#]1QIsa[a] reads mhšwkym, an Aramaic participle of šwk, to hedge or fence in. It is a secondary confusion of hē with ḥet of MT maḥšok.

[##]MT pesel and massēkâ are to be read as collective nouns; G, Syr. translate them as plurals.

---

[11]See D. N. Freedman, "Isa 42:13," CBQ 35 (1973) 225-26.

There is no agreement as to the extent of the literary unit or units in chs. 41-42 (see above Table 1).
Clifford, for example, understands 41:1-42:9 to be a
literary unit built up out of a large-scale parallel
structure beginning with a summons to trial (41:1, 5-7;
41:21-22b) and concluding with Israel's vindication
(41:8-20; 42:1-9).[12] Beuken, on the other hand, delimits a unit to ch. 41 structured by an inclusio formed
by the two legal proceedings around a central section
of salvation oracles.[13] Since similar trial speeches
and oracles vindicating Israel are scattered throughout
the early chapters of Deutero-Isaiah, the burden is on
the critic to prove his case through detailed analysis
of structure and form. We will argue that 41:1-20 and
41:21-42:17, each introduced by a trial speech against
the foreign gods, are two parallel halves of a single
compositional unit.

Each half of this extended composition has its own
formal and structural integrity. Isa 41:1-20 is composed of three pairs of stanzas of nearly equal length:
12 (8+4), 11 (5+6), and 14 (6+8) bi/tricola. The four
middle stanzas are linked by the recurrent verbs $^c\bar{a}zar$
(vv. 5, 10, 13, 14), yārē' (vv. 5, 10, 13, 14) and
ḥāzaq (vv. 6-7, 9, 13). The slightly longer outer
stanzas form a chiasm, with the concluding statement of
Yahweh's purpose, "in order that they might see
(yirĕ'û) and know... that the hand of Yahweh has done
this" (41:20) directly answering the question in 41:4
"who has acted and done this?" While the nations upon
seeing Cyrus's advance build idols (v. 5), through

___

[12]Clifford, Fair Spoken, 89.

[13]W.A.M. Beuken, "Mišpāṭ: The First Servant Song and
its Context," VT 22 (1972) 12-13.

Israel's restoration they will "see and know" that it
is Yahweh who has acted in history.

Isa 41:21-42:7 is similarly composed of three pairs
of stanzas, each pair of roughly equal length: 15
(8+7), 12 (5+7) and 16 (7+9) bi/tricola respectively,
corresponding to the three pairs of stanzas of
Isa 41:1-20.[14] These stanzas are united by a common
refrain: the ridicule of the idol-gods who are the butt
of the prophet's argument throughout. Each of the
first two stanzas composing the trial speech ends with
declarations that the gods are nothing (41:24,29). The
fourth stanza concludes the mission of the servant with
the notice that Yahweh will not let his praise be
ascribed to idols (42:8). Finally in 42:17 the works
of Yahweh transforming the desert are contrasted with
the fate of the idolators, who are consigned to humiliation.

Goldingay was the first to adduce the parallel
structure of this unit.[15] Accepting the prevailing
view that the prophet delivered short oral utterances,
he attributes the parallelism of what he calls "sequen-
ces" to their redactional arrangement by the prophet or
a collector. However, the uncovering of a tightly
interwoven structure linking these supposedly independent units makes the very supposition that they were
originally disparate oral sayings less tenable. More
likely, this structure was the conscious artifice of a
writing prophet who built his compositions with several

---

[14]The variation of these numbers may be due to
uncertainties in text and scansion. If v. 27 is removed as a gloss, the stanza lengths are 32, 30, and 32
cola. If the b:b:l cola in vv. 24, 26b and 29 are read
as l:l, the lengths would be 31, 30 and 32.

[15]John Goldingay, "The arrangement of Isaiah XLI-
XLV," VT 29 (1979), 289-294.

stanzas. Note that this composition is hardly mechanical; the prophet alternates stanzas with l:b meter
(41:11-13 and 42:14-17) opposite corresponding stanzas
in balanced meter.

Each unit opens with a trial scene whose context is
the conquering advance of Cyrus. Corresponding to
41:1-4,5-7 where Yahweh challenges the nations to recognize his sovereignty behind this historical event
but they refuse and vainly build idols, in 41:21-24,25-
29 Yahweh directly challenges the gods of the nations
to foretell history and thereby prove their ability as
causal agents, but they cannot and fall silent. In the
next two stanzas of each unit, 41:8-10,11-3 and 42:1-4,
5-9, Yahweh supports his servant and invests him with
power and authority over the nations. Isa 41:8-11
confirms the vocation of the servant-Israel and corresponds to the presentation of the servant in 42:1-4;
both begin with noun clauses "You Israel are my servant"/"Here is my servant..." The correspondence extends to the role of the servant before the nations: in
41:8-10,11-13 the servant-Israel is called out from the
nations and will experience the defeat of his oppres-
sors, and in 42:1-4,5-9 the servant is to bring Yahweh's **mišpāṭ** to the nations and deliver the oppressed.
In the final two stanzas of each unit, 41:14-16,17-20
and 42:10-13,14-17, Yahweh marches out to war amidst
the rejoicing of nature, and the desert is transformed
to make a way in the wilderness for Israel's return.
Here we differ from Goldingay, who includes Isa 41:14-
16 in his second section as a salvation oracle addressed to the servant-Israel even though it describes
the transformation of nature and hence belongs properly
in the third section. These findings are summarized in
Table 2.

TABLE 2

Parallel Structure of Isa 41:1-20 and 41:21-42:17

A. Trial speech: Yahweh the plaintiff versus the
   nations or their gods

41:1-4,5-7   (26 cola) | 41:21-24,25-29   (34 cola)

Address to the nations | Summons to the nations
Trial of the nations | Trial of their gods
Who acts in history? | Who foretells history?
Cyrus comes | Cyrus comes
In fear, they build idols | Useless, they don't answer

 yiggĕšû | yiggĕšû, haggîšû
 niqrābâ, qārĕbû | qorĕbû
 rî'šôn | rî'šônôt
 'ahărôn | 'ahărîtān
 hēᶜîr | haᶜîrôtî
 yiqrā'êhû (of Cyrus) | yiqrā' (of Cyrus)

B. Yahweh's purpose for his servant

41:8-10   (23 cola) | 42:1-4   (30 cola)

Servant-Israel identified | Servant presented
Helped and supported | Given God's spirit
Called from ends | Mission to bring justice
   of the earth | to nations

41:11-13 | 42:5-9

God upholds Israel | God upholds his servant
Defeat of oppressors | Delivers the oppressed
Opponents reduced to | Idol-gods not to be
   nothing | glorified

 ᶜabdî | ᶜabdî
 bāhartîkā (bis) | bĕhîrî
 tĕmaktîkā | 'etmok bô
 mahăzîq yĕmînekā | 'ahzēq bĕ-yādekā
 hehĕzaqtîkā |
 qĕrā'tîkā | qĕrā'tîkā
 ṣidqî | bĕ-ṣedeq

C. Yahweh transforms nature amidst rejoicing,
   acknowledged by humanity

41:14-16 (28 cola)	42:10-13 (32 cola)
Israel to thresh mountains	Yahweh the warrior
Israel rejoices	Nations and nature rejoices

41:17-20	42:15-17
Yahweh answers	After restraint, Yahweh acts
Turns desert into garden	Turns good land into desert
	Leads exiles on the way home
Yahweh does this	These are things Yahweh does
All people recognize	Idolators are shamed
God's power	

tithallāl	tĕhillātô (bis)
ḥādāš	ḥādāš
lō' 'e^cezbēm	lō' ^căzabtîm
'āśîm	'āśîm
'ăgam mayim	'ăgamîm
nĕhārôt	nĕhārôt
^cāśĕtâ zō't	'ēlleh had-dĕbārîm ^căśîtîm

The parallel structure and common vocabulary of
41:1-20 and 41:21-42:17 suggest that together they form
two halves of a single literary unit. It may be demarcated from the following unit 42:18-43:7 which, despite
a few verbal links such as ᶜiwwĕrîm, ᶜabdî and 'aḫărîš,
takes off in a new direction--a lawsuit against Israel.
It has a different structure, with 6 stanzas or two
triplets of 12 (4+3+5) and 12 (4+4+4) bi/tricola each.
Yet it is also possible to construe this lawsuit as
concluding a tripartite unit 41:1-43:7, similar to the
collocation of a lawsuit against Israel and a trial of
the gods in 43:8-44:5 (see below).

b. Isa 41:1-20 and Traditions of Yahweh's Victory over
the Nations in the Jerusalem Cult

The first half of the diptych begins with a trial
speech, 41:1-4(5), whose supposed form-critical independence hinges on a questionable emendation. Westermann and Schoors correctly view the second colon
yaḫălîpû kōḫ as a dittography, probably a marginal
correction from the preceding verse (40:31).[16] Then
they transpose v. 5c (reading the verbs as imperatives
with 1QIsaᵃ) into this verse, and reconstruct:

	syllables
Be silent before me, O coastlands,	[7]
O Nations, <draw near and come forward>.	[11]
Let them [the gods] approach, then speak,	[8]
together let them draw near for judgment.	[8]

This suggestion suffers from inferior metrical balance
in the first bicolon and requires the unusual coinci-
dence of two presumably random scribal transpositions
on the same verse. Moreover, it appears to be preju-

---

[16]Schoors, I am God your Savior, 209-213; Westermann, 62-63.

diced by efforts to separate out vv. 1-5 as an independent formal unit by removing from v. 5 words which
apparently introduce the following description of idol
manufacture. Our reconstruction of v. 1, removing the
dittography but leaving v. 5c where it is:

Be silent before me, O coastlands,	[6]
let the nations [ ] approach.	[6]
Let them consult together,	[7]
let us gather for judgment.	[7]

is nearly identical in form to the summons in 45:21.
These opening words are apparently addressed only to
the nations, with no mention of their pagan gods.[17] In
v. 5 these same nations tremble with fear at Yahweh's
historical theophany manifest in Cyrus's Blitzkrieg and
again gather together, this time intending to defend
themselves by building idols.

The opening stanza is thus an integral part of a two
part trial scene which combines an argument for God's
sovereignty in history now manifest in the rise of his
instrument Cyrus with ridicule of the nations' futile
idolatry. First Deutero-Isaiah points to Cyrus, a
threat recognized by all in Babylon, and by rhetorical
questions mî hē^{c}îr and mî pā^{c}al (vv. 2, 4; cf. 42:24)
declares that Yahweh is the power behind his advance.
It is Yahweh who stirs him up, calls him, gives up
nations before him, and enables him to subdue kings.
In the traditional imagery of the divine warrior, Cyrus
is the captain of Yahweh's host, the agent of his
"vindication" who marches "in Yahweh's ranks"
(lĕ-raglâw). Cyrus's advance leads him on "a path his
feet have not trod," with the implication that it is

---

[17]But see Schoors, 209; H. E. von Waldow, "Anlass
und Hintergrund der Verkündigung des Deuterojesaja,"
diss. Bonn, 1953, 43-44. They detect an address to
both the nations and their gods.

Yahweh, not Cyrus, who is directing the line of march.
Yet while the nations were invited in v. 1 to come to
trial (lĕ-mišpāṭ niqrābâ) and are challenged to accept
Yahweh's arguments, ironically in vv. 5-7 they have
come together (<yi>qrĕbû wĕ-ye'ĕtāyûn) to make idols.
Idol manufacture is the desperate act of the fearful
(yîrā'û) and trembling (yeḥĕrādû) nations in v. 5 who
have heard reports of the irresistible onslaught of
Cyrus and frantically set to work as if they could
avert the onrushing storm.

The description of the manufacture of idols is also
linked semantically to the following words of reassurance. Verses 8-13 form one of the many passages in
Deutero-Isaiah affirming Israel's vocation as Yahweh's
servant. While in v. 5 the idolators fear, in v. 10
Yahweh tells Israel to "fear not" ('al tîrā'). The
trembling nations are called "the ends of the earth"
(qĕṣôt hā-'āreṣ) in v. 5, and in v. 8 Yahweh has
grasped Israel "from the ends of the earth" (miq-qĕṣôt
hā-'āreṣ). The idol makers strengthen (yĕḥazzēq) and
help (yaᶜăzōr) each other. They fasten their idol
(yĕḥazzĕqēhû) and say of its workmanship, "it is good"
('ōmēr lĕ- ... ṭôb hû'). In contrast, in vv. 9-10
Yahweh himself helps Israel (ᶜăzartîkā), grasps her
(heḥĕzaqtîkā), and says to her, "you are my servant"
('ōmar lĕ- ... ᶜabdî 'attâ).

This verbal repetition continues into vv. 11-13,
which is constructed in qinah meter.[18] In spite of the

---

[18]For recent studies of this meter, see F. M. Cross,
"Studies in the Structure of Hebrew Verse: The Prosody
of the Psalm of Jonah," in The Quest for the Kingdom of
God: Studies in Honor of George E. Mendenhall, ed. H.
B. Huffmon, F.A. Spina and A.R.W. Green (Winona Lake:
Eisenbrauns, 1983) 159-67. Cf. "Studies in the Struc-
ture of Hebrew Verse: The Prosody of Lamentations 1:1-
22," in The Word of the Lord Shall Go Forth (Winona
Lake: Eisenbrauns, 1983) 129-53.

change of meter, this stanza is not to be separated
from vv. 8-10; in fact the prophet often varies the
meter between subunits of his long compositions.[19] In
the background of this stanza are community laments
such as Ps 35:4,26 where in an almost identical construction in qinah meter the psalmist calls for the
defeat and humiliation of his enemies. Deutero-Isaiah
has used the same phrases and meter but has changed the
verbs from jussives to imperfects and added the exclamatory particle hēn, thereby transforming a wish of the
psalmist, "may they be shamed and humiliated, those who
seek my life" (Ps 35:4) into a confident prediction,
"Now they will be shamed and humiliated, all who rage
against you" (Isa 41:11a). By this and similar transformations of psalms of lament, the prophet often comes
to employ 1:b::1:b meter in words of promise and hope
(cf. 42:15-17, 54:14-25).

Verses 14-20 constitute a pair of stanzas which,
while form-critically salvation oracles, dispute with a
disbelieving Israel that has been reduced to the status
of a "worm" (cf. Ps 22:6) and impoverished without the
means to travel over the deserts to return to Israel.
Vv. 14-16, which describe Yahweh's making "worm Jacob"
into a threshing sledge to thresh the mountains, open
by repeating the words 'al tîrĕ'î and 'ănî Căzartîk of
v. 13. Beuken aptly describes its rhetorical relationship to the preceeding stanzas as "ascending parallelism."[20] Its image of Israel threshing the mountains
and the picture in vv. 17-20 of Yahweh turning the

---

[19]I.e. Isa 40:25-26, a stanza of 1:b meter in 40:12-
31. Cf. Lawrence Boadt, "Isaiah 41:8-13: Notes on
Poetic Structure and Style," CBQ 35 (1973) 20-34.

[20]Beuken, VT 20 (1972) 12.

desert into irrigated land are complementary. Both
stanzas conclude with the epithet "Holy One of Israel."

We further seek a formal basis for the integrity of
Isa 41:1-20 in the literary forms and cultic traditions
which the prophet inherited and which structured his
work. The opening trial speech is not a preexilic rîb
against Israel, but rather recalls the trial of the
gods in Psalm 82. Yet the compositional unit as a
whole draws upon the Zion and royal traditions of the
Jerusalem cult, where Yahweh defeats his raging enemies
and then goes forth to be acclaimed as king with atten-
dent rejoicing and fertility.[21] We discern in both Isa
41:1-20 and 41:21-42:7 features of a pattern which has
been noted in a number of psalms of this tradition.

The royal psalm 89 contains a series of rhetorical
questions (vv. 6-9) comparing Yahweh to the other gods
of the divine council which bears a certain resemblance
to the rhetoric of Deutero-Isaiah's trial speeches:
"who in the skies is comparable to Yahweh? Who is like
Yahweh among the divine beings?" These questions are
answered by a recital of Yahweh's mighty deeds (vv. 10-
15), acclamations of his salvation for Israel (vv. 16-
19) and proclamation of his covenant with David as Yahweh's servant (vv. 20-38), these comparable to the
prophet's words of reassurance in Isa 41:8-13 (and
42:1-9). The Zion psalms 46 and 48 exhibit notable
similarities to Isa 41:1-20; they are structured with
notices of the vain raging and defeat of the enemy
sandwiched between praises of Yahweh's victory. At
their opening they share with Isa 41:2-4 the motif of
Yahweh's war. Then the hostile nations gather but are
discomfited upon seeing Yahweh's might (Ps 48:6-7), a

---

[21]See Pss 2, 46, 48, 89, Isa 17:12-14, 29:5-8,
Mic 4:11-12.

scene comparable to the vain scurrying to build idols
in Isa 41:5. Both conclude praising Yahweh's victory
(Pss 46:11-12; 48:10-15). Yahweh helps Israel (^{c}zr
Ps 46:2,6; Isa 41:10,13) who need not fear (lō' nîrā'
Ps 46:3); Yahweh defeats all who would fight with
Israel (Ps 46:10; Isa 41:11-12); and his might reaches
to the ends of the earth (^{c}ad qĕṣê hā-'āreṣ Pss 46:10,
48:11; Isa 41:5,9). These psalms conclude with a call
to rejoice at Yahweh's victory (Ps 48:12; Isa 41:16).

The cult of preexilic Jerusalem also depicted Zion
as the place of judgment.[22] This is explicit in the
enthronement psalms (96:13; 98:9) where Yahweh the king
judges (špṭ) the nations. Prophetic texts such as
Isa 2:2-5/Mic 4:1-3 where from Zion Yahweh "judges
between the nations," and Joel 4:9-21, which depicts
the nations gathered together beneath Zion at the ^{c}emeq
yĕhôšāpāṭ where Yahweh will sit in judgment (šām 'ēšēb
lišpôṭ), also have connections to the cult.[23] There
Joel quotes an earlier tradition from the Judean redaction of Amos which prefaces the oracles against the
nations with the words "Yahweh roars from Zion, and
from Jerusalem he utters his voice, the pastures of the
shepherds dry up, the top of Carmel withers" (cf. Mic
1:2-9). Evidently Zion was the place from which to
give oracles against the nations. However, this tradition speaks of judgment as Yahweh's theophany as the
divine warrior and the nations' submission to his rule
rather than the juridical process against the gods as
found in Ps 82. While Deutero-Isaiah adds specifically

---

[22]John Gray, "The Kingship of God in the Prophets
and Psalms," VT 11 (1961) 1-29.

[23]Hans Wildberger, "Die Völkerwallfahrt zum Zion:
Jes II 1-5," VT 7 (1957) 62-81; J. W. Ahlström, Joel
and the Temple Cult of Jerusalem (Leiden: Brill, 1971).

juridical language to his depictions of the trial of
the nations, the martial imagery of Yahweh's conquests
through Cyrus in 41:2-3 (and likewise in 42:25-26) is
an expression of the underlying Zion tradition.

The images of Israel threshing and the storm-wind
scattering the mountains in vv. 14-16, of Yahweh's
enemies blown away like dust in v. 2, and their being
reduced to nothingness in vv. 11-12, employ language of
Yahweh's theophany in the storm which was also integral
to the tradition of the Zion cult. In Pss 46:10 and
48:8 the enemies and their weapons are smashed and
scattered by the east wind. Other passages depicting
the storm-theophany from Zion afford even better parallels: the nations become like chaff (**daq, mōṣ** Isa 29:5,
17:13); Israel, empowered with sharp blades, threshes
them (Mic 4:13); they are chased and scattered on the
mountains before the storm wind (**sĕ^cārâ** Isa 29:6). The
other figure of annihilation in the tradition of Yah-
weh's defense of Zion depicts Israel's foes as suddenly
disappearing, "they will become as nothing and void"
(Isa 41:12); they become like a dream (Isa 29:7-8), to
exist no more (**'ênennû**, Isa 17:14).

In the Jerusalem cult the defeat of Yahweh's enemies
becomes the occasion for God's processional return to
Zion. The image in vv. 16b-20 of Israel crossing the
desert, its fructification and attendant rejoicing,
belongs to the second movement of the traditional mythic pattern of the victory of the storm god, who comes
home in procession after having first battled and defeated his foes.[24] Yahweh's defeat of the nations

[24]See Frank Moore Cross, Canaanite Myth and Hebrew
Epic: Essays in the Religion of Israel (Cambridge:
Harvard, 1973) 162-63. He defines the underlying mythic
pattern as (a) the Divine Warrior goes forth to battle
against chaos; (b) nature convulses as God manifests

through Cyrus and his leading the exiles through the
wilderness to Zion represent one of Deutero-Isaiah's
many adaptations of this tradition from the Jerusalem
cult.[25]

The finding that Deutero-Isaiah has drawn upon the
preexilic tradition of Zion as Yahweh's fortress abode
from which he appears in the storm to judge his foes
gives a formal basis for the integrity of Isa 41:1-20
which complements the unity discerned through study of
its rhetorical features. However, Deutero-Isaiah has
modified this inherited tradition of the Jerusalem cult
in order to accomodate his altered situation in Babylon. While Zion had been the place within whose midst
(bĕ-qirbāh) God had dwelt (Ps 46:6) and where the nations gathered to meet their judgment, now in exile the
nations gather for judgment (lĕ-mišpāṭ niqrābâ 41:1)
and encounter Yahweh at an undefined place. Due to the
situation of exile, the circumstances of Yahweh's conquest are reversed: Yahweh does not defend his immovable (bal timmôṭ Ps 46:6) fortress Jerusalem, but comes
in power to conquer Babylon whose priests have rallied
around their immovable idols (lō' yimmôṭ). The exilic
context also leads Deutero-Isaiah to accentuate the

---

his wrath; (c) God returns to take up kingship and is
enthroned upon his mountain; (d) the Divine Warrior
utters his voice from his temple and gives forth fertilizing rains, nature rejoices and is fruitful. Paul
Hanson has further subdivided the ritual pattern into
nine parts: the threat of the amassing enemies, combat
by the Divine Warrior, his victory, salvation for God's
people, a shout of acclamation, a procession to the
temple, God's universal reign, a festive banquet to
which all are invited, and fertility and peace to the
land. He charts Pss 2, 9, 24, 29, 46, 47, 48, 65, 68,
76, 77:17-21, 89b, 97, 98, 104, 106:9-13, and 110
according to this pattern. Cf. Dawn of Apocalyptic
(Philadelphia: Fortress, 1975), pp. 300-310.

[25]Cf. Isa 34-35; Cross, 170-74.

element of the victory procession; more than a celebration, it becomes the purpose of Yahweh's conquests to provide a means for the exiles to return to Zion. Hence he even subsumes the traditional imagery of the thunderstorm in service of the procession; the mountains and hills are threshed not as a manifestation of Yahweh's wrath, but rather to ease the exiles' perilous journey home (cf. Isa 40:4, 49:11, 35:8).

c. Isa 41:21-42:17: Judgment of the Nations and Confirmation of the Servant

This second half of the compositional unit likewise opens with a trial speech addressed to the nations, but here the idol-gods in particular become the object of Yahweh's words and deeds throughout the unit. Yahweh challenges the nations in vv. 21-24 to bring forward their gods, that they might demonstrate their power in history by explaining the past and predicting the future. Torrey questions **rîběkem** in v. 21 as he does the parallel 34:8: he expects a nomen agentis as the subject of **yaggîdâ** in v. 22.[26] The text emended to **rabêkem,** the idol-gods who are "your advocates," could have produced MT by metathesis.[27] Similarly, we render **Căṣûmôt,** a feminine plural adjective meaning "mighty," "terrible," as an agent "contenders."[28] The feminine

---

[26]Torrey, 317-18; Simon, 79, 247.

[27]Cross, personal communication.

[28]Other exegetes have pointed to Prov 18:18 where **Căṣûmîm** is used in parallel with **midyānîm** as the "contentions" in a lawsuit. Cf. L. Köhler, Deuterojesaja Stilkritisch untersucht, BZAW 37 (Giessen: Töpelmann, 1923) 14; Muilenburg, IB 5, 460; and Schoors, 215.

plural suggests "mighty goddesses," but that could be a
later demythologization of an original ᶜăṣūmêkem.
Torrey's emendation to ᶜăṣabbêkem, "your idols," is
unnecessary. The idol gods then become the butt of the
prophet's argument throughout Isa 41:21-42:17; their
mention serves as a sort of refrain at the conclusion
of many of its stanzas (41:24, 29, 42:8, 17).

However, the focus of Yahweh's contention is not the
gods themselves but an audience which he seeks to
convince of his claims. Vv. 22b-23 is composed of 3
interconnected bicola, each a conditional sentence
where a question or demand upon the gods in the protasis is followed by a reason "that we may know" in the
apodosis. The prosodic structure of the strophe is
unified by repetition of the verbs nēdĕᶜâ and haggîdû,
the series of temporal nouns, and an inclusio formed by
two short sentences with nominative pronouns mâ hēnnâ
and 'attem 'ĕlōhîm. Such complex prosodic units are
common in Deutero-Isaiah and continue in post-exilic
poetry where the individual bicolon even tends to lose
its integrity. The prophet piles up these conditional
sentences one after another for emphasis, challenging
the gods: did they previously foretell what has come to
pass?[29] Can they predict the future? Can they do good
or ill? Each challenge is posed in order that "we," an
audience of spectators at the trial, "may know" and may
be convinced to abandon worship of foreign gods: "an
abomination is he who chooses you" (v. 24).

---

[29]See textual notes on the emendation of haggîdû to
higgîdû, suggested by Schoors. The gods are not being
asked to interpret past events after the fact, but
rather whether they had previously foretold them.

The second stanza renews the argument using the occasion of the coming of Cyrus. Yahweh has aroused him (ha^cîrōtî) from the north and called ('eqrā') his name from the east; language reminiscent of 41:2 where Yahweh also arouses (hē^cîr) Cyrus and calls him (yiqrā'ēhû). Verse 26 resumes the pattern of conditional sentences with apodosis in the first person plural: Yahweh asks whether anyone had foretold Cyrus's arising, that "we," the audience, might say ṣaddîq, "he is right." The term ṣaddîq is often a juridical formula, a declaration of the rightness of one party by the judge or by common assent.[30] Its referent is not Cyrus, whose march is certainly righteous in the sight of Yahweh, but specifically mî higgîd, the gods at trial. Here it is the court, that is the assembled audience, that would say "he is right" to any god whose witnesses had accurately predicted the rise of Cyrus.[31] While v. 27 may be reminding the audience that Yahweh had always foretold past events by sending his prophets (měbaśśēr) to Jerusalem,[32] none of the gods can sustain a similar claim with regard to Cyrus. The question of the presumed audience in the trial, which by assent justifies one of the contending parties, is an issue to which we will return when considering the significance of the trial speech motif for the place of the nations in Deutero-Isaiah.

The third and fourth stanzas, often treated separately as the first servant song and its appendix, are an integral part of the compositional unit. Extensive

[30]Cf. 1 Sam 24:18; 2 Kgs 10:9; Jer 12:1; Ezek 18:9.

[31]Schoors, 214f.

[32]A conjecture since the verse is hopelessly corrupt.

verbal parallels between the servant of 42:1-4 and   the
servant-Israel of its counterpart passage 41:8-10 have
been noted in Table 2.   There are also verbal and
thematic linkages between 41:21-29 and 42:1-9.   The
particle hēn at the conclusion of each of the first two
stanzas (41:24,29) opens 42:1 and sets up a literary
contrast[33] between the idol gods, who cannot answer
Yahweh's charges and hence will not be declared ṣaddîq,
and the servant, who brings forth mišpāṭ to the nations
and who is called in righteousness (bĕ-ṣedeq 42:6). As
only Yahweh is justified as the God who directs history, so only Yahweh's servant can bring forth justice
upon the earth. This contrast extends throughout these
stanzas.   While the idols are empty wind (rûḥ 41:29),
Yahweh gives the spirit (rûḥ) of life to humanity
(42:5) and his prophetic spirit (rûḥî) to his servant
(42:1).   The idol gods are chosen by men (41:24) but
Yahweh chooses the servant (42:1,6).[34]   While Cyrus
comes with sound and fury trampling rulers in the   mud
(41:25), the servant is will come quietly and is himself bruised and humbled, a "broken reed."[35] Finally,
42:9 picks up the earlier themes of Yahweh's ability to
foretell the former things and the new things and
Yahweh's incomparability to idols.

---

[33]Compare the similar contrastive or comparative use
of repeated hēn in 50:9,11, 54:15,16, and 55:4,5, and
the linking function of hēn/hinnēh in 49:21-22.   See
Muilenberg, JBL 88 (1969) 14-15.

[34]Melugin, 100f.

[35]We cannot accept Melugin's forced suggestion (99)
that the language of the broken reed and the smoldering
wick refers to Israel's traditional reliance upon Egypt
(Isa 19:6, 36:6). The verbs "to break" and "to extin-
guish" can hardly be understood as denoting reliance or
trust.   The servant's suffering and humility is a consistent theme (cf. 49:4, 50:4-9, 52:13-53:12).

Other verbal and thematic connections join the servant passages to the following stanzas 42:10-13,14-17.
Extensive verbal repetition includes tĕhillāt-
(42:8,10,12), 'iyyîm (42:4,10,12,15), kābôd (42:8,12),
and yiśśā' [qôl] (42:2,11). The theme of waiting and
perseverance that will ultimately be rewarded in 42:4[36]
reappears in the figure of Yahweh restraining himself
for a time in 42:14, the image of a light to the nations (42:6) reappears in the figure of Yahweh leading
the blind and illuminating their way (42:16), and the
spurning of idols, as was mentioned, recurs at the
conclusion of the servant passages (42:8) and the way
through the wilderness (42:17).

These stanzas portray the vocation of the servant
rather than specifically a commission--they follow no
clear commissioning genre.[37] Baltzer has rightly recognized here a scene in the divine council.[38] This is
consistent with their place in a larger composition
which opens with trial scenes also arraigning the gods

---

[36]v. 4a has occasioned diverse interpretations.
Torrey (325f.) translates the verbs yikheh and yārûṣ
"rebuke" and "oppress" in order to fit with mišpāṭ of
the companion colon, thereby creating interesting wordplay with the previous adjective kēhāh with the usual
sense "to be dim." But they are correctly understood
by most to refer to the servant as persevering through
weakness and burdens, a theme found in 40:28-31 and
used of the servant in the other songs. As the servant
perseveres, the coastlands wait (yiḥēlû). The element
of struggle is emphasized by the parallel adverbs "certainly" (lĕ-'ĕmet) and "until" (ᶜad) which form a counterpoint with the negative lō'.

[37]See Melugin, 65-69,98,100f.

[38]Klaus Baltzer, "Zur formgeschichtlichen Bestimmung
der Texte vom Gottes-Knecht im Deuterojesaja-Buch," in
Probleme biblischer Theologie: Gerhard von Rad zum 70.
Geburtstag, ed. H. W. Wolff (München: Kaiser, 1971) 30-
31; North, The Suffering Servant, 142.

of the divine council (cf. Ps 82). The servant's vocation is to be understood in its context: his exaltation
and mišpāṭ contrasts with the judgment of the gods of
the nations in the preceding trial scene, and his
mission to liberate the prisoners is connected with the
return over the desert in the following stanzas.   In
the corresponding first half of the diptych, Isa 41:8-
13 similarly confirms the servant-Israel's favored
status as recipient of divine help in contrast to the
panicky and idolatrous nations, and likewise this help
would come through a transformation of nature.

Several of the motifs in 42:1-4,5-9,10-13 are shared
by the Cyrus oracle and royal oracles in general.   As
the servant brings mišpāṭ and protects the "bruised
reed," and as the coastlands wait and then rejoice at
his advent, so in the royal ideology of Judah the king
treats his subjects with justice and his accession was
greeted with rejoicing.[39] As in the Cyrus oracle (Isa
45:6) and the ideal of Judean kingship,[40] the servant's
authority is to extend to the ends of the earth ("the
coastlands"). Similarly in Judean royal oracles the
king's presence is likened to a light,[41] and he receives a covenant.[42] Mowinckel, Elliger and Schoors
have even argued that 42:5-9 was originally a Cyrus

---

[39]Cf. Isa 9:6; 11:4; Ps 72:2-4,11-12. The Cyrus
cylinder, reflecting the Mesopotamian version of this
royal ideology, makes similar statements about Cyrus.

[40]Pss 2:1,10; 72:8-11; Isa 8:23.

[41]Isa 9:1.

[42]1 Sam 23:5; 2 Sam 7:12-16; Pss 89:3,19-37; 132:11-
12. For a discussion of the disputed term běrît ᶜām,
see below, pp. 259-62, 276-79.

oracle reapplied to the servant;[43] Lindblom and Mowinckel have suggested that the prophet's disappointment
with Cyrus and the failure of the exilic community to
return to the land led him to conceive the servant as
"a kind of anti-Cyrus figure," whose faithfulness to
Yahweh and whose teaching ministry will accomplish what
Cyrus in his martial glory was unable to do.[44] On the
other hand, Melugin makes a case for the redactional
equation of the servant, Israel and Cyrus in 41:1-42:13
as conjointly responsible for Yahweh's conquest of the
nations.[45] Such hypotheses all point to the fact that
here Deutero-Isaiah depicts the servant with the tradition of Davidic royal theology.[46]

The finding that traditions of the royal cult lie
behind this servant passage agrees with our determina-
tion that these traditions are the antecedents of the

---

[43]S. Mowinckel, He that Cometh, 190, 245 n. 5;
Schoors, ETL 40 (1964), 35-39. Westermann (p. 101)
does not share this view.

[44]Lindblom, The Servant Songs, pp. 18, 52-74;
McKenzie, xlvii; Mowinckel, 190, 244-6.

[45]Melugin, 102. On the other hand, he rejects any
specific identification of the genre with a royal
oracle: "The prophet employed in general the style
customarily used for commissioning various kinds of
officials" (p. 67).

[46]Baltzer ("Zur formgeschichtlichen Bestimmung," 33-
34) would reject the royal background of this passage
in favor of the judicial function delegated to the
prophet as Yahweh's "vizier" on the basis of texts such
as Ps 68:7 where Yahweh himself liberates the prisoners. There is a certain fluidity between prophetic and
royal theologies since both originate as coordinate
offices of Yahweh the king. Yet Baltzer, by his prior
excision of the servant song from its context, ignores
the pattern of the royal cult which is evident in the
compositional unit.

extended diptych of which it is a subunit, Isa 41:1-20,
41:21-42:17. In the latter half there is no raging or
trembling of the nations, but in accordance with an
alternate tradition of Yahweh's victory over the nations at Zion, the enemy which is brought to judgment
simply vanishes (41:28-29).[47] The subsequent appearance of the servant is derived from the role of the
king in the preexilic cult, particularly as attested in
Pss 2 and 89. Psalm 89 prefaces the bestowal of a
divine grant upon David Yahweh's servant (vv. 20-38)
with a proof of Yahweh's sovereignty by rhetorical
questions comparing Yahweh to the gods in the divine
council (vv. 6-9), answered by a recounting of Yahweh's
mighty deeds (vv. 10-15). Psalm 2 similarly follows
the order of Isa 41:21-42:9: Yahweh first defeats the
raging nations (vv. 1-5) and then grants grace and
international dominion to his king (vv. 6-9). Note
that while Ps 2 is often adduced as a formal antecedent
to the servant song Isa 42:1-4, it actually partakes of
a tradition antecedent to the larger unit. At the
autumn festival reenactment of Yahweh's battle with his
enemies preceded his enthronement as king along with
confirmation of his Davidic representative.[48] It can
be said of the compositional unit 41:1-20,21-42:17 as a
whole that Deutero-Isaiah is drawing upon the traditions of the Jerusalem cult which formed the basis for
the theology of Davidic kingship in order to depict
Yahweh's rule over the nations and their gods as the

---

[47]See Isa 17:14; 29:7 and the discussion of 41:11-
12, above.

[48]Sigmund Mowinckel, The Psalms in Israel's Worship,
tr. D.R. Ap-Thomas (Nashville: Abingdon, 1962) 106-57;
Cross, Canaanite Myth, 155-63. Cf. Pss 76:9-10; 96:13.

basis for the servant's exaltation. The finding that
this antecedent tradition influences the function of
the servant passage within its context supports the
view that the servant passage is integral to its compositional unit and was not composed as an independent
song later to be incorporated at a secondary redaction.

The following hymnic passage (42:10-13) is related
to the enthronement psalms. While its geography may
have a political referent--the regions which rejoice at
God's attack are the coastlands and the desert regions
which had been crushed by Nebuchadnezzar's armies--it
also echoes cultic traditions. The roaring Sea, the
mythological enemy, had been subsumed under Yahweh's
sovereignty in Israelite tradition.[49] Also in the
background is the march of the divine warrior from
Sinai, Edom, Midian, and the southern deserts.[50] As
Yahweh's mythological domains, both the Sea and the
southern deserts would rejoice at Yahweh's new conquests.

Hymnic passages such as 42:10-13 sometimes have been
seen as marking the conclusion of redactional units in
Deutero-Isaiah and as significant signposts to the
book's overall structure.[51] Our compositional analysis
suggests that this view is partly mistaken. While
Isa 44:23, 48:20-21 and 55:12-13 do conclude their
respective units, neither 45:8, in the midst of the
Cyrus oracle, nor 49:13, at the transition between the
servant and Zion in the unit 49:1-28, fit this asser-

---

[49]Pss 96:11; 98:7; cf. the earlier tradition in Pss
46:3-4; 89:10-11; 93:3.

[50]Hab 3:3,7; Judg 5:4; Deut 33:2.

[51]Westermann, 28; Mettinger, A Farewell to the Servant Songs, 18-21, 24-28; Melugin, 81-82.

tion; they rather conclude subunits within larger compositional unities. Isa 42:10-13 does not form the conclusion of its compositional unit; neither should this hymnic stanza be abstracted as an independent oracle or as part of a skeleton upon which the other oracles are arranged.

We have demonstrated that the traditio-historical roots of the entire unit Isa 41:1-20,21-42:17 lie in the traditional complex of the Jerusalem cultus. The compositional unit as a whole and its constituent hymn of praise in 42:10-13 are from the same antecedent tradition. In that myth and ritual pattern, the call for nature to rejoice followed upon the enthronement of Yahweh and his earthly representative the king. That order--conflict with the nations, installation of the servant, and the rejoicing and transformation of nature--is also preserved in Deutero-Isaiah. Thus if these hymns of praise are seen to conclude many of Deutero-Isaiah's oracles, this fact may be due more to the motif's location as the final component of the underlying ritual pattern than to a redactor's design. In Deutero-Isaiah's adaptation of this preexisting tradition, he may either retain the traditional order or utilize the pattern within a larger structure.[52] Here 42:10-13 does not conclude its unit because the motif of the transformation of nature continues into vv. 14-17.

The qinah meter and much of the language of Isa 42:14-17, like 41:11-13 discussed above, is similar

---

[52]E.g. 45:8 at the end of the second movement of the Cyrus oracle is set within a larger envelope construction formed by 44:24-28 and 45:9-13; 49:13 comes at the end of the first half of a bipartite unit, ch. 49, which deals first with the servant and then with Zion.

to laments such as Ps 35:22, "Look, O Lord, and do not
keep silent ('al tehĕraš)," and Ps 40:15 (cf. Ps 35:4),
"let them be turned back and ashamed (yissōgû 'āḥôr wĕ-
yikkālĕmû), those who delight in doing me harm."
Westermann has sensitively analyzed this stanza and
noted the parallels to 41:17-20, which likewise alludes
to the people's lament that Yahweh has not answered
them, affirms God's new attitude of help, and describes
God's intervention in strikingly parallel terms.[53]   He
calls the correspondence between these two passages
"curious" because his method of isolating short stanzas
as independent units robs the observation of much of
its significance.   In fact these stanzas correspond to
one another because they occupy the corresponding positions in their respective halves of the compositional
unit. The contrasting reversals of nature, one (41:17-
20) turning deserts into fertile land and the other
(42:14-17) transforming rivers into deserts, exhibit
each of the two modes of the theophany of the divine
warrior, either turning a bountiful land into desola-
tion or bringing fertility to the desert (cf.
Ps 107:33-37).[54]   Here both theophanies are in the
service of Israel, providing a way for her to cross the
desert and return to Zion.   With these complementary
theophanies, each transforming nature and reversing the
status of weak Israel versus the idolatrous nations,
the two halves of the composition 41:1-20,41:21-42:17
each come to a close.[55]

---

[53]Westermann, 106.

[54]Cross, 162-63.   Deutero-Isaiah develops and joins
both types of theophany in the diptych chs. 34-35.

[55]Compare again chapter 49, which concludes with a
similar reversal of status (49:24-26).

2. Isa 43:8-44:5: A Trial of the Gods Introduces Yahweh's Lawsuit Against Israel.

Isa 43:8-44:5, like Isa 41:1-42:17, could be described as a sequence of alternating and parallel "trial
speeches" and "salvation oracles." The initial trial
speech is a trial of the gods, it is followed by words
proclaiming a new exodus for Israel over a revivified
desert; the second trial speech is directed against
Israel accusing her of cultic neglect of Yahweh, it is
in turn followed by a corresponding promise of Israel's
restoration as a people devoted to Yahweh upon a renewed and fruitful land. At the same time, the entire
unit takes on the form of an extended prophetic lawsuit
against Israel, as the opening trial of the nations
sets the stage for Yahweh to admonish Israel to live up
to its ordained role as witness and servant in an
international context.

43:8-13

Bring forth[a] a people which is blind yet has eyes,	9
and which is deaf yet has ears.	9
All nations have gathered together,	8
and all peoples have assembled.	8
	1:1::1:1

Who among them [the gods] could foretell[b] this?	7
did they announce to us the former things?[c]	7
Let them designate their witnesses that they might be	
justified;	10
let them testify,[d] that people might say,	
"It is right."	9
	1:1::1:1

You are my witnesses--oracle of Yahweh--	7
my servant whom I have chosen.	7
That you may know, believe me,	5/5
and understand that I am He.	10
Before me no god was formed,	7
and after me there will be none.	6
	1:1::(b:b):1::1:1

```
I, I am Yahweh,                                                   8
    and besides me there is no savior.                           8
As I myself[e] foretold, so I saved;                             9
    when I proclaimed there was no stranger among you.  9
Then you were my witnesses, [    ][f] and I was God;     8
    also henceforth[g] I am He.                                  8
None can deliver from my hand,                                   6
    I act--who can thwart it?                                    7
                                            1:1::1:1::1:1::1:1
```

43:14-15
```
[                                      ][h]
```

43:16-21
```
Thus says Yahweh--                                          rubric
Who makes a way in the sea,                                      6
    a path in the mighty waters;                                 7
Who brings forth chariot and horse,                             6
    army and warrior together,                                   6
They lie down,      never to rise;                             3/4
    extinguished,      quenched like a wick:                   3/5
                            b:b::b:b::(b:b):(b:b)
```

```
"Remember not the former things,                                 7
    nor consider things of old.                                  9
Behold, I am doing a new thing,                                  8
    now it sprouts forth, do you not perceive?[i]        9
Yea, I will make a way in the wilderness,                        7
    paths[j] in the desert.                                      7
                                            1:1::1:1::1:1
```

```
The beasts of the steppe will honor me,                          9
    the jackals and the ostriches,                               7
For I will give[k] water in the wilderness,                      7
    rivers in the desert,                                        7
To give drink to my chosen people,                               7
    my people,[l] whom I formed for myself,                      7
    that they may declare[m] my praise.                          7
                                            1:1::1:1::1:1::1:1
```

43:22-28
```
It was not to me that you called, O Jacob,[n]                    8
    neither did you weary yourselves for my sake, O
        Israel.                                                  8
You did not bring[o] your holocausts of sheep,                  10
    and your sacrifices[p] did not honor me.                    10
I did not force you labor with grain-offerings,[q]      8
    nor make you toil by demanding frankincense.                9
Not for me did you buy aromatic cane with money;                9
    the fat of your sacrifices was not to satisfy me. 10
```

On the contrary, you made me labor by your sins,   10
    you wearied me with your iniquities.   10
                        1:1::1:1::1:1::1:1::1̄:1

I myself am He   8
    who blots out your transgressions for my own sake; 9
    your sins I choose to remember no more[r].   8
                                          1:1̄:1

Remember,[s] let us argue together;   8
    declare[t] your case, that you may be justified.   8
Your father[u] of old sinned;   8̄
    your mediators have transgressed against me;   8
    your leaders desecrated my sanctuary.[v]   8
So I delivered Jacob to annihilation,   7
    Israel to revilings.   7
                            1:1::1:1:1::1̄:1

44:1-5

But now hear, O Jacob my servant,   9
    and Israel whom I have chosen,   8
Thus says Yahweh, your maker,   8̄
    who formed you in the womb, your helper:[w]   10
Fear not, O Jacob my servant,   7
    Jeshurun whom I have chosen.   7
                            1:1::1:1::1̄:1

For I will pour water on the thirsty land,   7
    streams on the dry ground;   7
I will pour[x] my spirit upon your descendants,   8̄
    my blessing upon your offspring.   8
They will spring up like the verdant moringa tree,[y]   7
    like willows by the watercourses.   8
                            1:1::1:1::1̄:1

This one will say, "I am Yahweh's,"   8
    that one will call himself[z] by the name of Jacob; 8
Another enrolls himself[aa] as Yahweh's,   8̄
    surnames himself[bb] by the name of Israel.   8
                                      1:1::1̄:1

TEXTUAL NOTES

[a]Where we, following MT, read **hôsî'**, 1QIsa[a] reads
the plural and 1QIsa[b] has the first person singular. G
ἐξήγαγον can be read either as first person singular or
third person plural. The first person verb could have
arisen by attraction to the first-person divine address

in 43:1-7 where Yahweh is the creator of Israel (43:1);
the plural by attraction to the following verbs.

[b]Read the plural **yaggîdû** with 1QIsa[a]; MT and G read
the singular. These imperfect verbs have a past dura-
tive tense and aspect.

[c]Read with MT the plural **yašmî[c]ûnû** against G and
Vulg. 1QIsa[a] **yšmy[c]w** arose from the plural by haplography of a **nûn**, likely in a text where the following verb
was rendered a converted perfect.

[d]Reading **yašmî[c]û** with 1QIsa[a]; MT has **wĕ-yišmĕ[c]û**.
See comments.

[e]G omits the first person pronoun; G[OL] corrects to
MT. We read the short form **'ănî** _metri_ _causa_.

[f]Omit **nĕ'um yhwh** _metri_ _causa_; it could have arisen
from attraction to v. 10a. G ὑμεῖς ἐμοὶ μάρτυρες κἀγὼ
μάρτυς λέγει κύριος ὁ θεός could have originated from
MT by transposition of **nĕ'um yhwh** and secondary expansion.

[g]G has ἀπ᾿ ἀρχῆς; Targ. **mn[c]lm'**; Vg. _ab_ _initio_. Westermann adds **mē-[c]ôlām** before **gam miy-yôm** to create an
8-6-6 tricolon. But the versions are reading **mē-[c]ôlām**
in place of **miy-yôm**, and we should avoid the temptation
to create a conflation. We prefer MT **miy-yôm** for the
temporal contrast with **'ên bākem zār** in the previous
bicolon.

[h]An intrusive fragment.

[i]Following 1QIsa[a], we omit the verbal suffix of MT
tēdā[c]ûhā _metri_ _causa_. In poetry the object would be
understood.

[j]Read **nĕtîbôt**. 1QIsa[a] has **nĕtîbîm**, while MT **nĕhārôt**
is due to contamination from v. 20.

[k]The imperfect **'ettēn** of 1QIsa[a] improves the meter.

[l]We transpose MT **ᶜam** with **ᶜammî** of the previous colon. G reads a suffix here, and this emendation improves the meter.

[m]The singular **yĕsappēr** yields a better meter. 1QIsa[a] **wyw'mrw** is secondary modernizing.

[n]G "I did not call you... I did not make you weary," reverses subject and object and reads the following verb **yg**[c] as a hiphil under the influence of v. 23b "Don't think that I made you serve..." It does, however, correctly understand **kî** as continuing and emphasizing the first negative.

[o]G omits the verb.

[p]1QIsa[a] and G prefix with the preposition **bĕ-**, probably by attraction to the following **bĕ-minḥâ** and **bi-lbônâ**.

[q]1QIsa[a] reads **lw' ᶜśyth ly' mnḥh**. G omits the entire colon due to homoeoarcheton.

[r]This is a tricolon. **ᶜōd** as attested in 1QIsa[a] improves the meter, and we further improve scansion by reading the long form of the pronoun **hû'â**. G is defective and lacks **lĕmaᶜanî ḥaṭṭō'tēkā**. An alternative reading as a bicolon would require the deletion of an **'ānōkî** as a dittography to give a balanced meter; but such an emendation would damage the parallel to v. 11 (see discussion).

[s]We read **hazkîr**, omitting the suffix on MT as a dittography of the following **nûn**. In this we have support from G: σὺ δὲ μνήσθητι καὶ κριθῶμεν. The issue to be remembered and recounted is not Yahweh, but Israel's sins. 1QIsa[a] reads the plural **hzkyrwny** and

yḥdyw for yaḥad. We accept the latter reading metri causa. G also transposes ḥaṭṭō'têkā from its original place following lĕmaᶜan in the previous verse, and some mss omit yaḥad.

ᵗHere sappēr is an infinitive construct functioning as an infinitive absolute since it follows the pattern of infinitive followed by nominative pronoun.

ᵘG reads the plural "fathers" and omits the verb.

ᵛWe emend MT 'ăḥallēl śārê qōdeš to []ḥillēlû śārê<kā> qodšî based upon G: καὶ ἐμίαναν οἱ ἄρχοντες [+ σου Gᴸ, GＱ] τὰ ἅγιά μου. śārê qōdeš is a late designation for a priestly office (1 Chr 24:5). However, the parallel structure is much improved in the G: three leadership offices in Israel are the subjects of three verbs for transgression. In MT, where this colon is the first of a tricolon describing Yahweh's punishment, its object, the "chiefs of the sanctuary", seems out of place in conjunction with the formulaic pair "Jacob"/"Israel. 1QIsaᵃ supports MT.

ᵂMT yaᶜzĕrekkā is probably a corruption of a participle ᶜōzĕrĕkā due to metathesis of wāw (confused in MT with yōd) and ᶜayin.

ˣ1QIsaᵃ begins the colon with kn, written supra lineam.

ʸMT bĕbên has long been a difficult crux. Most commentators emend the preposition bêt to kāp, following 1QIsaᵃ, G, Targ. G paraphrases "like grass (ḥāṣîr) among (bên) waters." Allegro[56] identifies byn as a

---

[56]J.M. Allegro, "The Meaning of byn in Isaiah XLIV,4," ZAW 63 (1951), 154-56; ZAW 64 (1952), 249-51. Cf. Schoors, 79 n. 1.

species of tree, cognate with Syriac **bînâ**, "tamarisk;"
Akk. **binu**, "tamarisk;" Arabic **bânon**, "moringa." He
would additionally emend **ḥāsîr** to **ḥāṣōr**, a **qatāl* form,
but this is unnecessary since in Hebrew **qātîl** is also
an adjectival form, and **ḥāsîr** is the adjective "green"
though often employed as a substantive. North identifies the <u>moringa</u> as a tree "remarkable for the intense
greeness of its leaves."[57] Hence we read **ka-bîn ḥāsîr**,
"like the verdant moringa tree."

[z]With G, Sym., read **yiqqārē'**, a niphal.

[aa]See discussion.

[bb]Read a pual **yĕkunneh** with Syr, Targ, G[O]. Other G
witnesses omit, probably a haplography due to the following **kh**; no G mss read an active form.

*   *   *   *

Form critics distinguish Isa 43:8-13 as a trial
speech, 43:16-21 as a salvation oracle, 43:22-28 as a
trial speech against Israel and 44:1-5 as a salvation
oracle. Verses 14-15 are probably a misplaced fragment
which cannot be translated with any certainty. Exegetes giving attention to literary structure have
variously delimited either one or two units, with some
agreement that 43:8 or 9 marks the beginning of a unit
and that 44:5 concludes a unit (see Table 1).

---

[57]North, <u>The Second Isaiah</u>, 133; North further makes
reference to **bēn pōrāt** in Gen 49:22 which he repoints
to **bîn pĕrāt**, but this latter conjecture is unlikely--
Joseph is rather likened to a "young steer" **ben parat**.
A suggestion by Guillaume ("A Note on the Meaning of
byn," <u>JTS</u> n.s. 13 [1962], 109-10) connecting **byn** to
Arabic **bînon**, "a region or tract of land," and translating "like a field of grass" must be rejected, since
bînon is probably a secondary nominal formation from
the preposition **baina**, "between," a cognate of Heb.
bēn; cf. Arabic **bain**, "interval."

Verbal repetition is one feature that binds together
all four subunits of Isa 43:8-44:5. Throughout Israel
is characterized as Yahweh's servant (43:10, 44:1-2),
the people Yahweh has chosen (bāḥar) and formed (yāṣar)
for himself (43:10,20-21; 44:1-2). The theme of Yahweh's watering the parched land so that nature sprouts
(ṣāmaḥ) and God's people may drink appears in 43:19-21
and 44:3-5. The contrast between the former things
(rī'šōnôt 43:9,18; 'ābîkā hā-rī'šōn 43:27), the sins
which brought on Yahweh's judgment, and the new thing,
a redeeming act of Yahweh that is to happen now (ᶜattâ
43:19, 44:1), is a polarity that structures the entire
unit. Deutero-Isaiah exploits the dialectic between
them in his various uses of the verbs zākar and sipper.
The "former things," will no longer be remembered ('al
tizkĕrû 43:18), yet with the imperative hazkîr Israel
is asked to recount her past sins and their consequences before Yahweh declares that henceforth he will no
longer remember them (lō' 'ezkōr 43:25). Similarly,
Israel is challenged to know Yahweh and his redemption
(tēdĕᶜû 43:10,19) and testify as Yahweh's witness
(43:10); yet first she is to recount (sappēr 43:26) her
past transgressions. Then through the promised redemption Israel will declare (yĕsappēr 43:21) Yahweh's
praise and confess (yō'mar) "I belong to Yahweh"
(44:5).

Yet verbal repetition and consistent thematic features do not exhaust the criteria for determining a
unit's compositional structure. They are not sufficient conditions for compositional unity because much
vocabulary and themes are common to large portions of
Deutero-Isaiah. Delimitation of the unit is assured
only by additional formal and rhetorical criteria: (1)
the presence of an overall chiastic or parallel stan-

zaic structure and (2) coherence with an established
form or traditional genre.

Isa 43:8-44:5 is a poem in four alternating stanzas
of 22, 20, 20, and 16 cola in a large-scale parallel
structure. The initial trial speech against the nations (43:8-13) is followed by the proclamation of a
new exodus and transformation of nature in 43:16-21;
likewise the second trial speech 43:22-28, this one
against Israel, is followed by another proclamation of
a transformation of nature in 44:1-5. Each of the two
trial speeches can be similarly analyzed into two
parts. The initial controversies, whether with the
gods (43:8-10) or with Israel (43:22-24), are followed
by proclamations of Yahweh's sovereignty which begin
with formulae Yahweh's self-identification: "I, I am
Yahweh" who acts in history (v. 11) and "I, I am He"
who forgives sins (v. 25). The second and fourth
stanzas which describe Yahweh's act transforming nature
also have a parallel structure: (a) opening address
formulae "Thus says Yahweh" combined with words of
praise (43:16-17; 44:1-2), (b) announcements of
Yahweh's act (43:18-19; 44:3-4), and (c) the response
of creation (43:20) and the people (43:21; 44:5) who
express their gratitude to God.

Finally, compositional analysis is mindful of underlying forms which may run through the entire unit or be
limited to an individual stanza. As a trial speech
against the gods of the nations, Isa 43:8-13 is of the
same form and partakes of the same antecedent traditions of the Jerusalem cultus as Isa 41:1-4 and 41:21-
29. In these trial speeches Yahweh arraigns the gods
of the nations and strips them of pretensions to divinity (cf. Ps 82). The scene opens in vv. 8-9 with a
summons to Israel, described as blind and deaf, and to

the gods of the nations, who are challenged as in the
other trial speeches of this genre to predict the
events of history. Yahweh calls upon the gods of the
nations to bring forth witnesses, presumably their
adherents among the assembled nations, in order to
justify themselves.[58] The syntax of v. 9b is ambiguous; who is the subject of these verbs? By reading
yašmî^{c}û with 1QIsa^{a}, the first verb of each colon
(yittěnû, yašmî^{c}û) describes actions of the defendant
gods and their adherents who are to designate witnesses
and to put forth their case. But the second verb in
each colon describes parallel actions of the jury or
audience which the gods solicit: it is petitioned for a
favorable verdict (wě-yiṣdāqû) that it might confirm
the truth of the gods' claims (wě-yō'měrû 'ěmet). As
with the similar appeal to the jury or audience for
vindication in 41:26 (wě-nō'mar ṣaddîq), it is safe to
assume that their witnesses are silent and Yahweh's
case stands; the gods' claims to divinity are rejected
(43:10c-11).

The traditions of the preexilic royal cult which
were noted for the diptych 41:1-42:17 would call for
notice of Israel's redemption and the procession of the
divine warrior to follow judgment upon the nations.
Isa 43:16-21, which proclaims a new exodus and a way
through a newly watered desert, fits this pattern.
God's servant Israel is vindicated in contrast to the
defeat of the nations and their gods. The trial speech
and the depiction of the journey through the desert are
evidently constituent subunits of a single traditional
pattern rather than two independent forms. A detailed
treatment of Isa 43:16-21 is deferred to pp. 77-81.

---

[58]Cf. Isa 44:9.

However, Isa 43:8-13 contains a second element
absent from the trial speeches in Isa 41: a reproof of
Israel for failing to fulfill its proper role as witness. The second trial speech of this unit, 43:22-28,
is entirely directed against Israel. The trial speech
against Israel stems from a different tradition than
the trial of the gods; its origins can be traced to the
preexilic prophetic **rîb** or covenant lawsuit, originally
a Northern tradition. Harvey has properly recognized
Isa 42:18-25 to be a truncated variation on the prophetic lawsuit.[59] However, 43:22-28 is so lacking in the
characteristic features of the prophetic lawsuit form--
notably the absence of a setting in the divine
council--that its origins in this genre have been
obscured. The relationship is clarified when this
subunit is viewed in its context, as elements of the
prophetic lawsuit extend through the entire compositional unit.

The prophetic lawsuit is in fact a significant
formal antecedent for the entire compositional unit
Isa 43:8-44:5. Texts including Mic 6:1-8, Isa 1:2-20,
Deut 32, and Ps 50 display the covenant lawsuit form or
modifications thereof,[60] to which one may add

[59]Julien Harvey, _Le plaidoyer prophétique contre
Israël après la rupture de l'alliance_ (Bourges: Desclee
de Brouwer, 1967) 58-59.

[60]See G. Ernest Wright, "The Lawsuit of God: A Form-
Critical Study of Deuteronomy 32," in _Israel's Prophetic Heritage,_ ed. B.W. Anderson and W. Harrelson (New
York: Harper & Row, 1962) 26-67; J. Harvey, "Le 'Rîb-
Pattern,' réquisitoire prophétique sur la rupture de
l'alliance," _Bib_ 43 (1962) 172-96; H. Huffmon, "The
Covenant Lawsuit in the Prophets," _JBL_ 78 (1959), 285-
95; E. Würthwein, "Der Ursprung der prophetischen
Gerichtsrede," _ZThK_ 49 (1952) 1-16. There are various
proposals as to the origin of the genre: Huffmon follows the form-critical analysis of Gunkel-Begrich de-

Jer 2:2-4:4[61] and Ezek 20:1-44. Each contains most of
the elements, in order, of a common structure:[62] (1) In
the introduction the scene is set in which Yahweh as
plaintiff invokes elements of nature, heaven and earth,
to hear his case.[63] (2) Then he states his charge,
often with a summons and with questioning. This charge
summarizes the proper covenant relationship between God
and Israel, i.e. father and son, which had been vio-
lated.[64]   (3) Yahweh the plaintiff recites his mighty
deeds of old, notably the exodus, to show the basis of
his claim against Israel.[65]   (4) He gives the indictment by reciting Israel's apostasy, especially the
history of apostasy of the fathers, often mixed with
refutations of the defendant's replies.[66] There is a
particular concern for cultic apostasy and insincere
sacrifices connected to this Gattung. (5) The sentence

---

fining the **rîb** as an oral genre stemming from secular
lawsuits; Würthwein's attempt to connect it with the
cult in Jerusalem leads to confusion with the trial of
the nations discussed above; Harvey sees a prophetic
imitation of international treaties; and Wright looks
for a background in a league covenant renewal festival
later adopted by northern prophetic circles.

[61]Cf. Muilenberg, JBL 88 (1969) 5, on Jer 2:2-4:4 as
displaying a single genre.

[62]Descriptions of the elements vary; this list is
taken from Wright, "Lawsuit," 52.

[63]Deut 32:1-2; Isa 1,2a,10; Jer 2:12; Mic 6:1-2;
Ps 50:1-6. In Ezek 20:1-3 it is replaced by the setting of the elders inquiring of the prophet.

[64]Mic 6:2b-3; Deut 32:4-6; Isa 1:2b-4; Jer 2:2-5,9;
Ps 50:7; Ezek 20:4a.

[65]Mic 6:4-5; Deut 32:7-14; Jer 2:6-7a; Ezek 20:5-
7,9-12.

[66]Mic 6:6-7; Deut 32:15-18; Isa 1:10-15; Jer 2:7b-
8,10-11,13,20-28,32-34; Ps 50:7-21; Ezek 20:8,13-32.

follows, bringing judgment upon Israel or justifying Israel's current distress.[67] (6) We must add a sixth subunit, which Wright considers to be an expansion of the lawsuit form but which Harvey recognizes to be integral to it:[68] the admonition to repentance or a promise of hope.[69] Wright remarks that the hopeful conclusion of Deut 32, where Yahweh for his own sake gets vengeance upon his enemies and redeems an undeserving Israel, is characteristic of the covenant lawsuit's secondary adaptation by the prophets in Northern Israel where it was used in a penitential and instructional setting.[70] We would rephrase Wright's analysis and assign this final subunit to the mature form of the covenant lawsuit as utilized by the prophets. The Gattung was a dynamic entity which went through an evolution, and while it may be possible to reconstruct its "original" form in a premonarchic covenant-renewal festival or even in a secular trial at the gate, in prophetic circles the form itself came to reflect a penitential and/or hortatory purpose.

Although the trial speech against the gods of the nations at the beginning of Isa 43:8-44:5 is a form quite distinct from the prophetic lawsuit, Deutero-Isaiah, the consummate artist, crafts this trial speech to do double duty. It has integrity as a trial of the gods, and in addition it serves as an elaborate intro-

_____

[67]Deut 32:19-25; Isa 1:5-9; Jer 2:14-19,30,35-37; Ezek 20:33-39; Ps 50:22.

[68]Harvey, Bib 43 (1962) 177-180.

[69]Deut 32:35-43, Mic 6:8, Isa 1:16-20, Ezek 20:40-44; Ps 50:14-15,23; Jer 3:1-4:4.

[70]Wright, "Lawsuit," 56-66.

duction for a lawsuit against Israel by providing its
characteristic setting against an audience of witnesses.
Once the gods of the nations have been rebuked, they
recede into the background and are not heard from
again. They become as silent observers, functioning
much as the olden gods heaven and earth in the classical **rîb**, while Yahweh upbraids Israel for not fulfilling her specific calling. The trial of the nations is
a suitable setting for a lawsuit against Israel because
Israel's purpose, as Yahweh's chosen servant and witness, is precisely to manifest Yahweh's sovereignty in
the sight of the nations (43:9-10,21).[71]

In vv. 10-13 Yahweh reminds Israel of her true
calling as "witness" and "servant," recalling an age of
faith prior to the exile when "there was no stranger
among you" (43:12a). Then Israel had recognized Yahweh
as Savior and as the God who had foretold what he would
do. This is a typical feature of the second element of
the lawsuit, where Israel is reminded of her covenantal
relationship in former times before her rebellion:
"sons I have reared and brought up" (Isa 1:2), "Do you
thus requite Yahweh, you foolish and senseless people?
Is He not your Father who created you, who made you and
established you?" (Deut 32:6), or "I remember the devo-
tion of your youth, your love as a bride..." (Jer 2:2-
3). In the tradition of these earlier prophetic lawsuits, Deutero-Isaiah accuses Israel of falling from
intimacy with God even though God has not changed: "you
were my witnesses, and I was God, but also henceforth I
am He" (43:12-13). But Israel had become blind and
deaf (43:8).

---

[71]Cf. Isa 48:9,11.

Isa 43:16-21 should contain the third subunit of the
rîb, the recitation of Yahweh's mighty deeds of old.
The motif of remembrance is present.[72] However, as we
noted, this subunit is primarily a proclamation of
salvation associated with the conflict-victory pattern
of the Zion traditions which inform Deutero-Isaiah's
trial of the gods, and hence it is a suitable continuation of the trial speech in 43:8-13. In conformity
with the tradition of the trial of the gods and unlike
the prophetic lawsuit against Israel, this is a proclamation of a new act of salvation and not a recollection
of the epic past. Nevertheless, as with the initial
trial speech against the gods, Deutero-Isaiah has
crafted this subunit to serve a double purpose. The
statement of God's past and present saving deeds functions as would the historical prologue of the covenant
lawsuit against Israel: it sets up the grounds for the
accusation in vv. 22-28. The proclamation of a new
exodus, founded upon the power of the same God who
conducted Israel on the first exodus, establishes
Yahweh's case as plaintiff, as the One who is ever able
to save at His own choosing.

In keeping with the cultic traditions behind the
trial of the gods, this restatement of the exodus
recalls Ps 77, an older cultic elaboration of the
exodus with ritual motifs of the storm-god's victory
over Sea:

12. I will remember (**'ezkōr**) the deeds of Yahweh,
        yea, I will remember (**'ezkĕrâ**) your wonders of old.
    I will tell of all your works,
        I will meditate upon your mighty deeds...

---

[72]Cf. Deut 32:7 where the poet asks the young
Israelite to "remember the days of old" in order to
know the righteous judgment and vindication of Yahweh.

17. The waters saw you, O God,
       the waters saw you and writhed,
       yea, the deeps trembled.
18. The clouds poured out water,
       the skies gave forth voice,
       yea, your arrows sped all about.
19. The noise of your thunder was in the whirlwind,
       lightnings lit up the earth,
       the land trembled and shook.
20. Your way was through the Sea (bay-yām darkĕkā),
       your paths in the mighty waters (bĕ-mayim rabbîm),
       your footprints were not observed.[73]
21. You led your people (ᶜammekā) like sheep,
       by the hand of Moses and Aaron.

In both Ps 77 and Isa 43:16-21 the exodus is depicted
as a path or way through the "sea" and the "mighty
waters," a poetic doublet influenced by the tradition
of the storm god defeating his enemy Sea. This motif
is explicit in the psalm where the waters writhe and
tremble at Yahweh's attack, and is echoed in the Isaiah
text (43:20) where Yahweh's theophany in the storm
brings fructifying rains to the desert. Both texts
conclude with a reference to the epic tradition of God
leading his people in the wilderness and giving them
water from the desert rocks. Deutero-Isaiah is drawing
upon the companion mythic and epic traditions which had
merged in the royal cult. Yet he explicitly contra-
dicts the theme of the psalm; he calls upon the people
not to remember them.

    In the pre-exilic cult, the remembrance of "the
former things" had inspired trust in Yahweh who would
uphold the cause of his people, so much so that earlier
prophets had attacked Israel's false self-assurance
which relied on Yahweh's cultic presence without the

---

[73]This figure also influences the depiction of
Cyrus's march in Isa 41:3, further evidence that
Deutero-Isaiah knew of this psalm.

requisite righteousness.[74] But with the exile such
remembrance by itself could not sustain hope. With the
temple's destruction the cultic celebrations of salvation history had ceased, to be replaced by fasts and
lamentations accompanied by recitations of a history of
apostasy, as, for example, the contemporary exilic
version of the Deuteronomistic History (Dtr$_2$).[75] This
is precisely Deutero-Isaiah's position in the following
indictment of Israel in the rîb (vv. 22-28): Israel's
cult had been false, and if there was anything for
Israel to remember about the former days, it would be
her continual violations of covenant (43:26). Hence
the "former things" (ri'šōnôt) in 43:18 stand in an
ambiguous relation to the exodus, a salvation which
from the vantage point of the exile with its "return to
Egypt" had come to naught.[76] Rather, in line with its
meaning elsewhere,[77] the "former things" refer to the
entire sweep of Israel's history, from the exodus whose
glory had been tarnished by exile to the more recent
judgments upon Israel for her transgressions
(43:9,12,25-28) which had been foretold by the
prophets.[78]

---

[74]Amos 3:2; 5:18-24; 9:7; Jer 7:1-15.

[75]Cf. Zech 7:5-14; Isa 58:1-9; Pss 74, 106.

[76]Hos 9:3; Deut 29:68. See Richard E. Friedman,
"From Egypt to Egypt: Dtr^1 and Dtr^2," in Traditions in
Transformation, Turning Points in Biblical Faith, ed.
B. Halpern and J. D. Levenson (Winona Lake, IN: Eisen-
brauns, 1981).

[77]Isa 41:22,27; 42:9; 44:6; 46:9; 48:3.

[78]The "former things" in this passage has often been
understood to refer to the saving event of the exodus
in light of the apparent typology of exodus/new exodus.
See B. W. Anderson, "Exodus Typology in Second Isaiah,"

The former things, robbed by events of any positive connotations in themselves, retained meaning for Deutero-Isaiah only as proofs of Yahweh's power to bring to pass his word. Wherever the prophet recalls the former things in order to convince his audience that Yahweh is sovereign in history, the God who brings to pass what he announces, his context is the announcement of a "new thing," i.e. Cyrus's conquest of Babylon[79] and the return of the exiles.[80] Deutero-Isaiah, like the Deuteronomistic Historian, emphasized the predictive element of prophecy as evidence of Yahweh's reality as the Lord of history. The fulfillment of past prophecy, though often the disastrous realization of words of judgment, became the basis for

---

in Israel's Prophetic Heritage, ed. B. W. Anderson and W. Harrelson (New York: Harper & Row, 1962) 185-88; Antoon Schoors, "Les choses antérieures et les choses nouvelles dans les oracles deutéro-isaïens," ETL 40 (1964) 24,44; I am God your Savior, 94-5. Schoors himself recognizes this meaning of the former things to be at odds with the meaning of ri'šōnōt in the trial speeches as Israel's prophesied judgments. Only von Waldow ("Anlass und Hintergrund," 240) recognizes that ri'šōnōt in 43:18 has a wider reference to the situation of exile and is not limited to the old exodus/new exodus typology. C. R. North, "The 'Former Things' and the 'New Things' in Deutero-Isaiah," in Studies in Old Testament Prophecy, ed. H. H. Rowley (Edinburgh: T & T Clark, 1950) 111-126, puts forward a doubtful hypothesis of earlier lost prophecies of Deutero-Isaiah predicting the rise of Cyrus. Our view of the former things as Yahweh's acts both saving and judging Israel accords well with recent attempts to view Deutero-Isaiah in its canonical context as commenting on and supplementing the words of his namesake. See Brevard Childs, Introduction to the Old Testament as Scripture (Philadelphia: Fortress, 1982) 328-29.

[79]Isa 41:1-4,21-29; 43:9-10; 45:20-21; 46:8-11; 48:1-16.

[80]Isa 42:5-9; 42:18-43:7; 43:19-21.

confidence in Yahweh's new promises of salvation.[81]

Deutero-Isaiah's "new thing" differed from the
memories of the exodus enshrined in the cult not in
form, but only in its newness. The promised manifestation of Yahweh's might is both the enactment of a
cultic processional way and a recollection of the exodus. In the Jerusalem cult where these motifs had
already merged, historical memory had become one with
the temporally fluid world of myth and ritual. The
prophet may therefore project the exodus motif into the
future in announcing Israel's imminent eschatological
redemption. Through the new exodus, Israel will once
again know (v. 19) of Yahweh's mighty and gracious
deeds and thereby make a good witness: "the people whom
I formed for myself that they might recount my praise"
(43:21). At the same time, Yahweh's saving deed, whether recollected in the cult or confidently anticipated
in the near future, may serve as the basis for the
indictment of Israel in the covenant lawsuit; Israel
should already know her relationship to the saving God
(43:26).

Isa 43:22-28, the trial speech against Israel
proper, functions as the fourth section of the prophetic lawsuit--the indictment. The specific grounds of
the indictment are cultic abuses and insincere sacrifice. This is the only passage in Deutero-Isaiah concerned with sacrifices, and its subject matter is
characteristic of covenant lawsuits.[82] There is no

---

[81]Cf. Isa 44:7-8; 48:3-8; 55:10-11. Cf. W. Brueggemann, "Isaiah 55 and Deuteronomic Theology," ZAW 80
(1968), 197; G. von Rad, Studies in Deuteronomy, trans.
D. Stalker (London: SCM, 1953) 78-91.

[82]Cf. Mic 6:6-7, Ps 50:7-15, Isa 1:10-15 and
Ezek 20:13-32.

inconsistency in the change of subjects in v. 23b.;
just as Israel's cultic acts did not in actuality serve
and honor Yahweh, so Yahweh had never asked for such
things.[83] Furthermore, v. 25 makes clear that Yahweh's
forgiveness and redemptive purpose is entirely his own
and by no means coerced by the sham faithfulness of
Israel. That Israel's redemption is unmerited is another theme common to the prophetic lawsuit; Yahweh acts
unilaterally "for the sake of my name, that it should
not be profaned in the sight of the nations."[84]

Verses 26-28 contain the other major element found
in indictments of covenant lawsuits, the behavior of
the ancestors.[85] This recounting comes in reply to the
implied protestations of Israel in v. 26.[86] The
"father of old" has been surmised to be Jacob, the
ancestor of the cult at Bethel whose shrine according
to Dtr_2 and Hos 12:3-5 became the occasion of Ephraim's
sin.[87] Yet Deutero-Isaiah has no truck with Bethel or
the Northern Kingdom. He draws widely upon Penta-
teuchal and other Israelite traditions which could
provide a host of other candidates: Aaron, ancestor of
the Jerusalem priesthood, comes immediately to mind.
The identity of this ancestor remains an open question.

---

[83]Evidently prophetic traditions considered the
sacrificial system to be an innovation of the royal
cult that had not been a part of the original Mosaic
covenant; cf. Jer 7:20-21. Our translation is indebted
to North, The Second Isaiah, 42.

[84]Ezek 20:14,22,44, cf. Deut 32:26-27.

[85]Cf. Deut 32:15ff., Jer 2:8,30, Ezek 20:8,13-30.

[86]Cf. Isa 1:18; Jer 2:23,29; Ezek 20:31.

[87]Westermann, 133; Cf. B.J. Van der Merwe, Penta-
teuchtradisies in die prediking van Deuterojesaja,
diss., Groningen, 1955, 132-39.

By melîṣ, a word ordinarily denoting a secular inter-
preter (Gen 42:23; cf. the Abydos inscription KAI
49,17), or an official envoy or māl'āk (2 Chr 32:31,
Job 33:23), Deutero-Isaiah is referring to cultic officials and prophets, those intermediaries responsible
for right worship. Similarly the "princes who defiled
my sanctuary" are the preexilic priesthood. Thus the
tricolon lists the sins of the leaders of Israel's cult
and continues the theme of cultic improprieties begun
in vv. 22-24. The fifth section of the lawsuit, the
sentence, is compressed into v. 28bc.

Finally, in 44:1-5 Deutero-Isaiah concludes the
lawsuit by announcing Israel's redemption and pointing
to the return to Zion, a change in Israel's fortune
introduced by wĕ-ᶜattâ. Concluding this lawsuit
against Israel with a salvation oracle has a parallel
in Isa 42:18-43:7. There the concluding salvation
oracle likewise opens with the transitional word
wĕ-ᶜattâ. This temporal adverb presumes a change from
an earlier state of despair[88] and sets up several
contrasts: the former state of destruction (hērem
43:28) is healed and the land once again becomes fruitful (44:3a,4); the priesthood, the mĕlîṣîm and śārîm
whose sins had defiled the sanctuary (43:28),[89] will be
restored with the appearance of people newly dedicated
to Yahweh (44:5); and Israel, who in the past had
neglected to call upon Yahweh (43:22-23), would soon
call themselves Yahweh's people (44:5).

---

[88]Westermann, Isaiah 40-66, 134. Cf. Isa 43:1.

[89]Cf. Ezek 22:26, Zeph 3:4.

The compositional context of this stanza leaves no
warrant for reading the final verses as a prophecy of
proselytes joining the people of Israel, as some would
contend.[90] We noted that at 43:16-21 he proclaims
Israel's redemption as a new exodus, when once again
the wilderness will flow with sweet water. 44:1-5
picks up the theme of water in the wilderness once
more, and, as in 43:20-21, the objects of Yahweh's
salvation are twofold: nature and Israel. Just as the
water poured on the dry ground in v. 3a yields flour-
ishing trees in v. 4, similarly the spirit and blessing
poured on Israel's offspring in v. 3b yields a multitude of people who call themselves Israel and give
allegiance to Yahweh. Israel's failure to call
(qārā'tā) in 43:22 is remedied, for now the people are
not ashamed to be called (yiqqārē') "Israel." If those
who take on new names were proselytes, they become part
of the people of Israel with no apparent distinction.
Yet elsewhere (Isa 49:7,22-23; 55:3-5) the kings and
nations who come to Israel remain distinct and subservient. The description of the Israelites taking on new
names refers rather to the fact that in Babylon many
Jews--Sheshbazzar, Zerubbabel, Esther and Mordecai
among those attested in the Bible--had adopted Babylonian names. Further evidence of Babylonian name-giving
in Jewish families has been gleaned from the Murashu
documents from Nippur.[91]

---

[90]So Elliger, Jesaja II, BKAT 11 (Neukirchen, 1970),
391-94; Simon, 113; Westermann, 136-8; North, 132-4,
Whybray, Isaiah 40-66, 95. It is denied by Torrey,
344.

[91]See Michael D. Coogan, "Life in the Diaspora: Jews
at Nippur in the Fifth Century B.C.," in The Biblical
Archaeologist Reader, IV, ed. E.F. Campbell and D.N.
Freedman (Sheffield: Almond Press, 1983), 249-56.

The image in v. 5 describes not only a reconstitu-
tion of the people Israel, but probably also alludes to
their function as a new or renewed priesthood, one
which will remedy the sins of Israel's former
"mediators" and "leaders". The verb 'essōq nowhere
else has rûḥ as its object. When yāsaq is used of a
person it often refers to an anointing with oil, to
invest authority on priests[92] and kings.[93] The rûḥ of
Yahweh in Deutero-Isaiah, when it does not mean
"breath" or "wind" as in 40:7, 41:29, comes out of the
tradition of rûḥ as the power of prophecy.[94] Here the
collocation of 'essōq and rûḥî probably alludes to the
investing of Israel with the authority and spirit of
prophecy, restoring the role of priest and of "mediator." We can similarly understand the difficult colon
wě-zeh yiktōb yādô la-yhwh. Most emend yādô to bě-yādô
as suggested by G[OL], Aq., Thdt.: χειρὶ αὐτοῦ. 1QIsa[a]
reads ydwhy, an Aramaic third person singular suffix on
the dual. But the unusual grammar of MT, lacking a
preposition cal or bě- which is otherwise required for
the indirect object of kātab either to signify the
tatooing a mark of slave ownership on the hand[95] or the
wearing of phylacteries (Deut 6:8), encourages us to
look elsewhere. The investiture of the Levites in
Exod 32:26-29 provides a ready alternative. There
Moses, disgusted with the people dancing about the
golden calf, stands at the entrance to the camp and

---

[92]Cf. Exod 29:7; Lev 8:12,15; 14:26.

[93]Cf. 1 Sam 10:1; 2 Kgs 9:6.

[94]Cf. Isa 42:1; cf. Num 11:29; 1 Kgs 22:23.

[95]Elliger, 393.

calls out, "who is for Yahweh?" (**way-yō'mer mî la-yhwh**). The Levites respond, and once they had slaughtered the transgressors, Moses says to them: "you have consecrated yourselves to Yahweh this day" (**millě'û yedkem hay-yôm la-yhwh**). The Chronicler uses the expression **yādô** la-yhwh either with the verb **millē'** or **nātan** (1 Chr 29:5; 2 Chr 29:31; 30:8) of people making offerings to the temple, and there it does not refer exclusively to priests or Levites, but to all who support the cult. In this idiom, **yād** refers to the self and not to a literal hand. Isa 44:5 uses the same phrase to refer to a people who will offer themselves to the service of God, perhaps a new priest-hood replacing the corrupt old **śārîm** and **mělîsîm**, who "enroll themselves to Yahweh." Thus the culmination of the promised restoration is a people collectively serving the new temple. Deutero-Isaiah's **rîb** ends pre-cisely at the same point as the lawsuit in Ezekiel:

> For on my holy mountain, the mountain height of Israel, says the Lord God, there all the house of Israel, all of them, shall serve me in the land; there I will accept them, and there I will require your contributions and the choic-est of your gifts, with all your sacred offer-ings. As a pleasing odor I will accept you, when I bring you out from the peoples, and gather you out of the countries where you have been scattered, and I will manifest my holiness among you in the sight of the nations. (Ezek 20:40-41).

As in Ezek 20:41, Deutero-Isaiah's lawsuit against Israel is prosecuted in the context of the nations. For Deutero-Isaiah and Ezekiel, who both lived in exile, the nations were always in the background as the standard by which Israel was measured. Deutero-Isaiah understood Israel's covenant responsibility as a voca-

tion to be Yahweh's servant (43:10; 44:1,2) and witness
(43:10,12) before the nations of the world, as Yahweh's
own chosen people (43:1,7,21; 44:2,5). As Yahweh's
servant and witness, Israel could testify to Yahweh's
glory before the nations only by first dedicating herself wholly and sincerely to God. The structure of Isa
43:8-44:5 makes this point explicit. As a prophetic
lawsuit like Mic 6:1-8, it exhorts Israel to its proper
covenant relationship. But at the same time this
exhortation is set within a trial where all the nations
have been assembled.

Thus Isa 43:8-44:5 evinces extensive rhetorical
parallelism with two distinct trial speeches and two
announcements of a new exodus and transformation of
nature. It combines two distinct preexilic traditions,
the conflict-victory over the nations from the royal
cult and the prophetic lawsuit, playing them off one
another with grace and irony. The trial of the nations
becomes the setting for a prophetic lawsuit against
Israel. The proclamation of Israel's salvation which
typically follows upon the judgment of the gods also
subsumes the mighty acts of the covenant lawsuit's
historical prologue. The motif of remembrance of
Yahweh's mighty acts from both the lawsuit and the Zion
traditions is inverted and related to the remembrance
of Israel's past transgressions and Yahweh's acts of
judgment. Throughout this unit, the twin themes of
judgment and salvation, corresponding to the two traditions of the prophetic lawsuit against Israel and the
cultic judgment upon the gods of the nations, are held
in dialectical tension.

3. Isa 45:14-25: A Trial Speech Inviting the Nations to Accept Yahweh's Universal Sovereignty

This unit contains a trial speech directed to the nations which concludes with one of the prophet's most striking universalist statements, an admonition to all nations to turn and receive Yahweh's salvation. It is followed by Yahweh's self-imprecation that surely all the world's peoples will recognize his sovereignty. The trial speech and admonition conclude a unit which begins with an eschatological vision of the nations bearing tribute to Jerusalem. It is a unit crafted with an extensive rhetorical structure, most notably an envelope construction formed by two confessions of the nations in vv. 14d-17 and 24-25.

45:14-17	meter
Thus says Yahweh:	rubric
Workers[a] from Egypt and traders from Ethiopia,	10
Sabeans, bearing[b] tribute,	8
Will come over to you and become yours,	9
they will follow after you;	5
In chains they will come over [ ][c]and fall prostrate,	10
they will petition you:	6
	1:b::1:b::1:b

"Surely in your midst is God, and there is none other,[d] 6
    nothing else is God.   4
Surely you are the invisible God,   8
        the Go[ ]d of Israel, the Savior.[e]   6
They are ashamed, even embarrased, [   ][f]   7
    those who make images.[g]   5
Israel is vindicated by Yahweh,   8
    a salvation everlasting;   6
You shall not be ashamed, nor embarrased,   10
    forever and ever."   5
                          1:b::1:b::1:b::1:b::1:b

45:18-19

For thus says Yahweh-- rubric
Creator of the heavens, 5
He is God; 4
Fashioner of the earth and its maker, 7
he established it; 4
He did not create it as chaos;[h] 6
he fashioned it to be inhabited: 5
x:b:b::l:b::l:b

"I am Yahweh and there is no other-- 7
I did not speak in secret, 6
in a place in the dark underworld; 5
I did not say to the offspring of Jacob, 8
'seek me[i] in chaos.' 6
I am Yahweh who speaks justice, 7
and announces vindication." 5
l:b:b::l:b::l:b

45:20-21

"Come and assemble yourselves; 7
gather yourselves together,[j] 6
survivors of the nations! 6
They do not know, 4
who carry about their wooden idols; 6
Who pray to a god 6
who cannot save.[k] 3
l:b:b::b:l::l:b

Declare and present (your case), 7
yea, take counsel[l] together![m] 6
Who announced this long ago? 6
who foretold it of old?[n] 5
Was it not I, Yahweh? 6
there is no other God[o] besides me; 9
Righteous and saving God, 6
there is none other than I." 4
l:b::l:b::b:l::l:b

45:22-25

"Turn to me and be saved,[p] 9
all the ends of the earth! 4
Because I am God, and there is no other, 7
by myself I swear. 4
From my mouth goes forth vindication; 7
a decree[q] that is irrevocable: 5
'To me every knee[r] shall bend, 6
every tongue shall swear.'" 6
l:b::l:b::l:b::l:b

"Truly with Yahweh," let it be said,[s]   8
    "is victory and might.   5
To him will come in shame[t] $\overline{9}$
    all who were incensed at him;   4
In Yahweh shall triumph and glory   1$\overline{1}$
    all the descendents of Israel."[u]   5
                                     1:b::1:b::1:b

TEXTUAL NOTES

[a]With North[96] we emend MT **yĕgîc**, "produce," to **yĕgîcê**, "workers," and MT **sĕḥar**, "merchandise," to **sōḥĕrê**, "traders." In parallel with the Sabeans, all three subjects of this description of a pilgrimage are groups of people.

[b]Where MT has **middâ** 1QIsa[a] reads **middôt**. In Neh 5:4 **middâ** means "tribute", a loan word from Akk. **mandattu**, and that is apparently what is meant here. Therefore we suggest an emendation of MT **'anšê**, "men," to **nōśĕ'ê**, "bearers," in which case the MT could have arisen by a metathesis. The idiom **'îš middâ**, "man of stature," (cf. 1 Chr 11:23, 20:6, 2 Sam 21:20 [emended]), appropriate for the Ethiopians and their Sabean neighbors, "a nation tall and smooth" (Isa 18:2,7), could have encouraged acceptance of this corruption.

[c]See discussion.

[d]G: καὶ ἐροῦσιν οὐκ ἔστι πλὴν σοῦ; ἔστι is an inner-Greek corruption of ἔτι, and the preceding Hebrew consonants have been read as **'mrw**.

[e]Westermann and Spykerboer consider this verse to be intrusive. MT **'attâ** marks a change of addressee from Jerusalem to Yahweh; hence Duhm and others emend to **'ittāk**. Furthermore, it has a balanced 8:8 meter in a passage in 1:b meter; Torrey recognizes this latter

---

[96]Cf. North, _The Second Isaiah_, 155-6.

problem and omits **môšîᶜ**. We prefer to retain the verse
as authentic and look for expansion by an innocuous
mechanical scribal error rather than propose it to be a
conscious gloss. Suitable 1:b meter can be restored by
positing an original **'ēl** as in the first colon which
was later expanded to the idiomatic **'ĕlōhê**. The verse
is integral to the polemic against idolatry implicit in
vv. 15-17, the opening **'ākēn** is typical of confessions,
and there is repetition of the root **str** and **môšîᶜ** elsewhere in the unit.

ᶠWe omit MT **kullām yaḥdāw hālĕkû bak-kĕlimmâ** as a
secondary expansion. For the awkward phrase **kullām
yaḥdâw** G has πάντες οἱ ἀντικείμενοι αὐτῷ, which is
nearly identical to its translation of **kol neḥĕrîm bāk**
in 41:11. Yet G is a questionable basis for reconstruction and is almost certainly a secondary misreading of the consonantal MT--rendering **klmyḥdyw** as
klnḥryw. Proper Hebrew grammar requires that the niphal
of **ḥārâ** be followed by the preposition **bĕ-** as in 45:24
and 41:11. North seeks to obviate this difficulty by
assuming an original Qal participle of **nḥr**, "to
snort,"[97] but regardless, the verb in 45:24 and 41:11
takes the preposition **be-**. More likely, **klm yḥdw** is a
dittography of **niklĕmû ḥārāšê**, which could have been
read with **dālet/rēš** and **wâw/yōd** confusion as **n]klmy
ḥd[šy**. Lacking a b colon, one of the l cola would also
be a secondary and conflate variant. They are certainly quite similar, and the shape of the dittography
suggests that **hālĕkû bak-kĕlimmâ** was the secondary
expansion.

---

[97]Following Driver, _JTS_ 36 (1935), 398f.

gReading with 1QIsaᵃ ṣwrym, "images," for MT ṣîrîm,
"pangs." Cf. Ps 49:15: ketîb ṣyrm, qerē' ṣûrām, "their
form." The words are difficult, and G is of little
help, reading ἐγκαινίζεσθε πρός με νῆσοι which is probably interpretive of MT, reading dālet for rēš (ḥdš),
the yōd as a first person suffix, and 'iyyîm for ṣiyyîm
(lacking rēš).

hWhere MT reads tōhû 1QIsaᵃ has lĕ-tōhû; G ἐις
κενόν. The lāmed arose by dittography and under influence of lĕ-šebet. Bārā' can take two direct objects
without a preposition: cf. Isa 65:18. G omits the
following colon.

iFor MT baqqĕšûnî G has ζητήσατε ἐγώ εἰμι < *baqqĕšû
'ănî.

j1QIsaᵃ reads w'tyw in place of yaḥdāw.

kWestermann omits v. 20b, a condemnation of idolatry, as a gloss in accordance with his general attribution of idol passages to a later editor. But these two
bicola are essential to the prosody of a stanza which
is metrically identical to v. 19. They also repeat the
key word yōṣîᶜ (cf. vv. 21,22). For MT 'ēl G has the
plural θεούς, probably an inner-Greek corruption.

lG reads γνῶσιν < *ywdᶜw for MT ywᶜṣw. This is
probably an instance of modernizing.

mRead yaḥad instead of MT yaḥdāw metri causa.

nFor MT mē-'āz G reads τότε < *'āz due to haplography of mem.

oG omits both 'ĕlōhîm and the following 'ēl.

p1QIsaᵃ has the hiphil imperative whwšyᶜw in place
of the rare niphal hiwwāšĕᶜû in MT.

^q G < *dābāray, from wāw/yōd confusion of MT
(=1QIsa^a) dābār wĕ-. A metrically superior reading
omits the conjunction from MT.

^r1QIsa^a bwrk indicates a qutl biform of MT berek.⁹⁸

^sWhere MT has lî 'āmar Schoors reads li-yē''āmar
emphatic lāmed and imperfect niphal;⁹⁹ the niphal is
based upon 1QIsa^a ly' y'mr. Westermann reads lē'mōr
with G λεγῶν and transposes it to the beginning of the
line, but the Qumran reading is lectio difficilior and
does not require any transposition.

^tRead the plural yābō'û with 1QIsa^a and G. MT yābô'
may be due to metathesis of wāw and 'ālep. The pair of
verbs yābō'û wĕ-yēbōšû form a hendyadis.

^uG adds expansions ἐν τῷ θεῷ and υἱῶν.

The extent and form of Isa 45:14-25 are debated.
While North, Muilenberg and Clifford view it as a
complete unit, Bonnard, Torrey and Haran attach it to
the Cyrus oracle giving a unit 44:24-45:25 (see Table
1). By itself, 45:14ff. appears to lack a proper
introduction, and the reference to Zion implied by the
second person feminine singular suffixes in v. 14 is
unexpected. But following upon 45:13, where Cyrus
rebuilds Jerusalem "without price or reward," the image
of gifts coming to Jerusalem fits nicely. There are
also verbal connections: the phrase "I am Yhwh and
there is none other" is repeated in vv. 5, 6, 18, 21

---

⁹⁸See Kutscher (pp. 473-78) on evidence for a u-i
shift in Tiberian Hebrew, with Qumran preserving the
older vocalization.

⁹⁹Schoors, I am God your Savior, 236f.; Cf. M.
Dahood, "Hebrew-Ugaritic Lexicography," Bib 47 (1966),
407-8.

and 22, and the roots yšᶜ and ṣdq occur 15 times in
45:8-25.[100]   The hymnic v. 18 also may hark back to
44:24-26 and 45:6b-7. On the other hand, Isa 44:24-
45:13 is a well-crafted chiastic structure,[101] while
45:14-25 has its own distinct chiastic arrangement.
While discussing 45:14-25 as a unit, we recognize it to
be a companion chapter which was written to follow
immediately upon the Cyrus oracle.

Most form critics distinguish in 45:14-25 two or
three independent oracles: vv. 14-17 and 18-25 or vv.
14-17, 18-19 and 20-25. Verses 14-17 are addressed to
Zion and appear to be comforting her, while vv. 18-25
are addressed to the nations for the purpose of exhortation. Vv. 14-17 describe the future well-being of
Zion, while vv. 18-25 stress the efficacy of Yahweh's
word to come to pass and bring vindication. Westermann
considers vv. 14-17 to be a collection of fragments.[102]
Yet even form critics recognize that vv. 18-25 constitute a mixed oracle: Schoors analyzes it into a trial
speech (vv. 18-21) and an admonition directed at the
"survivors of the nations" (vv. 22-25); Westermann sub-
divides it into two disputations addressed to the
nations (v. 18) and to Israel (v. 19) followed by a
trial speech addressed to the nations (vv. 20-25).[103]
Since vv. 18-25 is already a mixed oracle containing
several genres, arguments against including vv. 14-17
on formal grounds loose force.

---

[100]Spykerboer, Structure and Composition, 135-136.
He sees 45:9-25 as an integrated subunit introduced by
the hymnic passage 45:8.

[101]See below, pp. 200-202.

[102]Westermann, 168-71; Cf. Schoors, 30.

[103]Westermann, 171-6; Schoors, 233-38.

The integrity of Isa 45:14-25 as a compositional
unit is supported by a number of structural and rhetorical features. First, we can identify a large scale
envelope construction, a type of literary architecture
of which Deutero-Isaiah is fond.[104] The parallel confessions of the nations and their submission to Yahweh
in vv. 14d-17 and 24-25 form a large inclusio framing
the trial speech (vv. 18-21). Second, 45:14-25 has a
four part stanzaic structure. Each stanza--vv. 14-17,
18-19, 20-21 and 22-25--is of approximately equal
length: 17, 14, 15 and 14 cola respectively,[1.] and
each is composed of two strophes.[106] Third, the oracle
is in qinah meter throughout. Of the unit's eight
strophes (two strophes in each stanza) some are pure
qinah meter with three or four 1:b bicola; others have
an initial 1:b:b tricolon (often including a rubric)
followed by two 1:b bicola. Fourth, pivotal to the
structure of this piece is the monotheistic statement,
repeated in various forms, "I am God/Yahweh, and there
is none other" (vv. 14d, 18d, 21cd and 22b). These
statements of self-identification point to a common
three-part rhetorical structure for each stanza: first

---

[104]cf. 44:24-45:13; 52:13-53:12.

[105]Note this count includes the emendation of
vv. 14-17 which results in removing 2 cola; see textual
note #f.

[106]The definition of prosodic units larger than the
bicolon or tricolon is complicated by the fact that
this poetry does not recognize a single level of organization, but often nests several levels together. Here
the "stanza" of 14-15 cola is built of a pair of
"strophes" or "stanzas" each of 7-8 cola. There is no
standard way to refer to these nested units. We will
arbitrarily call the larger rhetorical unit the stanza
and the smaller unit the strophe. The smallest unit
is, of course, the individual bicolon or tricolon.

a view towards the nations (vv. 14a-c, 20-21a and 22a)
or the inhabited earth (v. 18a-c); then the monotheistic statement "I am God and there is none other;" and
finally a word about Yahweh's righteous (ṣedeq and
môšîᶜ) attitude (vv. 19c, 21d and 23a) vindicating
Israel (vv. 17, 19b and 25). Fifth, there are connections in vocabulary: the frequent use of the root wšᶜ
(vv. 15, 17, 20, 21 and 22) including the rare niphal
(vv. 17 and 22), ṣdq (vv. 19, 21, 23, 24 and 25), bwš
(vv. 16, 17 and 24), yitpallēl of the nations who pray
to Zion (v. 14) and to their idols (v. 20), str of
Yahweh's hiddenness and revelation (vv. 15,19), and
nōśě'îm of the nations who carry their idols (v. 20)
and tribute to Zion (v. 14 [emended]). This structure
is summarized in Table 3.

    Torrey correctly scans v. 14 in 1:b meter, and is
led to omit baz-ziqqîm metri causa as a later expansion.[107] However, this emendation begs the question of
the role of the nations in this passage. It is more
likely that a dittography of the repeated 'ēlayik is
responsible for disrupting the meter. The alternative
without emendation would be to scan the verse in a
balanced short meter. But this is unacceptable as it
yields but a list of parallel items, a type of degener-
ate prosody found nowhere else in Deutero-Isaiah but
which becomes characteristic of late 5th century and
early 4th century poetry.[108]

---

[107]Torrey, 360.

[108]If scanned in balanced b:b meter, v. 14 is
composed of lists of three and six parallel elements:

	meter	
Workers from Egypt,	4	
merchants from Ethiopia	4	
and Sabeans, men of stature,	8	b:b:1

TABLE 3: Chiasm and Parallelism in Isa 45:14-25

45:14-17 17 cola	45:18-19 14 cola	45:20-21 15 cola	45:22-25 14 cola
Nations bear tribute to Jerusalem	Yahweh creates the inhabited world	Yahweh calls the nations to trial	Yahweh admonishes the nations to accept his sovereignty
yitpallālû		Idolators are ignorant mitpallĕlîm	
	'ănî yhwh wĕ-'ên ʿôd		kî 'ănî 'ēl wĕ-'ên ʿôd
	Yahweh speaks openly Yahweh speaks ṣedeq and mêšārîm	Yahweh foretells events	Yahweh's word is sure Yahweh speaks ṣĕdāqâ
Nations bow down			Nations bow down
Confession: 'ak bĕkā.... 'ākēn....			Confession: 'ak bĕ-yhwh...
...'ēl wĕ-'ên ʿôd		hălō' 'ănî yhwh wĕ-'ên ʿôd	
Yahweh is môšîaʿ		Yahweh is ṣaddîq and môšîaʿ	Yahweh is ṣĕdāqôt
idolators are shamed bôšû			idolators are shamed yēbōšû
salvation of Israel nôšaʿ tĕšûʿat	speaks to Israel zeraʿ yaʿăqōb		salvation of Israel zeraʿ yiśrā'ēl yiṣdĕqû

The stanza depicts a procession of the nations to
Jerusalem, referred to conventionally in the feminine
singular. The nations offer their tribute which becomes Jerusalem's property (lᵃk yihyû). Then they
worship her; our scansion reveals parallel short cola
'aḥărayik yēlēk, a Deuteronomic phrase connoting worship, and 'ēlayik yitpallĕlû, "they make supplication
to you." The same phrase hitpallēl 'el is used in
Solomon's prayer of the foreigner who makes pilgrimage
to Jerusalem and prays toward the temple (1 Kgs 8:42).
The description of representatives of the nations
coming in chains recalls Egyptian and Assyrian reliefs
of conquered peoples in audience before the pharaoh or
emperor. Here these vassals are not defiant; they
accept the new reality of power in Yahweh's imperium
and make a confession of his sovereignty (vv. 14d-17).

Westermann has emphasized the apparently abrupt
transitions between vv. 14, 15 and 16-17 and breaks up
these verses into separate fragments.[109] V. 14 is
addressed to Jerusalem, v. 15 he terms an "amen gloss"
addressed to Yahweh, and vv. 16-17, while resuming
discussion of the nations, refers to Israel, not Zion,
as the protagonist. While the nations in v. 14 confess
Yahweh, in v. 16 they are idolators. But Melugin
correctly discerns in vv. 14d-17 a single confession of

Will come over to you	5
and become yours,	4
Will follow after you,	5
come in chains;	6
Bowing down to you,	6
they will petition you:	6 b:b::b:b::b:b

On the list as a typological feature of later Hebrew
verse, see Paul Hanson, The Dawn of Apocalyptic (Philadelphia: Fortress, 1975) 46-48.

[109]Westermann, 168-71; Schoors, 30.

the nations, following the same form as that of vv. 24-
25.[110] Both speeches begin with **'ak** (vv. 14d, 24a) or
'ākēn (v. 15) followed by a confession of Yahweh's
sovereignty in the third person (vv. 14d-15, 24a) and
they conclude with curses upon idolators (vv. 16, 24b)
and affirmations of Israel's salvation (vv. 17, 24).
The opening **'ak** or **'ākēn** with a confession of Yahweh's
sovereignty, curses invoked upon the wicked using the
words **bwš** and **klm**, blessings for the righteous with
promises of vindication (**yěšûᶜâ, těšûᶜâ**), and the 1:b
meter, are all characteristics of the form of the
confession as found in Jer 3:22-25, Pss 27:1-6 and
56:12-14, and Jonah 2:8-10.

Recognition that the confession is a <u>Gattung</u> informs
our exegesis of the statements contrasting the victory
of Israel and the humiliation of idolators. These
should not be taken as Israel gloating over its
enemies, but rather as the confession of repentant
transgressors. Jer 3:22-25 is particularly instructive
in this regard. Like Isa 45:14-17 and 45:24-25, the
supplicants are themselves repentant idolators who come
(**'ātānû**) to Yahweh, condemn their idolatry as a lie,
declare that in Yahweh is the **těšûᶜat yiśrā'ēl**, and
speak of the shame and humiliation (**boštēnû,
kělimmātēnû**) of their own past idolatry. Similarly,
within Deutero-Isaiah's confession is also a polemic
against polytheism and image worship. Yahweh is recognized as the sole God and the "invisible god" (**'ēl
mistattēr**) while Yahweh's enemies are identified as the
craftsmen who make images (**ḥārāšê ṣûrîm**, v. 16).
Evidently the foreigners who make this confession of

---

[110]Melugin, <u>Formation</u>, 127 n. 25. Spykerboer (pp.
138-41) recognizes the confession but nevertheless
removes v. 15 as a gloss.

allegiance to Yahweh are at the same time repudiating
their prior religious affiliation and all their
brethren who still practice idolatry. Deutero-Isaiah
is employing the traditional form of the confession to
describe the oath by those survivors of the nations
(v. 20) who, having repented of their idolatry, now
recognize Yahweh as the sole God. Consequently they
also respect Jerusalem's and Israel's privileged status
in the government of Yahweh (cf. Isa 55:3-5) and come
bearing tribute.

The second stanza (vv. 18-19) sets up the ground for
Yahweh's claim upon the nations in the succeeding
verses. First, the initial messenger formula is
expanded in v. 18 with hymnic participial and nominal
sentences praising Yahweh as creator of the cosmos.
This creation was purposeful and orderly; he did not
create the world tōhû--perhaps referring to the desola-
tion of Jerusalem and the dispersal of Israel among the
nations. In the second strophe in this stanza, beginning with v. 18d, Yahweh speaks in the first person.
It is framed by a chiasm of identity formulae 'ănî yhwh
and ends with a pair of participial phrases which form
a larger inclusio with the participles at the beginning
of v. 18. Yahweh does not speak in secret, through a
barû diviner-priest hidden in the recesses of a pagan
temple as though from the underworld ('ereṣ ḥošek). On
the contrary, Yahweh's word is proclaimed openly, perhaps a reference to the proclamations of his prophets
and the published precepts of his tôrâ. These contrasts give content to Yahweh's word as ṣedeq, meaning
vindication of the weak and the righteous in a world
where Israel found itself oppressed, leading to a world
that Israel may inhabit in safety. It is likewise
mêšārîm, which in the Mesopotamian context meant an

equitable and just social order (mī̌sarum)[111] instituted
through a general amnesty proclaimed at the accession
of a new monarch. The institution of a righteous
social order governed by equitable laws was a royal
function and a constituitive element of both Mesopotamian and Israelite royal ideology.[112] Yahweh's word
brings order to a world of chaos (tōhû), vindication to
the oppressed, and a society governed by God's covenant
law.

In vv. 20-25 Yahweh calls to court the "survivors"
of the defeat of Babylon. As one of the most universalistic passages in Deutero-Isaiah, this trial speech
has engendered some dispute. Snaith wants to see the
"survivors" in this passage as Israelite exiles among
the nations, survivors of the deportations by Nebuchadnezzar who come from the "ends of the earth."
Hollenberg has proposed that they are "crypto-
Israelites" who had adopted Babylonian religion, the
"offspring of Jacob" in v. 19 who seek divine guidance
through Babylonian divination.[113]

Hollenberg comes to his view as a corollary to his
rather extreme hypothesis that "the nations" in
Deutero-Isaiah is everywhere equivocal, meaning either
gentile peoples or the Israelites among them. But this
so opens interpretation to the subjective opinion of
the exegete as to make any conclusion concerning the

---

[111]CAD 10,2 s.v. mī̌saru.

[112]Cf. Ps 72:1-4,12-14; and numerous Assyrian and
Mesopotamian royal inscriptions such as the Prologue of
the Code of Hammurapi I.32ff.: mī̌saram ina mātim ana
šūpîm, "to make justice prevail in the nation..."

[113]Snaith, "Teaching... Consequences," 160; Hollen-
berg, VT 19 (1969), 21-36; followed by Schoors, 234-36;
Martin-Achard, A Light to the Nations, 16-17; Holmgren,
With Wings as Eagles, 39-42.

role of the nations non-falsifiable. Moreover, there
is ample evidence that Deutero-Isaiah does distinguish
between Israelites and gentiles. In Isa 44:1-5, the
most arguable case for assimilated Jews reaffirming
their ancestral identity,[114] the prophet specifically
addresses them as Jacob/Israel. He similarly addresses
exiles who have been impressed by pagan religion as
Jacob/Israel in 40:18,27 and 46:3,5.

Snaith and Hollenberg rest their case largely upon
the apparently nationalistic content of the confession
in vv. 24-25, which includes condemnation of idolators
and praise of Israel. However, the parallel confession
in vv. 14d-17 is clearly spoken by the nations as they
come to offer tribute. We have identified the form of
these verses as that of a conventional confession of
faith, and it is characteristic of that form that
condemnation of the wicked and praise of the righteous
alternate in the mouths of the same penitents.

Their theory is further weakened by a close analysis
of the prosodic structure of these verses. The third
and fourth stanzas (vv. 20-21,22-23) are linked by
repeated imperatives summoning the nations to trial
(vv. 20a, 21a, 22a), moving from from a call to the
idolators who "do not know" in v. 20b to their interro-
gation in v. 21b to the call to repentance in v. 22.
Yahweh's self-identification to the idolators in the
first person in v. 21 is linked to his oath, also in
the first person, that they will submit to him in
v. 23. Moreover, vv. 22-23 form a strophe thick with
parallelism and chiasm: repetition of the verb nišbaᶜ
in alternate b̲ cola, the particle kî opening alternate
l̲ cola, the adjective kol repeated three times, verbs

---

[114] See above, p. 84.

of turning (pĕnû) and returning (yāšûb), and five
different first person pronouns. The very prosody
requires that the confession which will be spoken by
"every tongue," that is all peoples, be parallel to
"all the ends of the earth" that are called to be
saved; they form a chiasm as the first and last bicola
in their strophe of four bicola. Hence despite an
adduced parallel to Israel at the "ends of the earth"
in Isa 41:9, here the "all the ends of the earth" and
"survivors of the nations" must denote the gentiles.

Interpreting the "survivors" as Israelite fugitives
of Nebuchadnezzar would require that the deed (zō't)
which was declared from long ago (v. 21) be the exile
itself. Snaith notes that Babylon's downfall was a new
event first declared by Deutero-Isaiah and hence could
not be an event "declared long ago."[115] Schoors has
attacked this view, arguing that "this" (zô't) here as
in the other trial speeches (43:9; 48:14) must refer to
the coming of Cyrus.[116] The scene in v. 20 is identical to that in 41:1-7 (cf. 41:21-29), where the pagans
rush about building new idols to defend themselves, in
vain, from the onrushing tide of Cyrus and his forces.
Yahweh accuses the defeated gentiles of ignorance for
praying to idols who cannot save, and, as in other
trial speeches, Yahweh puts forward as evidence to

---

[115] One can also point to older Isaianic prophecies
such as 13:1-8, 17-22 and 14:4-21 as the canonical
context for asserting the prior prediction of Babylon's
downfall; see Childs, Introduction to the Old Testament
as Scripture, 328ff.

[116] Schoors, 224-5, 235-6. While he argues for the
advent of Cyrus as the occasion for this oracle, he
still comes down rather lamely against the universalistic interpretation, which he admits is "the most
obvious meaning of this text."

support the assertion of his sole divinity and lordship the fact that only he has foretold their doom. Note in addition that when Deutero-Isaiah speaks of the exile he describes Yahweh's aspect towards Israel as one of wrath and judgment,[117] but concerning "this" event (v. 21) whose survivors are the object of the lawsuit, Yahweh identifies himself as the savior.

Our identification of Isa 45:14-25 as a single compositional unit confirms Schoor's view that the oracle is anticipating the conquest of Cyrus and speaking to the survivors of his campaigns. In the opening stanza of this unit Jerusalem is restored and receiving the tribute of nations. By its context in the book of consolation immediately following upon the Cyrus oracle, Yahweh's vindication through Cyrus his champion is an established fact, and the chastened nations are invited to recognize and submit to the authority of the one true God. The actual occupation by Cyrus was peaceful, hence the oracle must be anticipatory. The prophet looks ahead to the destruction of Babylon, from which the survivors, confused and defeated, would seek a new source of help. That helper is none other than Yahweh, the one who stands behind Cyrus and whose sovereignty will be manifest in the new order.

The oath, "to me every knee must bend, every tongue shall swear," is among the clearest statements of the universal scope of Yahweh's lordship in the Hebrew Bible. From the rubble of the Babylonian world-empire about to be crushed by Cyrus, Yahweh announces the coming of his universal rule with all the confidence and authority of a world conqueror. Perhaps this conception of the nations paying homage to Yahweh's imper-

---

[117] Cf. Isa 42:18-25; 43:28.

ial rule in Jerusalem was influenced by the imperial
pretensions of Babylon with which Deutero-Isaiah was
familiar. There are also ample Israelite precedents
for this conception in the traditions of the royal
cult, which will be discussed in chapter 4.

This oath is introduced by the phrase 'ănî yhwh
wĕ-'ên ᶜod. As in v. 18, these words introduce
Yahweh's speaking as unique and true. Because Yahweh
is unique, he can swear by himself and not invoke any
other deity, and his self-imprecation is supremely
effective. In the following bicolon (v. 23a) Yahweh's
decree goes forth and does not return. The oath's
irrevocable character serves to substantiate the
opening vision in which the nations, some in chains,
come bearing tribute to Zion.

That oath is further called a decree of ṣĕdāqâ.
Westermann[118] and RSV wrongly translate ṣĕdāqâ as an
adverb, "truly," based upon the parallel phrase "a word
which will not return." However ṣĕdāqâ in this verse
is parallel to dābār; it denotes a decree, not its
manner of promulgation. It is the case that in Isa
48:1 lō' bĕ-'ĕmet wĕ-lō' bi-ṣĕdāqâ, "not in truth nor
in right," is the indirect object of nišbaᶜ. But
against this one reading, ṣĕdāqâ appears 5 times in
Deutero-Isaiah in parallel with a nominal form of the
root wšᶜ, and 10 times with a meaning in the range
"vindication," "victory," "security," or "power."
Blank has traced Deutero-Isaiah's particular shade of
meaning for this term from the primary sense of yiṣdaq,
to win one's case in a legal proceding.[119] The triumph
of right in the law court becomes in Deutero-Isaiah the

[118]Westermann, 171.

[119]Sheldon Blank, Prophetic Faith in Isaiah, 152-56.

triumph of Yahweh's right over the nations and their
gods.   Victory in a military sense is also a primitive
meaning of ṣĕdāqôt (cf. Judg 5:11, Mic 6:5).[120] For
Israel ṣĕdāqâ is vindication because, in the triumph of
Yahweh, Israel as Yahweh's servant will be liberated
from her thralldom to the idolators.   In Deutero-Isaiah
ṣĕdāqâ comes to mean the fulfillment of God's purpose
in history, a meaning not restricted to triumph over a
rival but including the establishment of Yahweh's sovereignty on earth and the universal enactment of
Yahweh's covenant law.   In this light, the stanza may
be viewed in relation to vv. 18-19 where Yahweh is the
one who speaks ṣedeq and mêšārîm, there the opposite of
uninhabited chaos and a false order supported by decrees uttered in secret to the privileged.   Blank's
rendering of the term "God's sure purpose" barely hints
at the richness of this concept.

The final confession by the nations (vv. 24-25) is
presumably the very words of the oath which "every
tongue shall swear" in the preceding verse.   In a
coherent strophe in three bicola, repetition of bĕ-yhwh
forms a chiasm connecting the first and third bicola,
and additional repetition of pairs of verbs and kol
joins the second and third bicola.   Semantic parallels
tie these verses to what precedes them: zeraᶜ yiśrā'ēl
with zeraᶜ yaᶜăqōb in v. 19; ṣĕdāqôt, meaning the
mighty victories of Yahweh, with ṣĕdāqâ in v. 23;
doubled verbs recalling the same pattern in the first
confession (vv. 16-17) and in the trial speech
(vv. 20, 21 and 22).   This confession is formally one
with the initial confession in vv. 14b-16.   The nations
confess as repentant idolators, and as is typical of

---

[120]On this meaning for ṣĕdāqôt, cf. Schoors, 53,
210-11, 236.

the form, the penitent nations invoke curses upon those who fail to honor Yahweh and praise upon righteous Israel.

By this confession of allegiance to Yahweh and the blessings and curses, the nations take an oath of covenant to Yahweh their new overlord. Finally, the chiastic structure of the unit indicates that the place where this oath will be fulfilled, where the nations will bow the knee and acknowledge Yahweh's sovereignty, will be Jerusalem.

4. The Trial Speech: Form, Context and Claims

a. Form-Critical and Tradition-Historical Considerations

The term "trial speech" as used by form critics is usually understood to refer to a self-contained spoken unit preserving and perhaps modifying contemporary or preexilic forms of speech. Yet form critics have been unable to come to a consensus as to either the tradition history or the Sitz im Leben of the two types of trial speeches--trial speeches against Israel (42:18-25; 43:22-28; 50:1-3) and trial speeches against the nations (41:1-5,21-29; 43:8-13; 44:6-8; 45:18-25)[121]-- in Deutero-Isaiah. Our analysis suggests that these trial speech Gattungen are better understood as components of larger formal or traditional complexes. The prophet's transitions between these trial speeches and

---

[121]So distinguished by Westermann, Isaiah 40-66, 15-18; Schoors, I am God your Savior, 239; Melugin, Formation, 43-63. Melugin (p. 137) also considers 48:12-15 to be a trial speech, but he is alone among recent interpreters.

their surrounding oracles are often artificial and
conceal the larger continuity of his poetry. A question which can be raised here only tangentially is what
effect this analysis of the trial speech as a constituent form within larger literary compositions rather
than itself an independent formal unit will have on
efforts to describe its genesis. It may be that the
tradition histories of the trial speech forms are also
inseparable from the tradition histories of the larger
units of which they are a part.

Regarding the background of the first type of trial
speech against Israel, form critics have taken two
major positions. Either Deutero-Isaiah is imitating
the speech forms of contemporary secular trials[122] or
he is utilizing the preexilic covenant lawsuit.[123] The
lack of any clear verdict or punishment and the evident
disputational purpose of Deutero-Isaiah's trial speeches represent substantial departures from the trial at
the gate. Thus, although Israel is indicted for her
past sins (42:24; 43:22-24,27; 50:1b), instead of the
usual sentence her punishment is a fait accompli
(42:22,25; 43:28; 50:1).[124] In line with his purpose
to persuade Israel that her distress was not from any
weakness on Yahweh's part but rather judgment consequent upon past sins (42:23-4; 43:26-8; 50:1), the
prophet may add a word describing Yahweh's willingness
to blot out sin (43:25) or his power to save by recal-

---

[122]J. Begrich, Studien zu Deuterojesaja, BWANT 77
(Stuttgart, 1938), 26-48; H. J. Boecker, Redeformen des
Rechtslebens im Alten Testament, (Neukirchen, 1964);
Schoors, 181-88.

[123]See H.E. von Waldow, "Anlass und Hintergrund,"
37-47.

[124]Schoors, 197, 239f.

ling the Exodus and the plagues of Egypt (50:2b-3).[125]
These speeches thus differ from the prophetic Gerichtswort whose purpose is to announce Yahweh's judgment
upon Israel, and likewise from the secular trial whose
purpose is also to render a verdict.   Instead Deutero-
Isaiah challenges his hearers to accept a claim about
Yahweh's lordship over their history.   Attempts to
derive the trial speech against Israel from the covenant lawsuit form also have encountered difficulties.
Although the purpose of the preexilic covenant lawsuit
is more commonly disputational, it has a number of
well-defined characteristics[126] which also do not
cohere with the trial speech form as narrowly delimited
by form critics.   Saddled with such difficulties,
Melugin finally doubts that the trial speech can be
understood as a real or imitated Gattung apart from
Deutero-Isaiah's preaching.   His opinion is typical:[127]

> It is noteworthy that Deutero-Isaiah always uses
> trial speeches for disputational purposes....
> Indeed, in converting the trial form from its
> normal function of dealing with violations of
> the established order to the purposes of dispu-
> tation, Deutero-Isaiah has divorced the trial
> from its traditional moorings.

From our compositional analysis of 43:8-44:5 we wish
to introduce a different perspective into the discussion of the origin of the trial speech against Israel
in Deutero-Isaiah.   The larger compositional unit of

[125]Schoors, 199, 201-2.

[126]See above, pp. 73-75.

[127]Melugin, 49-52. Schoors (pp. 197, 199, 239, 244)
similarly has to defend the designation trial speech
against those who would view some of these passages as
disputations.

which the trial speech is but one stanza may evince a
relationship to antecedent forms far more clearly than
does the trial speech as conventionally delimited. For
example, our analysis of Isa 43:8-44:5 showed that this
large unit, having the trial speech Isa 43:22-28 as but
one element, contains most of the elements of the
covenant lawsuit form.[128]   Covenant lawsuits such as
Mic 6:1-8, Isa 1:2-20, Deut 32 and Ezek 20 are themselves complex units with multiple stanzas and
elements, some of which form critics have separated as
trial speeches and salvation oracles. Deutero-Isaiah
is picking up a form which is not only complex, but
which had already gone through an evolution from

---

[128]Another prophetic lawsuit form can be discerned
in Isa 42:18-43:7, a unit in which the trial speech
42:18-25 is joined to the following salvation oracle
43:1-7 by the transitional phrase wĕ-ᶜattâ and various
rhetorical features, notably contrasts between Israel
trapped in prisons (bātê kĕlā'îm), burned (tibᶜar bô)
by fire, and with none to say ('ên 'ōmēr) "restore" and
Israel walking unscathed (lō' tibᶜar bāk) through the
fire, released from prisons ('al tiklā'î), and with
Yahweh to say ('ōmar) "give back." All six characteristic elements of the lawsuit form are present in this
unit, though some in truncated form: (1) Although the
setting in the divine council is lacking, Isa 42:18
opens with the characteristic invocation to trial
where, as in 43:8, Israel is called blind and deaf.
(2) Verses 19-20 state the initial charge in which
Israel's transgression is portrayed with reference to
her proper relationship to Yahweh as his servant.
(3) Verse 21, describing Yahweh's glorifying of tôrâ,
corresponds to the recital of Yahweh's mighty acts. In
this context, tôrâ in parallel with ṣedeq refers less
to the stipulations of the law than to Yahweh's deeds
in history which glorify the law by confirming its
attendant blessings and curses. (4,5) The following
indictment mixed with a description of Yahweh's punishment in vv. 23-25 is conveyed with repeated rhetorical
questions, another characteristic of this form.
(6) Corresponding to the final section, the word of
promise, is the salvation oracle 43:1-7. Cf. Julien
Harvey, Le plaidoyer prophétique contre Israel, 58-59.

distant antecedents--variously surmised as a secular
trial at the gate or a league covenant festival--into a
rhetorical form utilized by the prophets for penitential and instructional purposes.[129] The classical
covenant lawsuit, as distinguished from the judgment
oracle (Gerichtswort) and the secular trial at the
gate, does not generally conclude with a sentence;
rather there is an invitation to return (Mic 6:8;
Isa 1:16-18; Ps 50:22-23) or even, in the case of
Deut 32:35-43 and Ezek 20:40-44, a promise of salvation. From this perspective, the disputational character of the trial speeches and the lack of any sentence
is not such an innovation as assumed by form critics.
As derivative of the prophetic **rîb**, the trial speech in
Deutero-Isaiah is properly disputational. Furthermore,
it is neither the accidental arrangement of a collector
nor a specifically Deutero-Isaianic innovation that the
trial speeches 42:18-25 and 43:22-28 introduce words of
salvation.

Our special concern is the second type of trial
speech, the trial between Yahweh and the nations and
their gods. Again, the background of the trial speech
against the nations as a narrowly delimited form cannot
be determined with any certainty; Westermann's opinion
that these speeches are highly stylized creations of
the prophet is typical.[130] Von Waldow is correct to
look to cultic contests or trials between Yahweh and
the gods such as Psalm 82, where Yahweh as the execu-
tive deity disputes the right of the older gods of the
divine council to rule over the earth and then senten-

---

[129]Wright, "Lawsuit," 54-66.

[130]Westermann, Sprache und Struktur, 51-58; Melugin,
53-63.

ces them to death.[131] But an extensive demonstration
of the genetic relationship of the trial speech to a
preexilic Israelite tradition is only clarified when it
is considered in the context of its larger compositional unit.

In the case of the units which open with trials
against the nations, we have shown their traditional
background to be the autumn enthronement festival of
the Jerusalem cult. The evident verbal and thematic
connections of these compositional units to Pss 2, 46,
48, 77, 89 and prophetic passages out of the Zion
tradition support the autumn festival as the background
for these compositions. The ritual pattern of the
autumn festival--Yahweh's defeat of the raging nations,
the deliverance of Zion, the enthronement of Yahweh's
anointed, the victory procession to the temple and the
fertilizing rains--is repeated in each half of the
compositional unit Isa 41:1-20,21-42:17 and in 43:8-
44:5. There opening trial scenes proclaim Yahweh's
defeat of the nations through his lieutenant Cyrus in
order to refute the claims of their gods, then Israel
is redeemed and/or the servant is installed as the
recipient of **mišpāṭ**, and finally Yahweh leads his
people in procession to Zion over a fructified desert.
The pattern is inverted in 45:14-25 where the initial
procession of the nations to Zion in order to pay
homage to the divine king is substantiated by the the
ascription to Yahweh of their military defeat in the
following trial scene. These trial speeches, in which
Yahweh's forensic claims to sole sovereignty among the
gods are predicated upon his military victory as the
divine warrior, thus cohere well with the first move-

---

[131]von Waldow, 37-47.

ment of the ritual pattern where the nations challenge Yahweh's kingship and call forth his judgment. The added forensic language, perhaps with roots in the alternate tradition of the judgment of the divine council in Ps 82, is Deutero-Isaiah's modification of this tradition of the preexilic cult.

b. The Trial's Context in the Divine Council: A Forum for Arguing Universal Claims

The traditional mythological setting for both royal cult's contest between Yahweh and the enemy deities and the prophetic covenant lawsuit against Israel was the divine council. However, in both these traditions the motif of the divine council was multiform. The psalms of the cult include Ps 89:6-12 which, drawing on the Canaanite myth of creation,[132] mentions the gods of the divine council as Yahweh's subordinates and spectators to his victory over his enemy Sea. Psalm 82, on the other hand, draws on a mythological tradition of the rebellion of the astral deities (cf. Job 38:12-15; Isa 14:12-15) to depict Yahweh judging the gods of the council as his adversaries. There is also considerable fluidity between the gods of the divine council and the nations: in Pss 46 and 96 Yahweh's mythological adversaries become the nations themselves.[133]

In prophetic traditions the members of the divine council had a passive role as subservient beings in Yahweh's court (Isa 6:1-3; 2 Kgs 22:19-23). In the

---

[132]Cf. CTA 2.1.

[133]The equation of the gods with the nations is explicit in Deut 32:8. In Ps 46 the raging of the mythological Sea in vv. 3b-4 becomes the raging nations in v. 7; they are equivalent threats to the cosmic

developed prophetic lawsuit the council tended to become otiose; its function as witness to violations of
covenant could just as well be performed by "heaven and
earth" (Isa 1:2, Mic 6:1-2), natural features or "olden
gods" which had no living presence in the divine
council.[134]

Deutero-Isaiah exploits this variegated motif in his
several trial speeches against the nations and their
gods. Features of the divine council can be recognized
both in the arraignment and judgment of the assembled
foreign deities and in the council's passive role as
witness or audience for their lord Yahweh's decrees.
In Deutero-Isaiah's trial speeches the nations and
their gods are invoked with the repeated plural impera-

---

order established from Zion. Ps 96:7-9 imitates the
language of Ps 29:1-2 except that the heavenly scene at
the divine council in Ps 29:

29:1. Ascribe to Yahweh, O sons of El,
      Ascribe to Yahweh glory and might;
      Ascribe to Yahweh the glory due his name,
   2. Fall down before Yahweh at his holy theophany!

has been reinterpreted as the nations coming to the
temple:

96:7. Ascribe to Yahweh, families of the peoples,
      Ascribe to Yahweh glory and might;
   8. Ascribe to Yahweh the glory due his name,
      Bring an offering and come into his courts!
   9. Fall down before Yahweh at his holy theophany,
      Tremble before him, all the earth!

[134]See Cross, Canaanite Myth, 188-89. He recognizes
the essentially literary character of this introductory
formula in the Israelite adaptation of the rîb.   In
Canaanite culture the olden gods typically were listed
alongside the local pantheon as witnesses to treaties:
cf. the Sefire Treaty Inscription KAI 222.I.A.8-12,
Hittite treaties, and the Arslan Tash incantation; on
the latter see Cross and Saley, "Phoenician Incanta-
tions on a Plaque of the Seventh Century B.C. from
Arslan Tash in Upper Syria," BASOR 197 (1970) 42-49.

tives "hear," "approach" which are likewise used to invoke the witnesses in the covenant lawsuit (Mic 6:2, Isa 1:2, Deut 32:1). The form of repeated rhetorical questions with which Yahweh disputes with the foreign gods are similarly used to dispute with the gods of the divine council in Pss 82:2 and 89:6-9. The first person plural address, e.g. "that we may know" (Isa 41:22-23,26), is commonly used of Yahweh addressing his council: e.g., Gen 1:26 "Let us make humanity in our image," Gen 11:7 "Come, let us go down and confound their language," and Isa 6:8 "Whom shall I send, who will go for us."[135] As if reflecting the multiform nature of the divine council motif, in several of Deutero-Isaiah's trial speeches (Isa 43:8-9; 44:6-8) the nations and/or gods of the divine council are first briefly refuted, but then, functioning as if witnesses in the classical prophetic lawsuit, they recede into the background as Yahweh turns to take issue with Israel.

Cross regards the divine council in trial speeches in Isa 41-44 as an "ancient literary pattern used as an artistic device."[136] For Deutero-Isaiah the divine council is a literary setting without ties to any living cult or ritual. We concur that in the hands of Deutero-Isaiah the trial of the nations and their gods in the divine council becomes a literary device, a

---

[135]F. M. Cross, "The Council of Yahweh in Second Isaiah," JNES 12 (1953), 274-77. Some Ugaritic examples of the divine council speaking in the first person plural include: CTA 6.1.54, namluka ᶜattaru ᶜarīzu, "let us make Athtar the Terrible king;" and CTA 4.4.43, malkunū 'al'iyānu baᶜlu tāpiṭunū wa-'ên dū ᶜalênhū, "Our king is Baal the Conqueror, our judge, and there is none above him."

[136]Cross, JNES 12 (1953), 275 n. 3.

forum through which the prophet can address a real
audience. The trial speeches thus serve a disputational function, and the divine council is the literary
image by which the prophet can state his claims for
Yahweh's sole divinity in the teeth of the surrounding
polytheistic culture. The trial speech, with its fic-
tive audience of the assembled nations, is a literary
vehicle for the prophet to argue universal claims.

We now turn once again to specific texts. Isa 41:1-
4 addresses the nations, summoning them to trial and
challenging them to draw up a defense. Then Yahweh, in
the position of an advocate, asks a series of rhetorical questions which challenge the nations to recognize
that the oncoming march of Cyrus is his work. Verse 2
opens with the question "Who" not to identify Cyrus,
but Yahweh who stirs him up, calls him, gives up
nations before him, and enables him to subdue kings.
Instead, in vv. 5-7 the nations rush about building
idols, as if those would save them. While in v. 5 they
tremble at the visible rise of a new conqueror it is
not, as Westermann believes, because they recognize the
aweful grandeur of Yahweh's judgment.[137] Rather, their
building idols indicates that they obdurantly refuse to
recognize Yahweh's claim. The argument that Yahweh is
the power behind a foreign conqueror such as Cyrus is
not in itself a new claim; the theme and vocabulary are
drawn from the tradition of the 8th century Isaiah for
whom Assyria was a rod in Yahweh's hand (cf.
Isa 10:5).[138] But while for Isaiah of Jerusalem it was

---

[137]Westermann, Isaiah 40-66, 65f.

[138]Ironically, the preexilic tradition of Yahweh's
judgment upon the nations from Jerusalem behind this
composition is the very tradition which Isaiah of Jerusalem turned on its head in describing Assyria's judgment of Israel.

enough   that   Israel   believe   in   Yahweh's   international
sovereignty,   Deutero-Isaiah   argues this   claim   before
the nations.

The gods of the nations are defendants in the second
trial speech, Isa 41:21-29.   The nations are challenged
to bring forth their gods, here called "your advocates"
(rābêkem)   and "your mighty ones"   (ᶜăṣūmôtêkem).   Yet
the   focus   of Yahweh's dispute is not the   gods   themselves   but   an audience which he seeks to convince   of
his claim to sovereignty in history.   In vv. 22b-23 the
prophet   piles   up   conditional   sentences   one   after
another   for   emphasis,   each containing a question   or
challenge   to the gods in the protasis followed by   the
purpose "that we may know" in the   apodosis.   Yahweh's
challenge   to the gods to prove their efficacy in   history   by   predicting   the future is in   fact   aimed   at
convincing   "we,"   the   audience of spectators   at   the
trial,   to abandon their worship: "an abomination is he
who chooses you" (v.   24).   The pattern of conditional
sentences resumes in the second stanza,   where again it
is   the court,   that is the   assembled   audience,   that
would   say   "he is right" (ṣaddîq) to any god   who   had
accurately predicted the rise of Cyrus.   Evidently none
of   them can (v.   28),   and that is exactly the   point.
The   concluding   tricolon repeats the summation of   its
counterpart   in v. 24,   that the gods are   nothing   and
their worship is in vain.[139]

What   is the actual referent for this literary audience to which the prophet appeals?   The figure of   the
assembled   nations at the divine council is a   literary
device in order to involve an audience,   which is to be
convinced   of   a   claim.   This audience is also   in   a

---

[139]Schoors, 214f.

position to be tempted to choose other gods (v. 24).
Deutero-Isaiah's audience was in fact primarily Israel,
as the purpose of the trial speech was to convince the
exiles that it was fruitless to adopt the religions of
Babylon. His claim that only Yahweh can foretell the
future would only have been credible to an Israelite
audience; the Babylonians with their elaborate priestly
institutions for divining the future would have found
such a characterization of their gods ludicrous.
Indeed, the priests of Marduk also claimed that their
god had aroused Cyrus to avenge the neglect of his cult
by Nabonidus.[140] We conclude that while the image in
the trial scene may depict the members of the divine
council either as being arraigned before Yahweh or as
witnesses to Yahweh's judgments, as a literary motif
the image is sufficiently ambiguous that Deutero-
Isaiah's actual audience--the Israelite exiles for whom
he published his work--could identify themselves as
"we," spectators to the trial. Deutero-Isaiah has
adapted the tradition of the divine council, having
been shorn of any connections to living religious lore,
as a literary motif and a vehicle to involve his
audience of exiles in the disputation.[141]

---

[140]Cf. the Cyrus Cylinder, in ANET, 315b.

[141]The trial becomes a "language event," a term used
by the "new hermeneutic" school to describe words that
invite the reader's participation. See Robert Funk,
Language, Hermeneutic, and the Word of God (New York:
Harper & Row, 1966) and J. M. Robinson and J. B. Cobb,
The New Hermeneutic, New Frontiers of Theology 2 (New
York: Harper & Row, 1964). Cf. a similar understanding
of Isa 53, in which the audience is invited to identify
themselves with its personae, by David J. Clines, I,
He, We and They: A Literary Approach to Isaiah 53,
JSOTS 1 (Sheffield: JSOT, 1976) 62-64.

Yet the nations are also specified as present. They are addressed in 41:1, refuse to heed when they build their idols in 41:6-7, and in v. 21 they are called to bring their gods forward as advocates. In both trial scenes in the compositional unit 41:1-20,21-42:17 the audience includes the nations because the issues of Yahweh's speech are claims binding upon them and their gods. The motif of the divine council, including among its members the gods of the nations (Deut 32:8, Ps 82), was inherently universal, and hence it became in the hands of Deutero-Isaiah a suitable literary vehicle in which to press universal claims. Yahweh's divinity as a claim based upon parochial Israelite traditions of covenant and the promise to defend Zion had been discredited by exile and carried little weight in cosmopolitan Babylon. If Israel was to have confidence in the face of Cyrus's conquests that it would be spared (41:8-13), and even be able to return to its homeland (41:14-20, 42:7-8, 14-17), it would have to believe that Yahweh is sovereign over all other powers. The trial speech uses the motif of the divine council to set up the grounds for Yahweh's universal claims, claims which, while not credible to an actual gentile audience, appeared to be so by this literary conceit. In this way Israel, living among the nations, might be convinced of the universal sovereignty of Yahweh and thus have new grounds for hope.

The third trial speech 43:8-13 is noteworthy because Israel is given the role of witness before the forum of the assembled nations. After an opening summons to both Israel and the nations, in v. 9b the nations are challenged with a contrary-to-fact conditional sentence like those in the second trial speech. Here the apodosis giving the court's potential assent to a claim for

the idol-gods is in the third person: "that one might
say 'It is true.'" The gods are challenged to prove
their case through presenting witnesses, presumably
their adherents, but this is little more than a foil
against which Israel is called to the role of witness
for Yahweh. In spite of being described as blind and
deaf (v. 8), Israel has the role of witness for
Yahweh's claim. Primarily this role requires Israel to
understand, believe, and testify to God's sole lordship
(v. 10) which should be recognizable on the basis of
past experience with Yahweh's guidance and judgment
(vv. 11-12).[142]

In an actual trial it would be strange indeed for a
plaintiff to rest his case on the testimony of a witness who was blind and of questionable loyalty. But as
the introduction to a long covenant lawsuit (43:8-
44:5), this scene functions not only as a trial with
the nations, but as a setting to introduce and give a
context to Yahweh's rîb with Israel.[143] Israel's role
as an active, speaking witness continues to be a theme
throughout Isa 43:8-44:5, where Israel is several times
challenged to "recount" either her sins (43:26) or
Yahweh's praise (43:21). Finally at its conclusion
Israel will dedicate herself totally to God (44:5).

---

[142]See Westermann, 122f; Schoors, 224. They understand the prophet to mean that Israel is Yahweh's
witness in spite of blindness because it had experienced Yahweh's intervention in history. Yet how could
a blind Israel, who had not drawn lessons from that
history, effectively testify? The paradox is resolved
when the trial speech is recognized to be part of a
larger lawsuit which ends with Israel's knowledge and
faith restored.

[143]Spykerboer (Structure and Composition, 103f.) is
too extreme in denying any meaning to the trial of the
nations and focusing entirely on Israel.

The trial setting imputes a larger significance to Yahweh's lawsuit with Israel. Israel must be restored and purified in order to overcome her blindness in order to thereby properly manifest Yahweh's divinity before the nations.[144]

The circumstances of the trial scene, where conflicting claims were argued before the assembled peoples, corresponded to the actual situation of Israel living in exile. Within preexilic Israel, insulated from the views of distant peoples, Yahweh's lordship was evident in the institutions and symbols of nation and cult. But a people living in exile, having been stripped of its institutions and having lost any tangible evidence of God's favor,[145] was inevitably beset by doubts. They also could not but be sensitive to the opinions of their conquerors for whom Yahweh was but a local divinity of no consequence.

Thus the question of Yahweh's divinity became during the exile a claim to be argued, as people began to doubt his effectiveness and reality. It is instructive to compare the message of the 8th century Isaiah, who spoke to an intact nation and spelled out the attitude of faith which could preserve Judah in the face of the threat of superior foreign powers: "In returning and rest you shall be saved; in quietness and in trust shall be your strength" (30:5). Yahweh's reality was not then at issue; Israel's behavior and

---

[144]Cf. Isa 42:18-43:7 and 48:1-11. This recalls Ezekiel's frequent sayings that Yahweh will restore Israel for the sake of his name, or that that Yahweh's name not be profaned among the nations (Ezek 20:8b-9,14,22; 36:22-32). Cf. Blank, Prophetic Faith, 117-137.

[145]I.e. the promise of Zion's inviolability (Lam 4:12).

obedience to the covenant with Yahweh was. On the
other hand, while Ezekiel was equally concerned about
the people's obedience to covenant, his writings are
peppered with the recognition formulae "you will know
that I am Yahweh." Zimmerli relates this to a "token
of proof" in legal cases, as in Gen 42:34 when Jacob
tests his brothers' sincerity by asking "bring me your
youngest brother, that I may know that you are not
spies, but honorable men." The actions of Yahweh in
judging and saving Israel were not only significant in
themselves; for Ezekiel they also functioned as proofs
that he is God.[146] In the atmosphere of doubt prevailing during the exile, Israel thirsted for some evidence
of Yahweh's reality.

Countering this same atmosphere of doubt, Deutero-
Isaiah was equally insistent in claiming that Yahweh is
the living God, and his oracles continually identify
Yahweh as the only God and savior.[147] Like Ezekiel, he
had to remind people that Yahweh indeed had the power
to perform what he has promised.[148] For a community
beset by such fundamental doubts, he utilized the motif
of the trial of the gods as a suitable vehicle by which
to assert claims for Yahweh's existence and power. At
the trial Yahweh and the foreign gods each must bring
forward proofs of their divinity, and in this literary
context Deutero-Isaiah could argue Yahweh's case based
upon proofs from current events (Cyrus) and from the
historical efficacy of his word.

---

[146] Zimmerli, Ezekiel I, Hermeneia (Philadelphia:
Fortress, 1979), 37-38. Cf. Erkenntnis Gottes nach
dem Buche Ezechiel, ATANT 27 (Zürich: Zwingli, 1954).

[147] I.e. Isa 43:3,10-13,15; 45:18; 46:9; 48:12,17.

[148] I.e. Isa 44:26; 46:10-11; 48:3; cf. Ezek 12:23-
25; 17:24; 22:14; 24:14; 36:36. See Blank, 123-32.

The trial speeches also addressed a second cause of exilic doubt: Israel's immersion in a polytheistic culture. Living beside prosperous neighbors who worshipped at impressive religious establishments, the exiles could not help but be sensitive to these neighbors' opinions, especially since their low station contrasted with the prosperity and the cosmopolitan splendor of their captors' culture. Hence reassurance of Yahweh's imminent redemption of Israel necessarily included the element of international recognition. Ezekiel, particularly in his oracles against the nations, often named foreign nations as the subject of recognition formulae.[149] Deutero-Isaiah also portrayed the revelation of God's saving acts towards Israel as aimed at convincing the nations, "all flesh," that Yahweh is God. He employed a recognition formula akin to that of Ezekiel: "that all flesh may know that I am Yahweh your savior..."[150]

Likewise in the trial speeches, Deutero-Isaiah challenged his audience to have sufficient faith in Yahweh's reality to stand confidently for Yahweh in the midst of a pagan culture. He disputed claims of pagan religion which must have attracted many Israelites.[151] The nature of this dispute over truth claims meant that while these speeches were meant to convince apostate Israelites, they also made claims upon the gentiles.

---

[149]Ezek 21:10; 25:11,17; 26:6; 28:23; 29:6,9a,21; 32:16; 36:23. These recognition formulae are probably authentic with Ezekiel; his school added a number of others (36:36; 37:28; 39:23, etc.). See W. Zimmerli, Ezekiel 2, Hermeneia (Philadelphia: Fortress, 1983).

[150]Isa 40:5; 41:20; 45:6; 49:26b; cf. the hymnic passages 42:10-13; 44:23; 48:20; 41:17-20.

[151]Cf. Schoors, 239-40.

While the prophet did not call for a mission to actively evangelize the nations, he recognized that in polytheistic Babylon faithful Israel must necessarily stand
out as a witness by its very profession that Yahweh
alone is God.

Finally, it would be going beyond the evidence to
claim that in the trial speeches Deutero-Isaiah was
actually addressing a gentile audience. Granted, he
lived in exile among a cosmopolitan community, and in
accordance with this social location, his words could
have reached a mixed audience of Judean exiles and
their gentile neighbors. His circumstances living in
exile undoubtedly provided an opening towards a more
international outlook than would be expected from a
preexilic prophet who lived and worked within Israel or
Judah and worked for its welfare. But Deutero-Isaiah
wrote mainly to console Israel and to restore its faith
in Yahweh. If his words were not aimed at a gentile or
mixed audience, at least they were aimed at an Israel
painfully aware of the opinions and attitudes of their
gentile neighbors. In order that his writings be convincing to the exiles, they had to address the challenges and critiques of their "parochial" Yahwistic
faith which their Babylonian environment had placed
before them. Hence those foreigners were virtually his
audience in the trial speeches, whether or not they
actually read his writings. Some among the nations
would have to be seen as potentially convinceable that
Yahweh was sovereign if the disheartened Israelites
were to regain their faith.

c. From Claims at Trial to an Invitation to Universal Salvation

The distinguishing feature of the trial scene in Isa 45:14-25, addressing the "survivors of the nations," is its connection to the admonition that they turn and submit to Yahweh. In other trial scenes Yahweh sought in vain to convince the nations of the truth of his claims; now in a more confident voice God invites the nations to recognize his divinity and submit to his sovereignty in order that they might receive the benefits of salvation. In continuity with previous trial speeches, the addressees of this speech, also called "all the ends of the earth" (45:22), are the nations who have suffered defeat at the hands of Cyrus the new conqueror. As the nations and/or their gods are called to take counsel together and answer Yahweh's challenge to name another deity who has foretold the coming of Cyrus (v. 21), so now, recognizing Yahweh's ascendancy in Cyrus's victory, they are admonished to submit to his sovereignty and abandon their worship of idols.

In v. 22 Yahweh the advocate, his arguments made, invites the nations to give their assent. More than that, in v. 23 he makes an oath, which is the closest approximation of a verdict in any of the trial speeches. Israelite legal proceedings could end with one or both parties making an oath or covenant.[152] Here, bringing the trial to a conclusion, Yahweh makes an oath to enforce his claims. Indeed, by their bearing tribute to Jerusalem in vv. 14-17, the trial and assent of the nations in vv. 20-25 is a fait accompli upon Yahweh's historical victory through Cyrus. Or, from the perspective of the prophet writing prior to

---

[152]See Gen 31:32,44-50; 1 Sam 24:22.

these events, his vision of Jerusalem's future exaltation by the nations in vv. 14-17 will be the manifestation of Yahweh's oath in v. 23.

Thus having repeatedly argued for Yahweh's divinity
as a universal claim binding upon all in each of the
trial speeches, including the trial speech integral to
this oracle (vv. 20-21), Yahweh admonishes the nations
to turn and swear alliegiance to his covenant. The
nations' response is indeed an important aspect of each
of the trial speeches. One can discern a temporal
progression in their response: In 41:1-7 when Cyrus
only looms on the horizon, the nations ignore Yahweh's
arguments that he is responsible for Cyrus and instead
scurry about to build idols. In 41:21-29 Yahweh denies
that these idols can say or do anything. Israel in
43:8-13 is challenged to appear as Yahweh's witnesses,
and the idol makers as witnesses for the Babylonian
gods are confuted in 44:6-22. But it takes the advent
of Cyrus, who pillages the nations and rebuilds Jerusalem, to humble the nations sufficiently that they would
come to recognize Yahweh's claims. This is explicit in
the term "survivors of the nations" and implicit in the
arrangement of 45:14-25 after the Cyrus oracle. This
progression of the nations' responses to the trial
speeches is a literary device--evidence, we note, that
Deutero-Isaiah was a writing prophet who carefully
crafted and arranged his material--by which the prophet
indicates his perception of the nations' recalcitrance
and the necessity for their severe judgment and humiliation before they will submit to Yahweh's lordship.

That these chapters were all written in anticipation
of Cyrus's conquests is evident by the fact that Cyrus
did not pillage Babylon. Cyrus's leniency towards
Babylon--even embracing the Marduk cult--may have been

a source of disappointment to Deutero-Isaiah, who had hoped Cyrus would have done more to establish Yahweh's ṣědāqâ. Yet the trial speeches indicate that alongside the expected manifestation of Yahweh's historical vindication of Israel, partial responsibility for convincing the nations of Yahweh's sovereignty always lay with Yahweh's witnesses, with those who could argue Yahweh's cause. This prophetic mission to be an advocate for Yahweh among the nations outlived any disappointment with Cyrus.[153]

The universalism of the nations' oath in vv. 23-25 may be viewed as a universalizing of covenant. According to the oath Yahweh's blessing would flow to Israel and by extension to those faithful to Yahweh, and his curse to all idolators. While in Deut 30:15-20 God had laid out a choice of life and death, blessing and curse before Israel, here it is the nations who are offered that choice. The nations' oath summarizes in three bicola the content of Israel's covenant: exclusive allegiance to Yahweh, a curse upon those who reject him, and blessings for those who are faithful. By their oath the nations bind themselves to both the blessing and the curse.

Deutero-Isaiah, by setting the oath of the nations in a trial speech which has an ahistorical, literary setting, defines a new basis for the nations' covenant allegiance. Yahweh's claim to universal sovereignty at issue in the trial before the divine council is a universal claim, one broader than the older national

---

[153]This argues against the supposition of a sudden emergence of universalism late in the career of a supposedly nationalistic prophet, as does Stuhlmueller, "Deutero-Isaiah: Major Transitions in the Prophet's Theology and in Contemporary Scholarship," CBQ 42 (1980) 24-27.

covenant founded upon Yahweh's saving deeds at the
exodus and the conquest of the land of Israel. Since
the trial speech's origin can be traced back to the
cultic drama of creation where God defeats his
opponents and establishes his rule and law over the
cosmos--extended in the Israelite cult to include
Yahweh's historical victories whereby he establishes
his sovereignty in Israel--its claim for Yahweh's
cosmic sovereignty may be rooted ultimately in the
tradition's depiction of Yahweh as Creator. At the
same time, the claims actually put forward in the trial
speeches deal with Yahweh's historical deeds. This is
in fact consistent with Deutero-Isaiah's repeated emphasis on a theology of creation as the basis for
Yahweh's rule in history.[154] We conclude that the
claims for Yahweh as the sole Creator and Actor in
history become the foundation for the new universal
covenant expressed in the oath of the nations. As we
shall see below, this setting of a universal trial
would also lead to the universalizing of Israel's
covenantal prohibitions of idolatry to become binding
upon the nations.

[154]E.g., Isa 40:12-31; 44:24-28; 51:9-11.

CHAPTER 2
POLEMICS AGAINST IDOLATRY

The converse of the trial speeches meant to persuade Israel to faith in Yahweh are the polemics against the making and worshipping of idols (Isa 40:18-20; 41:5-7; 44:9-20; 46:5-7). Despite skepticism as to their authenticity among the previous generation of scholars,[1] recent studies by form critics and rhetorical critics alike have tended to affirm Deutero-Isaianic authorship for many of these polemics.[2] We are interested in these passages as instances of Deutero-Isaiah extending to the nations a prohibition against idolatry formerly incumbent only upon Israel. As with the arguments for Yahweh's sole divinity in the trial speeches, so with these attacks upon idolatry, the prophet is making tenets of Israelite faith into universal claims.

1. Isa 40:12-31: The Incomparability of Yahweh

Isa 40:12-31 is of interest to our study of the place of the nations because vv. 18-20 contain a polemic against the manufacture of idols.

---

[1]So Westermann, *Isaiah 40-66*; McKenzie, *Second Isaiah*; and Elliger, *Jesaja II*, among others.

[2]Among the form critics are Schoors, *I am God your Savior*, 252-3, 274; Melugin, *Formation*, 33-34, 93-94, and "Deutero-Isaiah and Form Criticism,' *VT* 21 (1971), 326-37. Recent studies emphasizing rhetorical structure include Clifford, "The Function of Idol Passages in Second Isaiah," *CBQ* 42 (1980), 450-64; and Spykerboer, *Structure and Composition*, 116-18.

40:12-17

```
Who measured the watersᵃ in the hollow of his hand,      7
    and marked off the heavens with a span?ᵇ             7
Contained the dustᶜ of the earth in a measure,           7
    and weighed the mountains with a balance,            7
    the hills with scales?                               7
                                            1:1::1:1:1
```

```
Who takes the measureᵈ of the spirit of Yahweh,          7
    is his confidantᵉ who instructs him?                 8
[ ]ᶠ Who advises and enlightens him,                     8
    teaches him the path of justice,                     9
[ ]ᵍ instructs him in the way of understanding?          8
                                            1:1::1:1:1
```

```
See, the nations are like a drop in the pan,             8
    they are accounted as dust on the scales,            8
    see, the coastlands weighʰ as fine dust.             8
Lebanon does not suffice for fuel,                       7
    its animals do not suffice for a burnt offering.     7
All the nations are as nothing before him,               8
    they are accounted by him less than emptinessⁱ
    and void.                                            9
                                       1:1:1::1:1::1:1
```

40:18-20

```
To whom do you liken God?                                7
    to what likenessʲ would you compare him?             7
                                                       1:1
```

```
An idol!ᵏ A craftsman casts it,                          6
    [ ]ˡ with gold he plates it,                         8
Chains of silver he smelts,ᵐ                             6
    he erects[] its cover[]ing.ⁿ                         6
A wood that will not rot he chooses,                     6
    a skilled craftsman he seeks out for it,ᵒ            8
    to set up an idol that cannot be moved.              7
                                       b:b::b:b::1:1:1
```

40:21-24

```
Do you not know?    Have you not heard?                  10
    Have you not been told from the beginning?           8
    Have you not understood from the foundationsᵖ
        of the earth?                                    10
                                            (b:b):1:1
```

He who sits above the vault of the earth, 7
who has peopled it[q] as with grasshoppers; 8
He who stretches out the heavens like a veil, 7
who spreads them like a tent to dwell in; 7
He who brings princes to nought, 8
who makes rulers of the earth as nothing; 9
l:l::l:l::l:l

Yea, scarcely are they planted, 5
scarcely are they sown, 5
scarcely has their stem taken root in the earth; 8
When he blows[r] upon them and they wither, 9
the tempest carries them off like stubble. 9
b:b:l::l:l

40:25-26

"To whom do you liken me that I should be his equal?" 10
says the Holy One. 4
Lift up your eyes on high and see: 10
who created these? 5
He who musters their host by number, 9
calling each of them by name; 7
By <his>[s] manifold power and mighty strength, 8
not one is missing. 4
l:b::l:b::l:b::l:b

40:27-31

Why do you say, O Jacob, 6
and talk, O Israel: 6
"My way is hid from Yahweh; 8
my right has passed without notice[t] from my God?" 9
b:b::l:l

Do you not know, 5
have you not heard, 5
Yahweh is the everlasting God, 7
the Creator of the ends of the earth. 6
b:b::l:l

He does not grow weary, he does not tire, 7
his understanding is unsearchable. 7
He gives strength to the weary, 6
to him who lacks power he gives abundant[u] energy. 7
Youths grow weary and tire, 10
young men fall, exhausted, 9
but those who hope in Yahweh shall renew strength. 9
They shall mount up with wings[v] as eagles; 7
they shall run and not tire, 8
they shall walk and not grow weary. 8
l:l::l:l::l:l:l::l:l:l

TEXTUAL NOTES

[a]1QIsa[a] has **my ym**, "waters of the sea," but MT **mayim** (with G) is preferable from the standpoint of meter and assonance. The suggestion of BHS and BH[3] **yammîm** has no support. G lacks the pronomial suffix of MT **bĕ-šoᶜŏlô**, "in his palm," but that is probably idiomatic rather than reflecting on the Vorlage.

[b]1QIsa[a] **bzrtw** adds the suffix under the influence of the first colon.

[c]G lacks ᶜ**apar** and misunderstands MT **kāl**, the Qal of **kwl**, as the adjective **kol**.

[d]Note the subtle wordplay on **tikkēn** of the previous verse. Here the word is often translated "to direct," but Clifford points out Prov 16:2 where Yahweh is said to take the measure (**tōkēn**, a Qal participle) of the spirit of a man.[3]

[e]On '**îš** ᶜ**ăṣātô**, see Isa 46:11 "a man of my counsel."

[f]Omitting the initial '**et** of MT, which is a direct object marker and not the preposition "with." The verb **nôᶜāṣ** denotes the activity of the counselor (cf. 1 Kgs 12:6,9) rather than of Yahweh, in parallel with the other verbs in this strophe.

[g]Omit MT **wa-yĕlammĕdēhû** daᶜat, absent from G, as a dittography.

[h]Reading plural **yiṭṭōlû** with G, Aq., Sym., Thdt.; the final **wāw** in MT has been transposed to the following **û-lĕbānôn**. The root **nṭl**, while attested in the Hebrew Bible as meaning to lift or carry, here means "to weigh," as attested in the noun **nēṭel**, "weight"

---

[3]Clifford, Fair Spoken, 77 n. 1.

(Prov. 27:3), and in Syriac. Since in weighing an object lifts or tips the scales, these two meanings are quite compatible. Clifford correctly translates the entire tricolon as an image of weighing, hence **delî** here means the pan of a scale, not the modern English idiom "a drop in a bucket."[4]

[i]1QIsaa reads **kĕ-'epes.**

[j]Spykerboer correctly argues for **dĕmût** as including both concrete and abstract senses and criticizes Elliger, who argues against the unity of vv. 19-20 with its context partly on the basis of a traditional Christian exegesis of **dĕmût** as an abstract term (cf. Gen 1:26) which a hypothetical later editor understood as a concrete image.[5] **dĕmût** does indeed refer to concrete statues (2 Chr 4:3), and in the Tell Fakhariyah bilingual inscription (ll. 1,15) **dumûtā'**, "statue," is the Aramaic equivalent of Akk. **ṣelem** and refers to the statue of the king. Here it is simply a synonym for **pesel** and leads directly into v. 19.

[k]The definite article in MT **hap-pesel** is a strong demonstrative, marking off **pesel** as the referent (in this case the direct object) of a prosodic unit of several bicola or tricola, and the object-verb-subject word order gives additional emphasis.[6] Placing the main referent of an extended prosodic unit as the first

---

[4]Clifford, loc. cit. Cf. D.W. Thomas, "'A Drop of a Bucket'? Some Observations on the Hebrew Text of Is. 40,15," ZAW 103 (1968), 214-221.

[5]Spykerboer, Structure and Composition, 36; Elliger, Jesaja II, 59-73.

[6]See Spykerboer, 42f., who also notes the extensive use of this rhetorical syntax in 40:12-26; cf. Elliger Jesaja II, 59-60,74.

word in the initial colon is typical of the prophet's
style, e.g. 44:12,13,16,17. He does the same with
inital pronouns, e.g. 40:12, 41:2; 43:9b.

[1]MT and all the versions have wĕ-ṣôrēp, but it has
all the appearances of a dittography triggered by ṣōrēp
in v. 19d. The versions have a further expansion
adding the verb ᶜāśâ. 1QIsa[a] reads hpsl wyᶜśh msk ḥrš
wṣwrp where msk could easily a corruption of MT nāsak
due to mem/nûn confusion. G reads μὴ εἰκόνα ἐποίησε
τέκτων ἢ χρυσοχόος χωνεύσας χρυσίον περιεχρύσωσεν
αὐτόν. Χωνεύσας, the aorist participle of χωνεύω
meaning "to cast metal," corresponds to nāsak of MT.
The bicolon suggested by G:

< *hap-pesel ᶜāśâ ḥāraš
  haṣ-ṣôrēp nāsak

is short (the second definite article is secondary, see
#k), and it is difficult to imagine how such wholesale
transpositions could have generated MT. 1QIsa[a] supports the order of MT and points to a conflation. We
may have a pair of ancient variants in both the verbs
ᶜāśâ and nāsak and the nouns ḥāraš and ṣôrēp.

[m]We read a perfect ṣārap where MT has ṣôrēp. BHS
suggests on the basis of the Targ. m'ḥyd lyh that we
read the rare verb rṣp, to fit or join together, but
that verb is associated with marquetry or tile work
rather than with casting metal. Our finding that ṣôrēp
of v. 19a of MT is an expansion is best explained as a
dittography of ṣôrēp in this verse. G is defective;
ὁμοίωμα κατεσκεύασεν αὐτόν may be a paraphrase of the
text straddling vv. 19-20 as < *ṣĕrāpāhû massēkâ[ ].

[n]See the discussion.

[o]G transposes lô after the following verb; 1QIsa[a]
has suffered metathesis and reads wbšqlw. The pronoun
lô refers not to the wood but to the idol.

PTorrey and North emend MT **môsĕdôt**, attested by all versions, to **miy-yĕsûdat** (cf. Ps 87:1). But MT can stand if the **min** prefix on **mē-rō'š** does double duty. 1QIsaᵃ lacks the definite article on **'ereṣ**.

qMT **yōšĕbêhā**, "its inhabitants," may be read as **yōšîbehā**, a Hiphil imperfect with feminine singular suffix "he peopled it." Note the alliteration here.

ʳFor MT **nāšap** 1QIsaᵃ reads ᶜšp with a **nûn** written as a correction above the line.

ˢWe read **'omeṣ** with G, Targ. and **kōḥ<ô>** with 1QIsaᵃ for MT **'ammîṣ kōḥ**. Torrey understands **mē-rōb 'ônîm** as denoting the astral deities, who are often called **gibbôrîm**; cf. Ps 103:20. But none of these terms for strength are elsewhere used of the heavenly host. While **rōb** can refer to the stars of heaven (Deut 1:10; 10:22; 28:62), **rōb kōḥ(ô)** is elsewhere attested as an expression for Yahweh's strength (Job 23:6; Isa 63:1). Furthermore, **mē-rōb** is often used with a counting term (i.e. **yissāpēr**) to denote a multitude beyond anyone's ability to count (Gen 16:10; 32:13; 1 Kgs 3:8; 8:5), while in this description Yahweh <u>can</u> count the stars in spite of their vast multitude because his power is far greater (cf. Ps 147:5).

ᵗG is conflate with two verbs for MT **yaᶜăbôr**. On the translation see comments.

ᵘMT ᶜoṣmâ **yarbeh**: ᶜoṣmâ is a <u>hapax</u> while the masculine <u>qutl</u> noun is well attested; the meter is improved if the **hē** is transposed to the following verb rendered as a hiphil perfect **harbeh**. G reads λύπην < *ᶜaṣṣēbâ which is the result of haplography: ᶜṣ[m hr]bh.

ᵛThe noun **'ēber** is an adverbial accusative of means. RSV aptly translates "they mount up with wings."

Isa 40:12-31 is a fine example of a unit which lends itself to an analysis of structural features. It should not be divided into smaller pieces,[7] but has integrity as a structually complete whole.[8] Schoors recognizes a large-scale parallel structure in four stanzas: vv. 12-17, 18-20, 21-24 and 25-26, but for form-critical reasons he is uncertain about the relationship of vv. 27-31 to the "perfect chiastic parallelism" of the structure that precedes it. Schoors distinguishes type A and B stanzas by the fact that while both begin with rhetorical questions, in the A stanzas the questions about Yahweh as creator serve as arguments for a second set of assertions about nations and rulers, while in the B stanzas the initial rhetorical questions themselves state the issue under dispute for which the following verses serve as evidence. As a unity depicting Yahweh's superiority to every rival, he diagrams the structure thus:[9]

---

[7]Melugin (Formation, 33-35, 90-93) analyzes four genre units: 40:12-17, 18-24, 25-26 and 27-31, but recognizes they are arranged in a coherent group; Elliger (pp. 45-47) finds three: vv. 12-17, 18-26 and 27-31; and North (The Second Isaiah, 89) two: vv. 12-26 and 27-31.

[8]Schoors, I am God your Savior, 257-8; cf. Muilenberg IB, 5, 415-19; Spykerboer, Structure and Composition, 49-51; Bonnard, Le Second Isaie, 93-97; Clifford, CBQ 42 (1980) 457. Torrey (The Second Isaiah, 301-302) views all of chapter 40 as a single poem.

[9]Schoors, 257-9. Spykerboer (pp. 49-50), while dependent on Schoors, introduces a slight modification by recognizing that the opening rhetorical questions of both the A and B stanzas tie them together.

```
I.  A.  12-17:  1.  The great creating God           Yahweh
                2.  Thus, before him the nations     not
                    are nothing      (Hymnic)         active
    B.  18-20:  1*. To whom liken God?               Yahweh
                2*. For the Idols are nothing         not
                                                      active

II. A.  21-24:  1.  The great creating God           Yahweh
                2.  Thus he makes princes            active
                    as nothing        (Hymnic)
    B.  25-26:  1*. To whom liken God?               Yahweh
                2*. For he created the star-gods     active
```

With this starting point, recognizing A and B stanzas
of different but complementary formal structure, we can
discern additional unifying aspects of Deutero-Isaiah's
design.

Verses 27-31 constitute a complete disputation. It
is form-critically the only complete disputation in
this literary unit because it has the initial statement
of complaint (v. 27) which is lacking in the other
stanzas. Westermann sees here a quotation of a community lament, "a charge brought against the deity" that
he hides himself (cf. Ps 44:25).[10] Along with the
change of person from plural to singular and the slight
change of theme from Yahweh's ability as sovereign to
his willingness to help Israel, these features have led
some to adjudge this unit to be an independent
oracle.[11] Spykerboer points out that the change of
person is not significant, since the prophet often
switches from the second person plural to singular when
he specifies his audience as "Jacob"/"Israel."   Laying
aside v. 27 for the moment, vv. 28-31 form a disputation of the A type with clear parallels to vv. 21-24.

---

[10]Westermann, *Isaiah 40-66*, 59.

[11]Elliger, 95; Melugin, 35f.

Both open with rhetorical questions "Have you not
known, have you not heard" (vv. 21, 28a) and hymnic
style praise of Yahweh as creator (vv. 22, 28b). From
creation to consequences in human affairs, vv. 29-31
state that Yahweh gives strength to the weak, the
converse of the assertion in vv. 23-24 of the previous
A stanza that Yahweh uproots the strong.

Having now defined three type A stanzas, the larger
structure of Isa 40:12-31 is further delineated in
Table 4. The A and B stanzas are of similar but not
identical lengths: 17, 14 and 18 cola for the three A
stanzas, 9 and 8 cola for the B stanzas. Since the
initial quotation of the lament in v. 27 is outside of
the parallel rhetorical structure detected by Schoors,
the third A stanza may be analyzed as 14 plus 4 cola.
However, stanza lengths are only a rough indication of
structure. This composition is striking in its inten-
tional variety of prosody from one stanza to the next.
Thus the first A stanza has alternating bicola and
tricola, the second A stanza has bicola framed by
(b:b):1:1 and b:b:1 tricola, the third A stanza begins
with alternating b:b and 1:1 bicola, and the second B
stanza even switches to 1:b meter. Deutero-Isaiah was
a consummate artist who never allowed the structural
regularities of his compositions to dominate his
poetry. This metrical variety should not, however,
obscure the significant verbal and thematic connections
between these stanzas. They are integral to their
construction and could not have been produced by a
serendipitous arrangement of shorter oracles by an
editor.

The first stanza, a type A stanza, begins with a
series of questions. Whether their answer(s) are God
(v. 12) or no one (vv. 13-14), the purpose of these

TABLE 4: The Structure of Isa 40:12-31

A

	vv. 12-17 17 cola	vv. 21-24 14 cola	vv. 27-31 18 cola
Disputed lament			b:b My way hid from God **derek mišpāṭ**
Rhetorical question	**mî** Who measured heaven? 3x Whom did he consult? 1:1:1	**hălōʾ** Do you not know? 4x Have you not heard? (b:b):1:1	**hălōʾ** Do you not know? **ʾim lōʾ** Have you not heard? b:b
Hymn to Creator	(Yahweh the Creator) 1:1:1 **mišpāṭ derek** **tĕbûnâ**	**yôšēb** Peoples the earth **nôṭeh** Spreads out heaven	**bôrēʾ** Reach is infinite **tĕbûnâ** unsearchable Does not weary
Consequence	hence nations are as nothing **kĕ-ʾayin tōhû** **hēn** 2x 1:1:1	**nôtēn** hence he makes rulers as nothing **lĕ-ʾayin tōhû** **ʾap** 3x Their root withers (b:b):1	**nôtēn** hence gives strength to the weak 3x Mount up as eagles verb- initial

B

	vv. 18-20 9 cola	vv. 25-26 8 cola
Rhetorical question	To whom do you liken God? **ʾēl**	To whom do you liken me? **qādôš** - the Holy One
Creator/creation	Craftsmen make Idols **nāsak** Description of manufacture	Yahweh created the Astral deities **bārāʾ** Description of muster
Reason/consequence	because wood will not rot skilled craftsman hence Idol will not move	because of Yahweh's strength hence none is missing

questions is to illustrate God's sovereign and independent creative power, to act without anyone's help or
advice.[12]   These rhetorical questions are each introduced by **mî**, and they are followed in vv. 15-17 by a
conclusion introduced by **hēn** and depicting the rela-
tively paltry scale of the nations in comparison to
Yahweh. As these questions are reminiscent of Job,
Melugin discerns here a wisdom genre and points to Job
40:25-32, where a series of rhetorical questions designed to show the might of Leviathan is followed in
41:1 with a conclusion likewise introduced by **hēn**.[13]
Nevertheless, this observation does not warrant isolating these verses as a separate genre unit. Job was
not an oral poet, and this wisdom genre was not an oral
genre, and hence its appropriation into Deutero-Isaiah
may best be seen as that of a literary motif rather
than as a genre in the strict sense with a distinct
Sitz im Leben which would demarcate an independent
unit.

The repeated interrogative pronouns (**mî**) answered by
repeated emphatic particles (**hēn**) is the major rhetorical device which structures this stanza, and this rhetorical demarcation between initial rhetorical questions and consequent assertions will continue through
the other type A stanzas. Additional verbal repetition
within the stanza includes **tikkēn** and **yôdîᶜennû** in the
rhetorical questions, a chiasm formed by **neḥšĕbû** in the
conclusion, and **mō'zĕnayim** once in the questions and
again in the conclusion. Further verbal repetition
looks ahead to the other two A stanzas: **mišpāṭ, derek**

---

[12]On this tangential dispute see Spykerboer, 33;
Schoors, 248.

[13]Melugin, 32.

and **tĕbûnôt** in the rhetorical questions describe, according to Beuken, the course of history as determined by God's will and insight both here and in the corresponding section of vv. 27-31.[14] The words **'ayin** "nothing" and **tōhû** "void" which state God's perspective on the nations recur in the second A stanza (v. 23) where they describe the fate of their princes.

In the second A stanza, as in the first, it is Yahweh's cosmic size that allows him to treat human rulers like grasshoppers or young plants. But the primary argument is based upon Yahweh's activities to populate the world--rendering **yōšĕbêhā** in v. 22a as a hiphil verb--and to extend the heavens as a protective environment to support life. Hence Yahweh, like a cosmic gardener, can plant or uproot princes at will, and as the one who extends the heavens, he can bring the storm or the sirroco winds to devastate the harvest (cf. Isa 40:6-8).[15]

Both the first and second A stanzas are structured by repetition of interrogative pronouns in the opening rhetorical questions and emphatic particles in the conclusion--in this latter stanza **hălô'** (v. 21) and **'ap** (v. 24) respectively. These interrogative and emphatic particles are each in short, staccato half-cola which frame the entire stanza. Now the rhetorical questions chiding the audience (v. 21) are distinct from the hymnic depiction of Yahweh as creator (v. 22). The middle of the stanza is structured by the initial

---

[14]See W.A.M. Beuken, "Mišpāṭ: The First Servant Song and its Context," VT 22 (1972), 8-11.

[15]Clifford (Fair Spoken, 81-82) has noted language of kingship in the description of Yahweh as enthroned (**yōšēb**) and rulers as taking root and sprouting like a shoot (Isa 11:1), but this adds secondary richness and does not govern the argument.

participles **hay-yôšēb, han-nôṭeh** and **han-nōṭēn**, each
introducing hymnic passages. The first two describe
Yahweh's grandeur as creator, and the third his consequent power over the rulers of the earth. Several of
these prosodic devices--the interrogative particle
hălô', the short lines and the pair of verbs **yd^c** and
šm^c in the opening rhetorical questions and the initial
participles in the hymnic middle section--are also
found in the third A stanza.

The third A stanza (vv. 27-31) opens with a pair of
parallel questions in vv. 27 and 28a. Each have initial
interrogative pronouns (**lammâ, hălô'**), b:b bicola, and
following 1:1 bicola containing the pair **yhwh/'ĕlōhîm**.
The first question quotes and contests a community
lament. The second rhetorical question is worded similar to the question in v. 21 and introduces a rebuttal
based upon Yahweh's power and greatness as creator. As
in the second A stanza, the hymnic descriptions of
Yahweh's creative acts and his consequent acts for his
people are introduced by Qal participles **bôrē'** (v. 28b)
and **nôṭēn** (v. 29). The conclusion in v. 31 lacks any
emphatic particles; instead it features the repetition
of initial verbs **ya^călû, yārûṣû**, and **yēlĕkû**. Here the
major unifying device is the threefold repetition of
the pair **yî^cap** and **yîga^c**.

The substance of the community's lament as stated in
v. 27bb is often translated "my right is disregarded by
my God." But **ya^căbôr** here means to "pass by unnoticed"
in parallel with **nistĕrâ** "is hidden." The complaint is
not that Yahweh is actively disregarding Israel's
oppression or that he has no desire to save, but rather
that Israel feels distant, "hidden" from God and far
from the center of his concern. Hence the rebuttal to
this plaint (v. 28) depicts Yahweh's infinite extension

in time (ᶜôlãm) and space (qĕṣê 'ereṣ). A related
issue is God's justice. Repeating words from the initial stanza, mišpãṭ and derek have become points of
contention, recalling the questions of v. 14, "who
taught Yahweh mišpãṭ, or instructs him in the way of
tĕbûnôt." Only Yahweh can judge what is mišpãṭ, for
"his tĕbûnâ"--another word introduced in the opening
stanza (v. 14)--"is unsearchable."

Besides recalling a theme of the first stanza, the
major argument of vv. 27-31 is that Yahweh gives
strength to the weak. The argument for Yahweh's
strength had been made in the preceding B stanza (vv.
25-26), whose terms for Yahweh's strength, rōb 'ônîm
wĕ-'omeṣ kôḥ(ô), are repeated throughout vv. 29-31.
Furthermore, the claim that God endows the weak with
power is the converse of the claim in the second A
stanza, that he makes powerful rulers into nothing. In
both stanzas Deutero-Isaiah draws upon the tradition of
the great reversal as a manifestation of Yahweh's theophany.[16] His will to reverse the fortunes of the
oppressed of the earth is also an aspect of his mišpãṭ,
one which is made explicit in 42:1-9.

The two B stanzas, though showing very different
prosody, are likewise intimately related in theme and
rhetorical structure. Each begins with a nearly identical opening question "to whom do you liken God/me?"
each denoting God not as Yahweh or Israel's God, but by
the striking non-specific terms 'ēl (v. 18) and qãdôš
(v. 25). The arguments of both turn on the issue of
creator and creation. Yahweh is incomparable to idols
because they are human creations of wood and metal (vv.
19-20) and to the astral deities because he is their
creator and commander (v. 26). In the second prosodic

[16]Cf. Isa 49:7,24-26; chs. 34-35; 42:14-17.

unit of each stanza this point is stated explicitly:
the idol is cast nāsak by the craftsman, while Yahweh
created bārā' the heavenly host--here denoted elliptic-
ally by 'ēlleh. Then comes an elaboration on their
creation, either in terms of the work of the craftsmen
to fabricate idols out of precious metals in vv. 19b-
20a or through a depiction of Yahweh marshalling and
naming his host in v. 26b. They conclude with an
ironic comment in which the worth of the creations,
stated in the negative, is attributed to the skill or
strength of their creators. The idol is solid, it will
not totter (lō' yimmôṭ) because its wood is not rotten
and its craftsman is skilled (ḥākām, v. 20b-d). The
astral deities are obedient, not one is missing ('îš
lō' neᶜdār) on account of Yahweh's strength and might
(mē-rōb 'ônîm wĕ-'omeṣ kôḥô).

These B stanzas are also rhetorically linked to the
following A stanzas, so much so that Melugin considers
vv. 18-24 to be a single unit, and Clifford analyzes
vv. 18-24 and 25-31 as comparable sections.[17] The
questions in vv. 21 and 28, "have you not known..." may
be referring back to the preceding descriptions of
idols and astral deities as well as forward to the
following depictions of Yahweh's transcendence and
sovereignty. The verbal repetition of 'ônîm and kôḥ
linking the B colon vv. 25-26 with the following A
colon 27-31 have already been mentioned. Similarly,
vv. 18-20 and 21-24 together set up a contrast between
inert idols and Yahweh the Creator and Savior, between
the activity of Yahweh who annihilates rulers and blows
them away like chaff (v. 23) and the idol that can do
nothing in its immovability (v. 20).

---

[17]Melugin, 33; Clifford, Fair Spoken, 79; CBQ 42
(1980) 459.

Isa 40:18-20, the stanza comparing Yahweh to idols,
contains a notorious crux at the beginning of v. 20.
The original text may be beyond recovery, and our new
attempt at a solution has its flaws, but we present it
with the hope that it may advance the discussion beyond
the present impasse. MT, 1QIsaᵃ ham-mĕsukkān tĕrûmâ is
traditionally rendered "he who is poor in respect of a
contribution," where mĕsukkān is taken as a pual participle of the alleged Hebrew root skn, "to be poor," or
repointed to the adjective miskēn, "poor." This reading
has been long deemed inadequate, and there have been
many attempts at emendation.[18] A second line of interpretation renders musukkān a kind of wood, cognate to
Akk. musukkanu, "mulberry." But Deutero-Isaiah is
familiar with kinds of wood, mulberry among them (cf.
41:19), and "the mulberry of the [wood] offering" is
clumsy Hebrew, without any prosodic unity to what sur-
rounds. Some have interpreted the Greek ὁμοίωμα κατεσκεύασεν αὐτόν as though it were reading ham-mĕkōnēn
tĕmûnâ, "he who would set up a likeness," but G was
more probably paraphrasing a text straddling vv. 19d-
20a: ṣĕrāpāhû massēkâ (see note #m).

Recent attempts at exegesis have sought alternative
meanings for the root skn: Trudinger employs the
Hebrew root skn meaning "to be familiar with" (Job
22:21, Ps 139:3) and gives the rather farfetched
rendering of mĕsakkēn as a Piel participle meaning

---

[18]See Trudinger, "To whom then will you liken God?,"
VT 17 (1967), 220-25; K. Elliger, Jesaja II, 60-62, 73-
81; T.N.D. Mettinger, "The Elimination of a Crux?, A
Syntactic and Semantic Study of Isaiah xl 18-20,"
VTSupp 26 (Leiden: E.J. Brill, 1974) 77-83; North, The
Second Isaiah, 82; Schoors, 253-55; H. D. Preuss, Ver-
spottung fremder Religionen im Alten Testament, BWANT
92 (Stuttgart: W. Kohlhammer, 1971) 193ff.

"connoisseur [of idols]."[19] Driver has explained
tĕrûmâ as a Hebrew rendering of Akk. tarimtu, a sacred
object, possibly a dedicatory offering.[20] Gray, followed by Schoors and Mettinger, translates "he who
would set up an idol," drawing attention to Ugaritic
skn, a term with one of its meanings the noun stela or
image.[21] However, Ugaritic skn appears to be an
Akkadian loan word (šiknu), and evidence of a produc-
tive West Semitic verb form is scanty. Neither could
this be a contemporary Akkadian influence, since the D
form of škn is almost unknown in Akkadian. North
rightly termed these readings poetically impossible,
and he calls the colon a gloss on the basis of 1QIsa[a],
where it was written in by a second hand. But what
would motivate such an obscure gloss?

All of these attempts at a solution assume that
vv. 19-20 have a bipartite rhetorical structure, with
ham-mĕsukkān in parallel with hap-pesel. But this is
not at all a necessary assumption, given the disarray
of the text. Our approach dispenses with the medieval
verse divisions and treats the disputed phrase as the
final colon of the bicolon begun in v. 19b. The following tricolon (v. 20b-d) stands complete, with
climactic parallelism typical of Deutero-Isaiah. On
the other hand, v. 19 appears incomplete; there is no
parallel to the technical term rĕtûqôt.

---

[19]Trudinger, VT 17 (1967) 220-25.

[20]G. R. Driver, "Linguistic and Textual Problems in
Isaiah XL-LXVI," JTS 36 (1935), 396-406.

[21]John Gray, The Legacy of Canaan, VTSupp 5 (Leiden,
E.J. Brill, 1957) 192; Schoors, 254; Mettinger, VTSupp
26, 81-82. Cf. UT, 449f;

North understands **rĕtŭqôt** as temple ornamentation not on the image itself, but "silver fence chains"[22] framing its cella and creating a separation between the image and its worshippers. This is the sense of **rattûkôt** in 1 Kgs 6:21, chains which were drawn in front of the **dĕbîr**, and also of the Jewish Aramaic cognate **ritkā'**, a chain fence. Alternatively it could refer to ornamental chain jewelery worn by the image, since the semantic range of **rtq** includes both the fettering of captives with chains (Nah 3:10) and the delicate chain work of a silversmith.[23] But Trudinger's notion[24] that the chains were to tie down the god "so it cannot be moved," while it may appear consistent with Deutero-Isaiah's theology, cannot be accepted. It is iconographically inconceivable that the great gods, who are variously portrayed as seated enthroned or standing often in active poses, would be held down by chains, symbols of a prisoner. It is also unlikely that malleable silver would be molded to make "fastenings" to hold the image to its base. Such a construction would be structurally weak and would con- flict with what is known of idols as built out of a core of wood or base metal overlaid with precious metal (Isa 40:19b speaks of the gold as pounded out into a thin covering) and fastened by hammer and nails (Isa 41:7).

---

[22]North, 86.

[23]The late Hebrew verbs **rtq** and **rtk** can convey the sense of welding by a silversmith, and Jastrow cites an attestation in <u>Cant.</u> <u>R.</u> IV.4 where the niphal means to join together the gold chains of the breastplate. Arabic **rtq** can mean to darn (stockings), perhaps also hinting at delicate work.

[24]Trudinger, <u>VT</u> 17 (1967) 224-25.

A suitable technical term of temple architecture or cultic ornamentation parallel to rĕtuqôt is not hard to come by: several nouns from the root **skk** denote cultic structures or ornamentation. The **sukkâ** was a booth constructed at the New Year's festival. In P a **māsāk** is the screen at the entrance to each room of the tabernacle, dividing its chambers and, like the Orthodox iconostasis, concealing their contents from all but the priests. The **mĕsuk(k)â** in Ezek 28:13 comes in the midst of a two part oracle against Tyre which describes the riches of the king of Tyre in an extended simile as the riches of El in the Garden of Eden on the mountain of God. The image is of El's holy abode, the cosmic mountain represented by Zion in the Israelite tradition and equally appropriate as a description of the sanctuary at Tyre.[25] The **mĕsuk(k)â** is a pectoral inlaid with precious stones, presumably the ornamentation worn by a divine image as it stood in a sanctuary paved with "stones of fire," and perhaps related to the ephod worn by the Israelite high priest.[26]

The evidence is insufficient to determine whether the bicolon describes the jewelery adorning the idol, including both silver necklaces and a gem-studded **mĕsukkâ** as in Ezek 28:13, or alternatively, the screens and fence chains decorating or concealing its cella as suggested by cognate terms in P and 1 Kgs 6:21. In either case, a noun from the root **skk** is a fitting

---

[25]The connection between the Garden of Eden and the Mountain of God is explored by Jon D. Levenson, Theology of the Program of Restoration of Ezekiel 40-48, HSM 10 (Missoula, Mt: Scholars Press, 1976), 25-36.

[26]Zimmerli translates "garment" and makes a comparison of the list of precious stones on the **mĕsukkâ** to the stones in the high priest's pectoral in Exod 28:17-20. See W. Zimmerli, Ezekiel II, 84.

complement to **rĕtūqôt**. While our knowledge of neo-
Babylonian temple furnishings is scanty, with many as
yet unidentified terms, it is well known that Mesopotamian idols were adorned with much jewelry. Hence we
cautiously propose an emendation in which the silver
chains[27] held up the idol's bejewelled breastplate, its
"covering" or **mĕsukkâ**.[28]

There remains the problem of the original form of
the text. An unlikely possibility is that MT **mĕsukkān**
is a noun with a preformative **mēm** and afformative ***-ān**.
But the collocation of a preformative **mēm** with this
afformative is exceedingly rare, found only in the
hapax **maššā'ôn** (from **nš'**).[29] Our suggested emendation
to **mĕsukkātô rōmēm**, "he erects its covering," could

---

[27]See above, n. 23.

[28]The contrast noted above between the idol's immovability in v. 20 and Yahweh's activity in vv. 21-24 may
be enriched by the proposed description of goldsmiths
fashioning the idol's jewelery. In Mesopotamian religion a god's ornaments were considered insignia and
symbols of the god's offices and powers (**melammu**,
parṣum, **me**). On such jewelery as both symbol and
actual bearers of power, see the Sumerian myth
"Inanna's Descent into the Netherworld," (ANET, 52-57)
where Inanna, upon entering the netherworld, divests
herself of her seven **me** and thereby loses all her
protection. Another such insignia conveying authority
is the Tablet of Destinies; c.f. the Akkadian "Myth of
Zu." But for Deutero-Isaiah, these symbols of the
idol's purported powers are, like the idol itself, mere
human artifacts. Yahweh's power to wreak destruction
requires no jewelery or insignia; it is inherent in his
having created the cosmos. The alternative reconstruction of v. 19c-20a as denoting the decorative screens
surrounding the idol brings out a different comparison:
the grand image of Yahweh creating his cosmic abode,
stretching out the heavens "like a tent to dwell in" in
v. 22b, would contrast with the man-made home of the
idol, a paltry cella decorated with mere curtains and
screens.

[29]GK #85u.

generate the consonantal MT by metathesis of a **mēm**
which was then confused with **nûn**, and with additions of
a final **hē** mater and a definite article.

Our compositional analysis finds Isa 40:12-31 to be
a tightly structured whole. It will not permit the
oft-suggested transposition of 41:6-7 to a position
following 40:20.[30] The depiction of idol manufacture
in 40:18-20 fits into a distinct structure as a B
stanza parallel to vv. 25-26, and any addition would
violate that structure. Furthermore, each of these
descriptions of idol manufacture has its own integrity
in conformity to its context. We have shown that the
depiction of the busy, even frenetic activity of the
craftsmen in 41:5-7 is specifically designed to describe the nations' fearful response to Cyrus whose
advent has just been announced in 41:1-4. It would be
out of place in this unit, where the focus is less on
the craftsmen's anxiety than upon the idols themselves
as products of human labor. Here the contrast is
specifically between the idols as creations and Yahweh
as Creator. This analysis also confirms the integrity
of the polemic against idolatry in vv. 18-20 as of a
piece with the unit; it can by no means be assigned to
a separate redactional stratum.

---

[30]So B. Duhm, <u>Das Buch Jesaja</u>, HKAT 3/1 (Göttingen:
Vandenhoeck & Ruprecht, 1902) 263-65; followed by
Schoors, 252-53. Westermann (pp. 61, 66) and Elliger
(pp. 65-81, 115) join these verses but consider the
entire stratum of idol passages to be secondary.

2. Isa 46:1-13: A Taunt and a Polemic against Idols in
    a Disputation with Israel

The structure of chapter 46, and hence the proven-
ance of its polemics against idolatry, is in dispute.
Melugin and Schoors follow most form critics who divide
the chapter into several originally independent genre
units: a salvation oracle in vv. 1-4, a disputation in
vv. 5-11, and a short salvation speech in vv. 12-13.[31]
Westermann and Elliger excise vv. 5-8, a polemical
description of the manufacture of idols, as a later
addition, yet preserve vv. 1-4, a taunt against idols
as things to be carried, as genuine. Departing from
other form critics, Westermann sees 45:18-46:13, less
vv. 5-8, as a loosely unified composition organized by
repeated imperatives.[32] In this sense he approaches
the position of Muilenberg and Clifford, who use rhetorical analysis to discern in chapter 46 a unified
composition.[33] We also consider chapter 46 to be a
well crafted and unified literary piece in four stanzas
(vv. 1-4, 5-7, 8-11, 12-13). Some structural features
of this chapter are illuminated by compositional analysis. We must also attempt to deal with the difficult
textual problem of the opening verses.

---

[31]Melugin, Formation, 131-35, Schoors, I am God your
Savior, 31, 274.

[32]Isa 45:20,22; 46:3,9,12. Cf. Westermann, Isaiah
40-66, 184.

[33]Muilenberg, IB 5, 535-36; Clifford, CBQ 42 (1980)
454-57.

46:1-4

```
Bel bows down, Nebo stoops,                                     7
    they are but idol[]s.                                       5
On beasts and on cattle                                         8
    they are borne[], they are carried,ᵃ                        7
    a burden on weary (animals).                                6
They stoop, they collapse completely;ᵇ                         8
    not able to rescue a burden,                                8
    they themselves go into captivity.                          8
                                    1:b::1:1:b::1:1:1
```

```
Listen to me, O house of Jacob,                                 7
    all the remnant of the house of Israel,                     7
who have been carried since birth                               7
    who have been borne since the womb.ᶜ                        7
Unto old age I am he,                                           6
    unto gray hairs I will carry.                               6
I have carried,ᵈ  and I will bear;                            5/5
    I will carry,  and I will bring to safety.               5/4
                        1:1::1:1::1:1::(b:b):(b:b)
```

46:5-7

```
To whom do you liken me and make me equal?ᵉ                   10
    do you compare me that we may be alike?ᶠ                   8
                                                               1:1
```

```
Those who lavish gold from the purse,                           7
    who weigh silver in the balance:                            7
They hire a goldsmith;  he makes itᵍ into a god,ʰ          5/4
    which they adore;  yea, they worship.                    3/4
They lift it on the shoulder,  they carry it;              7/4
    they set it down on its base,ⁱ  and it stands.          7/3
From its place it does not move;                                7
    though one cries to it,ʲ it does not answer;              8
    from his distressᵏ it will not save him.                   9
                    1:1::(b:b):(b:b)::(b:b):(b:b)::1:1:1
```

46:8-11

```
Remember this and take courage,ˡ                               8
    take it to heart, you transgressors,                       9
Remember the former things of old:                             8
    for I am God, and there is no other;                       8
    God, and none is like me.                                  8
                                            1:1::1:1:1
```

Foretelling the future from time past, 7
   from of old things not yet done. 7
Saying "My counsel shall stand, 7
   all that I intend I will do."[m] 6
Calling a bird of prey from the east, 6
   from a far country a man of my counsel.[n] 8
I have spoken, and I will bring it to pass, 4/5
   I have purposed it,[o] and I will do it. 4/4
l:l::l:l::l:l::(b:b):(b:b)

46:12-13

Listen to me, you stubborn[p] of heart, 8
   you who are far from vindication. 8
I have brought near[q] my vindication, it is not far; 9
   my salvation will not tarry. 9
I have put salvation in Zion, 9
   for Israel my glory. 7
l:l::l:l::l:l

TEXTUAL NOTES

[a]See the discussion; we read:

kōrē^{c} bēl qōrēs nĕbô
hāyû ^{c}ăṣabbî[]m
la-ḥayyâ wĕlab-bĕhēmâ
nĕśū'ôt[] <wĕ>-^{c}ămûsôt
maśśā' la-^{c}ăyēpâ

[b]This colon is missing from the Greek, which reads ὡς φορτίον κοπιῶντι καὶ πεινῶντι καὶ ἐκλελυμένῳ οὐκ ἰσχύοντι ἅμα. It appears to be translating a series of expansions on **la-^{c}ăyēpâ** of the previous verse and omitting all of MT except the final **yaḥdâw.** Since this last word implies the collocation of the two preceding verbs, we translate: "completely."

[c]With MT, we read passive participles **ha-^{c}ămusîm** and **han-nĕśu'îm** depicting Israel as one who is carried. 1QIsa[a] has an alternative reading with active participles and without the definite articles: **^{c}wmsym mmny bṭn wnwś'ym mny rḥm.** While active participles would be suitable were the bicolon a hymnic description of

divine providence continuing through v. 4, plural participles are out of place. The text of 1QIsa[a] has suffered a corruption by metathesis.

[d]MT and all versions read ᶜāśîtî, but the emendation to ᶜāmastî suggested by BHS is attractive, requiring only a simple haplography. ᶜmś is a biform of ᶜms as attested in the proper names ᶜamāśay and ᶜamāśā', both hypocoristics meaning "God has carried (through pregnancy)."

[e]Where MT has wĕ-taśwû, 1QIsa[a] reads wtśwy, a yōd/ wāw confusion.

[f]Reading nidmeh with MT and G; 1QIsa[a] has 'edmeh, also a plausible reading, Cf. Isa 40:25.

[g]The suffix on MT (and 1QIsa[b]) yaᶜăśēhû is an accusative of material: "He makes it [the gold and silver] into a god." 1QIsa[a] and G lack the object suffix; this alternative reading implies that the devotees paid the craftsman who then made an idol from his own materials (wood, bronze, with a thin veneer of precious metal).

[h]G has χειροποίητα, an euphemism.

[i]taḥtāw is the suffixal form of taḥat, "base," formed analogously to yaḥdāw. It stands parallel to kātēp "shoulder" and mĕqômô "its place". Cf. G.

[j]MT yiṣᶜaq 'ēlāw; 1QIsa[a] yzᶜq ᶜlyw evinces 'el/ᶜal confusion and the biform yizᶜaq for yiṣᶜaq.

[k]G reads ἀπο κακῶν, reading a metathesis *mṣrwt of MT miṣ-ṣārātô.

[l]The traditional rendering of this hapax legomenon hit'ōśăśû is either a hitpolel denominative of 'yś, "to behave as a man," or a hitpoᶜel from the root 'śś, "to establish, to found," which as a reflexive would mean "to be strong." Some emend to hitbōśăśû, but how could

such a pedestrian reading lead to the present MT? Schoors surveys other suggestions, none convincing.[34]

[m]1QIsa[a] reads a niphal y[c]śh, which could have arisen from MT 'e[c]ěśeh by haplography of the 'ālep and compensatory dittography of the preceding yōd of ḥepṣî. G agrees with MT.

[n]Reading c̆ǎṣātî with the qerē' and G. 1QIsa[a] has c̥ṣtw agreeing with the ketîb.

[o]With 1QIsa[a], we read an object suffix yāṣartîhâ, which is absent from MT.

[p]Where MT has 'abbîrê, G < *'bdy due to rēś/dālet confusion.

[q]MT qērrabtî; 1QIsa[a] reads a feminine adjective qrwbh, "my salvation is near."

Verses 1-4 contrast a depiction of idols carried on beasts as spoils of war with Yahweh who carries and supports Israel through all her trials. In its literary context, the idols going into captivity is another consequence of Cyrus's conquests, which we saw in 45:22 left only "survivors." As with 45:18-25 this oracle is anticipatory, since Cyrus in fact respected the Babylonian gods and honored their cults.

Immediately we are faced with a corrupt text in v. 1 which is nearly impossible to reconstruct:

kāra[c] bēl qōrēs něbô	Bel bows down, Nebo stoops;
hāyû c̆ǎṣabbêhem	They were their idols
la-ḥayyâ wě-lab-běhēmâ	for beasts and cattle.
něśu'ōtêkem c̆ǎmûsôt	What you carried are loaded,
maśśā' la-c̆ǎyēpâ	a burden for a weary [animal].

---

[34]Schoors, 274f.

After the first line the intellegibility of the text
breaks down. 1QIsa[a] is of no help, either following MT
or introducing its own corruption mšmy^Cyhmh or
mašmî^Cêhemmâ for MT maśśā' la-^Căyēpâ. The Greek text
diverges radically from MT at the fifth and sixth
cola.[35] The usual emendations of něśū'ōtêkem ^Cămûsôt
as něśū'ōt kěmô ^Cămûsôt or něśū'ōt kě-ma^Cămāsôt,
"carried like burdens," inspired by G ὡς φορίον, are
still quite prosaic.

Westermann[36] has seen a clue in the short b:b meter
(2+2 in the Ley-Sievers system) of the first colon and
surmised that Deutero-Isaiah was utilizing a verse form
employed in the description of the vanquishing of an
enemy in battle. The scene at hand is the defeat of
Babylon and the capture of her idols, who are led out
of the city, an appropriate occasion for this verse
form.[37] But Isa 46:1 does not readily scan as short
meter. Westermann's own rendering is imprecise,
requires extensive emendation, and retains much of the
prosaic character of MT. Furthermore, the passive
verbs něśū'ôt and ^Cămûsôt are not appropriate in a
verse form denoting activity and conquest, and Deutero-
Isaiah customarily builds his own short meter with
active verbs and short, staccato particles ('ap, kî,
'ên).[38]

Clifford has recently essayed another reconstruction
of a balanced quatrain of long cola:[39]

---

[35]See note #b

[36]Westermann, 177; also Muilenberg, 536.

[37]See, e.g. CTA 2.4.25-27 and Judg 5:27.

[38]Cf. Isa 46:4b,11b

[39]Clifford, CBQ 42 (1980) 455, n. 19.

```
kāraᶜ bēl qōrēs něbô [      ]              7
la-ḥayyâ wělab-běhēmâ něśū'ôt[ ]          11
ᶜămûsôt maśśā' la-ᶜăyēpâ                   9
qārěsû kārěᶜû yaḥdâw                       8
```

Bel bows down; Nebo dips low,
On beasts and cattle they are borne,
Carried as a load on weary animals.
They dip low; they bow down together.

Following Torrey, he removes **hāyû ᶜaṣābbêhem** as a
gloss, citing a similar prosaizing gloss on another
idol passage, Amos 5:26. This rendering has the merit
of treating **ns'** and **ᶜms** as parallel verbs as they are
in v. 3. However, the meter of Clifford's rendering is
still unbalanced, and the attribution of a gloss is
unnecessary. Our reconstruction is similar, but scans
these verses in a modified qinah meter appropriate to a
taunt of the impotent and defeated idols:

```
kōrēᶜ bēl qōrēs něbô                       7
hāyû ᶜăṣabbî[]m                            5
la-ḥayyâ wělab-běhēmâ                      8
něśū'ôt[] <wě>-ᶜămûsôt\ᵃ                   7
maśśā' la-ᶜăyēpâ                           6
```

The prosody an initial 1:b bicolon followed by an
1:1:b tricolon, a common variant in Deutero-Isaiah's
qinah meter (cf. 44:26b, 45:20a). Each 1 colon has
doubled nouns or verbs, and the b cola have parallel
derogatory terms "idols," "burden." The tricolon also
features a chiasm formed by **la-ḥayyâ** and **la-ᶜăyēpâ**.

The verbs in the first line are pointed in MT one as
a perfect and the other as a participle suggesting a
conflation of two contemporaneous traditions. 1QIsaᵃ
reads perfects, and G translates as aorists; we read
participles in agreement with the passive participles
in the fourth colon. The verbs in the fourth colon are
read with MT as passive participles in agreement with
the passive participles in v. 3 except that, as dic-

tated by MT, they are feminine plurals. Here a difficulty is the lack of agreement between the feminine
gender of these verbs (něśū'ōt, ᶜămûsôt) and the masculine gods and their masculine verbs in the opening
colon. It is unlikely that the verbs had the feminine
pack animals as their subject; the prepositions lě- are
most appropriate as datives of   agent for passive
verbs. The idols here are the subjects, bowing and
stooping in the first and last cola. Perhaps the
feminine/neuter gender of the verbs is meant to ridicule the idols as inanimate objects.[40] This unusual
formation may have become a source for later corruption. Our only emendations to the consonantal text are
to omit the hē in ᶜăṣabbêhem which may be the trace of
a variant reading ᶜăṣabbîm hēmmâ,[41] and the emendations
to the fourth colon, which have been corrupted in an
attempt to rationalize the feminine gender of the participles. No attempt at restoring acceptable prosody
can avoid some emendation of this corrupt and prosaic
text. Our proposed reconstruction preserves MT in its
present order with minimal changes.

After the taunt against the defeated idols, vv. 3-4
address Israel to make a comparison between Yahweh and
the idols by repetition of the verbs nś', ᶜms and mlṭ.
Idols are heavy objects that cannot move unless lifted
and carried by pack animals and are helpless to even
save themselves from exile, but Israel has been carried
and raised by God since birth, and he can surely act to
save his people. Together vv. 1-4 form the first
stanza, which in its mockery of the idols as things
carried on beasts connects with similar ridicule in the

---

[40]cf. Isa 41:21.

[41]cf. Isa 44:11 for an analogous use of hēmmâ.

second stanza, repeating the verbs **nś'** and **sbl**. As a
word of assurance addressing Israel with the imperative
šimᶜû, it forms a chiasm with the concluding stanza
(vv. 12-13) which also opens with the imperative **šimᶜû**.
There the image of the idols going into exile is reversed as Israel returns triumphantly to Zion.[42] This
stanza also forms an inner chiasm with the word of
assurance in the third stanza (vv. 8-11). Both stanzas
speak of Yahweh's support for Israel in the past--
carrying her from the womb (v. 3) and foretelling
things to come from of old (v. 10)--as continuing into
the future--carrying her unto old age (v. 4) and
sending Cyrus as deliverer (v. 11a). These proclamations of assurance based upon the continuity of God's
activity are summarized in parallel concluding bicola
(vv. 4b, 11b) in (b:b):(b:b) meter, each with internal
parallelism built by a series of transitive verbs in
the first person moving from perfects denoting God's
past activity (**ᶜāmastî, dibbartî**) to imperfects declaring God's deeds in the future (**'esbōl** and **'ămalleṭ,
'ăbî'ennâ** and **'eᶜĕśennâ**). The third stanza (vv. 8-11)
is similarly linked to the fourth stanza (vv. 12-13) by
the opening imperative phrases disputing the same
people, called "stubborn of heart" (**'abbîrê lēb**) in
v. 12 and "trangressors" who are to take it to heart
(**pôšĕᶜîm ᶜal lēb**) in v. 8. There are also parallel
figures of distance: in v. 11 Yaweh calls Cyrus "from a
far country" (**merḥāq**); in v. 13 Yahweh "brings near"
his salvation, which "is not far away" (**lō' tirḥāq**).

The second stanza parallels the first with its mockery of idols being carried and connects to the third
and fourth stanzas by setting up contrasts. The god

---

[42]See Clifford, *CBQ* 42 (1980) 454-57.

('ēl) smelted by the smith contrasts with Yahweh's declaration "I am El" (v. 9). The stanza's conclusion (v. 7b) is linked to the corresponding conclusions of the first, third, and fourth stanzas by the word 'ap and by contrasts set up by its triad of negatives: in the first colon the idol cannot move while v. 4b states that Yahweh can carry his people; the second colon declares the idol to be deaf and dumb while in v. 11b Yahweh speaks and foretells his intentions; and in the third colon the idol cannot save (lō' yôšîᶜennû) while in v. 13b Yahweh places vindication (tĕšûᶜâ) in Zion. The patterns of its concluding cola: noun-lō'-verb or verb$_1$-lō'-verb$_2$ are repeated in v. 13a of the fourth stanza, but with the opposite intent; while the idols cannot act, Yahweh's vindication will not wait.

The structure of chapter 46 may thus be described as tetrahedral, with chiastic and parallel linkages between each of its four stanzas vv. 1-4, 5-7, 8-11 and 12-13. This pattern is diagramed in Table 5. Hence there are no convincing reasons why vv. 5-7 should be bound to vv. 8-11 in a disputation distinct from the units vv. 1-4 and 12-13,[43] nor why vv. 5-7 should be excized as secondary along with other polemics against idolatry 40:18-20, 41:6-7 and 44:9-20.[44]

Thus the second stanza with its stereotyped satire of idol manufacture is integral to the balanced rhetorical structure of the chapter and to the several arguments which it puts forward. In relation to the other polemics against idolatry, this stanza opens with the same rhetorical question as in 40:18,25: "to whom will you liken me and make me equal?" and it is followed in

[43]Pace Schoors, 274; Melugin, 131-35.

[44]Westermann, 184.

TABLE 5:   The Structure of Isa 46

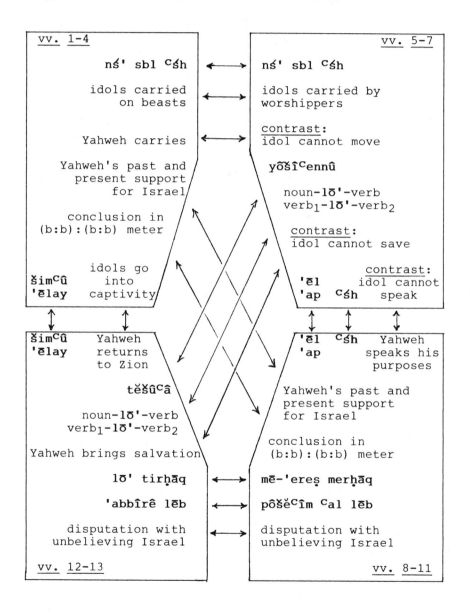

v. 8 by the same formula **zikrû zō't** as is found at the
reprise following the long polemic 44:9-20: **zĕkor
'ēlleh** (44:21). We have argued for the integral place
of 40:18-20 in the structure of 40:12-31, even though
there too its form is slightly different from the surrounding "A-type" stanzas. The function of the imperative **zĕkor 'ēlleh** in 44:21 is disputed, but here **zikrû
zō't** integrates vv. 5-7 into the chapter. Were the
initial cola of v. 8a to be omitted as allegedly a
later modification made to accomodate the editorial
addition of the idol polemic,[45] it would disrupt the
parallel to the disputation in v. 12. Arguments against
the passage's authenticity are thus weak. The stereotypical style of Deutero-Isaiah's polemics against
idolatry, instead of being an indication of a secondary
source, may be rather due to his own immersion in the
genre.

**3. Isa 44:6-23: A Satire on Idolatry Incorporated into
a Trial of the Gods of the Nations with Reassurance
for Israel**

The compositional unit Isa 44:6-23 frames a polemic
against idolatry (vv. 9-20) with an inclusio formed by
a trial speech (vv. 6-8) and a concluding word of
assurance with its attendant hymn (vv. 21-22,23). The
authenticity of Isa 44:9-20 has often been disputed;
even Muilenberg defers and considers these verses, if
the work of the prophet, to be out of context.[46] On

---

[45]So BHS.

[46]So Westermann, Isaiah 40-66, 146-46; Elliger,
Jesaja II, 414-16; Muilenberg, IB 5, 505.

the other hand, Spykerboer, Clifford, and Preuss[47] have recently defended the authenticity of Isa 44:9-20 in its present context. It has thematic similarities to the other idol polemics in Deutero-Isaiah just discussed which are clearly of a piece with their longer compositional units. While BH[3] and the RSV render it in prose, most exegetes now recognize it as verse,[48] and its vocabulary[49] and prosody is consistent with that of Deutero-Isaiah.

44:6-8

Thus says Yahweh, king of Israel	9
and its redeemer, Yahweh of Hosts:[a]	9
	1:1
I am the first, I am the last,	9
and besides me there is no God.	9
	1:1
Who is like me? Let him <take the stand>[b] and	
announce it;	9
declare and set forth his argument to me.[c]	10
Who has proclaimed of old things yet to come,[d]	9
or predicted for us[e] what is yet to take place?	9
	1:1::1:1
Do not tremble;	4
do not fear:[f]	4
Have I not proclaimed from of old?	7
yea,[g] I have foretold, and you are my witnesses.	9
Is there a god besides me?	8
there is no[h] rock, I know of none.	7
	b:b::1:1::1:1

---

[47] Spykerboer (Structure and Composition, 116-18) specifically answers the objections of Westermann. Cf. Clifford, CBQ 42 (1980) 450-64; Preuss, Verspottung, 208-15.

[48] So BHS, Westermann, Torrey, North, Muilenberg, Fohrer, Clifford.

[49] A recent and thorough textual study of Isa 44:9-20 is D. Winton Thomas, "Isaiah XLIV:9-20: A Translation and Commentary," Hommages à Andre Dupont-Sommer (Paris: Adrien-Maisonneuve: 1971), 319-30.

44:9-11

The makers of idols are all in vain,	8
their treasured objects do not avail.	9
They[l] are their [the idols'] witnesses; they do not see;	9
they do not think; therefore they look foolish.	9
Who fashions a god	4
and casts an idol	4
that cannot profit?	5
Yea, all its guild members[j] appear foolish,	8
the craftsmen, they are only[k] human.	8
Let them all gather together and take the stand,	9
let them tremble <and> be ashamed altogether.	8

1:1::1:1::b:b:b::1:1::1:1

44:12

The iron-worker beats out[l] iron	7
he works <it>[m] over the coals.	7
With hammers he forges it,	8
he works it with a strong[n] arm.	8
But even he grows hungry and his strength fails;	7
if he drinks no water, he grows weak.[o]	7

1:1::1:1::1:1

44:13

The wood carver measures[p] a line,	7
he traces out[q] its shape with a stylus,	7
he fashions it with chisels,	7
with a compass he guages its shape.	7
Then he fashions it like the image of a man,	8
like a glorified human to dwell in a temple.	8

1:1:1:1::1:1

44:14-15

He cuts[r] cedars for it,	7
he picks out an ilex[s] or an oak,	7
he nurtures it among the trees of the forest.	8
He plants a fir tree[t], the rain causes it to grow,	8
and it becomes suitable for people to burn.[u]	8

1:1:1::1:1

He takes some of them for heating,	7
yea, he kindles them and bakes bread;	7
He also fashions a god and worships,[v]	8
he makes it into an idol and falls prostrate before it.[w]	8

1:1::1:1

44:16-17

```
Half of it he burns in the fire,                             7
    upon <its coals>ˣ he roastsʸ meat,                       8
He eats the roast and is satisfied,                          7
    yea, he warms himself and says, "Aha!"                   8
    "I am warm, I see the fire!"                              7
                                        1:1::1:1:1̄:1
```

```
The rest of it he makes into a god,                          7
    into an idol,ᶻ and he falls prostrate before it.         6
He worshipsᵃᵃ and prays to it, [    ]ᵇᵇ                      9
    "Save me, for you are my god."                           9
                                        1:1::1̄:1
```

44:18-20

```
They do not know, they do not understand,                   8
    yea, something coversᶜᶜ their eyes                 
        that they cannot see,                                8
    their hearts that they cannot comprehend.                6
He does not take it to heart,                                6̄
    he lacks the knowledge or understanding to say:          9
"Half of it I burned in the fire,                            8̄
    Yea, I baked bread on its coals,                         9
    I roasted meat and I ate,                                7
The rest of it I make into an abomination,                  8̄
    I worship a decayed pieceᵈᵈ of wood."                    6
                          1:1:b::b:1::1:1:b::1̄:b
```

```
He herds ashes!                                              3
    a deluded mind has led him astray.                       6
He cannot saveᵉᵉ himself nor say:                            9
    "Is this not a lie in my right hand?"                    6
                                        b:1::1̄:b
```

44:21-23

```
Remember these things, O Jacob,                              6
    Israel, for you are my servant.                          8
    I formed you as a servant, and you are mine,             8
    Israel, you have not been forgotten by me.ᶠᶠ             8
I blot out your transgressions like a cloud,                 9̄
    your sins like a mist.                                   9
Return to me, for I have redeemed you.                       9
                                  1:1:1:1::1:1̄:1
```

```
Sing, O heavens, for Yahweh has acted,                       9
    Shout, O depths of the earth!                            7
Break forth into singing, O mountains,                       7
    the forest and all its trees!                            5
For Yahweh has redeemed Jacob,                               7̄
    in Israel he glorifies himself.                          7
                                  1:b::1:b::1̄:1
```

[a]1QIsa[a] adds šěmô, cf. Isa 47:4; 48:2; 51:15; 54:5.

[b]MT and 1QIsa[a] read yiqrā' wěyaggîdehā wěya[c]rěkehā; G has a different set of three verbs, reading a Vorlage *ya[c]ămōd wě-yiqrā' wě-ya[c]rěkehā. The prosody is improved if all four verbs are retained.

[c]1QIsa[a] reads lw' for MT lî.

[d]This common emendation to mî yašmî[c] mē-[c]ôlām 'ōtiyyôt is formed by redividing the consonants of MT and assuming a defectively written text.[50]

[e]MT lāmô presents difficulties. The poetic context parallel to the indirect object lî indicates that it is not a resumptive pronoun picking up the object of 'ăšer. Clifford[51] renders lāmô as a third person plural object pronoun referring to the nations to whom their gods allegedly speak. But sensitivity to the trial setting leads us to reconstruct a first person plural indirect object (cf. 41:22-23,26; 43:9). Schoors proposes reading the MT as lāmmû < *lamnū according to a proposal by Dahood,[52], but his poetic pronominal base *lam- is purely hypothetical; we would expect a suffixal form of *lāmō to be *lāmônû. The frequent occurences of lāmô where a first person plural suffix is indicated (e.g., Pss 44:11, 64:6, 80:7, Job 22:17, and perhaps Ps 28:8, Isa 26:16, and Deut 33:2) are better explained by the frequent confusion of mēm and nûn in paleo-Hebrew script. Westermann

---

[50]cf. BHS, Schoors, I am God your Savior, 230.

[51]Clifford, Fair Spoken, 107.

[52]M. Dahood, "Hebrew-Ugaritic Lexicography," Bib. 47 (1966), 409; Schoors, 231.

correctly emends to **lānû**,[53] and he has the support of G
ὑμιν, an inner-Greek corruption of ἡμιν.

[f]Reading **tīrā'û** with 1QIsa[a], G. MT has **tirhû** by
dittography of the following **hē**.

[g]MT **hišma^ctīkā** has a second person singular pronominal suffix which does not agree with v. 8 where Israel
is addressed in the plural. Schoors[54] divides off the
kap of the suffix and reads an emphatic **kî**. But then
the usual scansion which places **hišma^ctî kî higgadtî** in
the same colon leaves v. 8 with unbalanced prosody
(8-11-5-8-6). The proposed rendering of **kî higgadtî** in
the following colon gives a balanced 5-colon unit with
an initial b:b colon and structured by alternating
interrogative and demonstrative particles in the initial position of each colon: **'al, hălō', kî, hă-yēš,
'ên.** Note the alliteration of ^c**ayin, dālet, tāw,** and
a, î and **ay** vowels.

[h]Torrey, Clifford and BHS suggest on the basis of
the Greek emending MT **'ên** to **'im**, making a double
question **hă-... 'im.** But the evidence of G is ambiguous. MT continues the alternation of rhetorical
question and answer begun in the previous bicolon.

[i]**hēmmâ** in MT is written with puncta extraordinaria,
in 1QIsa[a] it is written supra lineam, and G omits the
entire colon. The pronoun had been lost from some
texts by homoeoarcheton, but it is not to be omitted,
since it gives better metrical balance. **Hēmmâ** contrasts with **'attem** in v. 8, contrasting these witnesses, the idol makers, to Yahweh's witness Israel. It
also parallels the **hēmmâ** in v. 11.

---

[53]Westermann, 138.

[54]Schoors, 232f.

j1QIsaᵃ reads a Qal participle ḥôbĕrâw, "those who join it," but MT ḥăbērâw correctly identifies the subject as a guild of craftsmen. Such guilds, attached to temples, were known to have existed in both Canaan and Mesopotamia. The suggestion that the verse is concerned with sorcery (repointing ḥăbārâw "his spells") is unacceptable and out of context.

ᵏMT mē-'ādām has a partitive mēm. G κωφοι, "deaf," is reading MT ḥārāšîm as ḥērĕšîm.

ˡMT ḥāraš barzel maᶜăṣād, lit. "The iron-worker, an axe," lacks a verb, since ḥāraš is a construct noun. G reads for the first bicolon: ὤξυνε τέκτων σίδηρον σκεπάρνῳ εἰργάσατο αὐτό; as BHS suggests, it is reading a verb yaḥēd, "he sharpens" from the root ḥdd. Since the previous verse ends with yaḥad (MT), G is probably reading a dittography; we cannot agree with Westermann and Thomas that this verb is original.[55] In conformity with Deutero-Isaiah's prosodic style, we expect the subject (ḥāraš barzel) of an extended prosodic unit (three bicola) to be introduced as the first word of the opening colon, for emphasis, as in v. 9 (yōṣĕrê pesel), v. 13 (ḥāraš ᶜēṣîm), v. 16 (ḥeṣyô) and v. 17 (šĕ'ērîtô). Hence it is unlikely that the original text had a verb at the initial position in this verse. We look for a verb in the term maᶜăṣad, attested here and in Jer 10:3 as a type of axe. Cognate languages including Ugaritic confirm that the root ᶜṣd has the meaning "to cut," though it is more often associated with pruning and the harvest--Arab. ᶜḍd "to lop off," mᶜṣd "a pruning hook," and perhaps Akk. eṣēdu "to harvest"--than with the work of a blacksmith. In

---

[55]Westermann, 145; Thomas, "Isaiah XLIV. 9-20," 324.

Hebrew the verb is attested only in the Gezer calendar,
yrḥ ᶜṣd pšt "the month of pulling flax," where the
context is difficult: flax was not cut with an sickle
like wheat, but pulled up by the roots to retain the
entire stalk. Talmon has suggested that pšt in the
Calendar did not refer to flax but to grass, which
would allow a translation "month of hay cutting."[56]
Tentatively we read with Muilenberg[57] a piel participle
mĕᶜaṣṣēd. There is no need to emend MT to mĕᶜaṣṣēb.[58]

ᵐMT û-pāᶜal is probably a corruption of yipᶜol.
Westermann and Thomas suggest inserting poᶜŏlô and
reading yipᶜal poᶜŏlô, thereby providing an otherwise
absent direct object and improving the meter. But
throughout vv. 12-13 the object is never otherwise
mentioned except as denoted by a pronominal suffix. G
reads a suffix; hence we read yipᶜolĕhû. G lacks
bap-peḥām.

ⁿWe move the suffix on MT kōḥô to the initial
position of the following colon as a contrastive conjunction.

ᵒG has ἐκλεξάμενος at the beginning of v. 13, a
Greek corruption of ἐκλυόμενος which would properly
render MT.

ᴾWhere MT nāṭâ kāw propersly lacks the suffix,
1QIsaᵃ and G read nāṭāhû qāw, "they take its dimensions."

---

[56]S. Talmon, "The Gezer Calendar and the Seasonal
Cycle of Ancient Canaan, "JAOS 83 (1963), 187.

[57]Muilenberg, IB 5, 512.

[58]Torrey, The Second Isaiah, 349.

^{q}MT yĕto'ărĕhû is an imperfect pō^{c}ĕl with suffix; see GK 64i. There is no reason to delete either this verb or its double in the fourth colon; the repetition of several key verbs is inherent in the prosodic style. But we do omit the suffix on the second yĕtō'ĕr metri causa. G reads "glue" instead of śered and omits the following two cola.

^{r}MT and 1QIsa^a read an infinitive likrot which is out of place as it stands. G reads an aorist indicative verb. Possible emendations are to omit the lāmed and read kārat or yikrot, to read an emphatic lāmed and a perfect indicative verb, or with Thomas,[59] to read [hālak] likrot which could yield MT by haplography. We choose the first of these; an initial preterite verb wĕ-yikrōt similarly opens v. 15ab (yiqqaḥ).

^{s}The identity of the tirzâ tree is uncertain; it is a hard wood (Arab. tazara, "to be hard); Thomas translates "ilex," RSV "holm tree."

^{t}MT has a diminuitive final nûn on 'oren which resembles a zayin to indicate two alternative readings 'oren "fir" or 'erez "cedar." 1QIsa^a 'wrn and G κυριός from *'adōn both favor 'oren; cedars have already been mentioned.

^{u}MT (G) wĕ-hāyâ is in sequence with nāṭa^c and yĕgaddĕl of the preceding verse: "to plant," "to grow," "to become." Otherwise, as the first colon of v. 15 it has no poetic connection with what follows, and could justly be regarded as a gloss. Gelston proposes to solve this problem with a needless transposition.[60]

---

[59]Thomas, "Isaiah XLIV. 9-20," 326.

[60]A. Gelston, "Some Notes on Second Isaiah," VT 21 (1971) 522.

1QIsa^a **whgh** is secondary.

^VRead the singular **yištaḥăweh** to agree with the following verb. It is not to be understood as an impersonal plural "for men to worship;" that would dull the satire and break up the action. The craftsman himself prays to his god in v. 17.

^WThis is the only clear attestation of **lāmô** as a third person singular pronoun in the Hebrew bible. Other possible occurences of this hypothetical poetic form are either in corrupt texts or can be better understood as plurals. However, this form cannot be easily dismissed as a textual corruption since a poetic third person singular pronominal suffix **-mô** is attested on other prepositions (^călêmô, pĕnêmô) in Job 20:23, 22:2, 27:23, and Ps 11:7.[61] Nevertheless, we emend to **lô** metri causa and by analogy with v. 17ab.

^XG reads *wĕ-^cal; MT wĕ-^cal ḥeṣyô may be an dittography. 1QIsa^a reads w^cl supra lineam. This popular emendation to ^cal gĕḥālāw is suggested by v. 19 and from a colon from 1QIsa^a absent from MT: w^cl gḥlyw yšb. yšb in 1QIsa^a is reading MT yśb^c.

^YThis and the following verb are transposed with G for sense.

^ZReading **pesel** with G γλυπτòν καì; MT reads **pislô**. 1QIsa^a reads **lblwy** ^cṣ, perhaps from attraction to v. 19.

^{aa}Read singular **yištaḥăweh** with 1QIsa^a. MT has plural; cf. note #v.

^{bb}Omit **wĕ-yō'mar** as a prosaizing expansion.

---

[61]GK #103g, n. 3; Joüon, #103f,m.

ccThe verb ṭwḥ is attested as an active transitive
verb "to plaster," "to coat" 10 times in the Hebrew
Bible, and in Mishnaic Hebrew and Ugaritic: CTA,
17.1.33, 17.2.22: ṭāḥu gagihū ba-yāmi ta'īti, "one who
will plaster his roof in the day of drenching rains"
(reading an active participle). Yet MT ṭaḥ is analyzed
based upon the hypothetical passive verb ṭḥḥ in BDB and
as rendered by most translations is a hapax legomenon
without support from cognates. If the verb were passive with "their eyes" as the subject, one would also
expect the plural, in spite of the infrequent use of
the third person masculine singular verb when it precedes plural or feminine subjects (GK #145.7a). The
subject of ṭaḥ as a transitive verb from ṭwḥ may be the
idol's splendor or the false notion of idolatry itself.

ddReading with 1QIsaa lě-balûy, a passive participle
from the root blh, "to decay." MT reads lěbûl cēṣ, but
the explanation of bûl as a passive of ybl, "a product," is grammatically difficult.

ee1QIsaa reads ywkyl, "His soul will not prevail."

ffMT tinnāśēnî is to be prefered over 1QIsaa tś'ny
and Torrey's supposition of a dual reading.

The outer inclusio enclosing the polemic against
idolatry (vv. 6-8, 21-23) begins with a trial speech
against the gods of the nations. As in similar trial
speeches, Yahweh challenges the gods of the nations to
appear in court: "Who is like Me? Let him take the
stand and declare his case..." Yahweh challenges the
gods to demonstrate their efficacy in human events by
predicting the future (41:22, 26; 43:9; 45:21). As in
the trial speech 43:8-13, Yahweh declares that the

Israelites are his witnesses, for Israel can testify
that Yahweh had indeed forewarned them of what was to
happen. But here is an additional, more direct point
of comparison concerning Yahweh's person, the phrase **mî
kāmōnî**, reminiscent of other polemics against idolatry
(cf. 40:18, 46:5).

With the opening stanza of the satire itself, vv. 9-
11, the object of the trial scene shifts from the gods
to the idol makers, called "them" (**hēmmâ, kullām**). In
v. 8 these craftsmen are ridiculed as blind and un-
thinking, and the ambiguous syntax **Cēdêhem hēmmâ** is
perhaps an intentionally ironic comparision between the
craftsmen and their deaf and dumb idols (cf. 46:7).
Their fate is to be humiliated (**yēbōšû**), the term
similarly employed to curse the idolators in 45:16,24.

At the same time, the verbal and structural corres-
pondences between these verses and the preceding trial
speech evince conscious craftsmanship. The call to
Israel as Yahweh's witnesses (**'attem Cēday**) is matched
by the challenge to the idol-makers as their god's
witnesses (**Cēdêhem hēmmâ**). Yahweh knows of no other
god (**bal yāda^Ctî**), and likewise the idolators are
accused of not knowing (**bal yēdĕ^Cû**). Repeated summons-
es (vv. 7, 11) to appear in court (note our rendering
of **ya^Cămōd** and **yiqrā'** as legal terms) are preceded by
assertions of the sole divinity of Yahweh (v. 6) and
the futility of idols (v. 9) respectively. There is
repetition of the verbs **yādā^C** (vv. 8cb, 9bb) and **yiphad**
(vv. 8a, 11bb). The second stanza's question in a
short (b:b:b) tricolon (v. 10) followed by an emphatic
hēn has its counterpart in v. 8a of the first stanza
where a word of assurance in a short (b:b) bicolon is
followed by a question (**hălō'**). This stanza which
formally opens the satire is thus distinct from but

connected to the trial speech which precedes it, and it
builds upon the trial setting by following up the
summons to the gods of the nations to trial by a summons to their craftsmen to face their own judgment.[62]

In the ensuing four stanzas, vv. 12, 13, 14-15 and
16-17, the satire develops in a measured pattern. In
vv. 12 and 13 the work of two craftsmen, the blacksmith
and the wood-carver, is described in parallel stanzas
of six cola. Each stanza opens by citing the name of
the craftsman.[63] Each is built up with pairs of verbs:
yip‎ᶜol in v. 12ab,bb; yĕto'ēr in v. 13ab,bb; yaᶜăśeh in
v. 13 ba,ca; or nouns: kôḥ in v. 12bb,ca. The stanzas'
second and third cola each have nouns preceded by the
preposition bĕ-, the latter a feminine plural mēm preformative (maqqābôt, maqṣuᶜôt), and their fifth and
sixth cola turn from the implements and activity of the
craftsman to the result of his labors: he grows faint;
he makes the form of a man.

The following two stanzas, each of nine cola, trace
the fate of wood used in building idols. The first of
these (vv. 14-15) develops sequentially towards an
ironic conclusion: the craftsman plants and cultivates
trees (v. 14) until they reach a size suitable for
burning (v. 15a); he burns some of their wood for fuel
(v. 15b); yet some of it he makes into a god (v. 15c).
The next stanza (vv. 16-17) amplifies the thought of
v. 15 and is built of two subunits, each beginning by
identifying the portion of the wood (ḥeṣyô, śĕ'ērîtô)

---

[62]Westermann's assertion that the words to summon
the idol makers to court "have lost all connection with
the purpose which they served in the legal process"
(pp. 148f.) is rightly contested by Spykerboer (pp.
122f.). The issue turns on whether 44:9-20 is considered in its context or in isolation (see below).

[63]See textual note #1 above, p. 168.

just as the craftsmen were so identified in vv. 12-13.
The phrase yištaḥweh... ᶜaśâ pesel wě-yisgod lě- is
repeated almost word for word in each stanza (vv. 15c
and 17a-b), as is the verb yaḥom. Each stanza ends in
a direct quotation of the craftsman in the first
person. Another notable poetic device in these stanzas
is alliteration of the same consonants in both stanzas:
ḥēt and mēm in vv. 15ba and 16bb; pēh, sāmek and lāmed
in vv. 15bb-c and 17a. Thus the entire satire through
v. 17 is highly crafted poetry, tightly organized, consistent with Deutero-Isaiah's style, and certainly
worthy of him.[64]

However, for vv. 18-20, the final stanza of the
satire proper, we had to consider hypotheses that would
place these verses as expansions by later hand(s). The
modified qinah (1:1:b::1:b) meter is not in itself
unusual for Deutero-Isaiah; we had noted a similar
variation between meters in the several stanzas of Isa
40:12-31. However, the apparently prosaic v. 20 is
more difficult. Clifford considers the verse to be
secondary and calls its style "judgmental" and "heavy-
handed" compared to the "restrained" irony of the rest
of the satire.[65] We do not find this verse any more
judgmental than the rest of what is undoubtedly the
most scathing satire in the Hebrew Bible, and on closer
inspection the prosody of this verse is can be seen to
continue the qinah meter established in vv. 18-19.
Like the preceding half-stanzas vv. 16, 17 and 18-19,
it ends with a direct quotation of words placed in the
mouth of the idolator. Neither are its exclamatory
phrases typical of deutero-prophetic glosses.

---

[64]Certainly not "doggerel" as opines North, 139.

[65]Clifford, CBQ 42 (1980) 463.

Westermann considers verse 18 to be intrusive. He
notes that the object of the satire changes to the
plural--to all the craftsmen together, but in v. 19 the
wood-carver is once again addressed in the singular.[66]
It may also be objected that Deutero-Isaiah does not
normally engage in repetition of the scale found in
v. 19, where the accusations made in vv. 15-17 are
restated in the mouth of the idolator.

Yet other evidence supports the unity of vv. 18-20.
They are unified by repetition of the key words lēb
(3 times, once in each verse) and lō' (8 times).[67] In
both vv. 18 and 20 it appears that something has
deceived the idol makers; we must read ṭaḥ in v. 18 as
a transitive verb[68] whose subject may well be the
"deluded mind" of v. 20. The device of putting words
in the mouth of the craftsman is consistent with the
direct quotes in vv. 16b, 17bb, 19b-c and 20bb. The
meter, as noted, is consistent throughout.

Furthermore, the satire begun in v. 9 requires a
conclusion beyond v. 17, a function fulfilled by this
stanza. The opening accusation is recalled by the
verbs yādĕ͏cû and mē-rĕ'ôt of v. 18 which repeat yēdĕcû
and yir'û of v. 9. In one stanza the opening accusation of vv. 9-11, represented in v. 18, and the satirical description of vv. 12-17, represented in v. 19,
are joined together. This evidence suggests that we
can retain vv. 18-20 as the satire's original conclusion.

---

[66]Westermann, 145.

[67]On the syntax of lō' dacat wĕ-lō' tĕbûnâ where the
verb to be is assumed, see Isa 52:3; 55:8.

[68]See above textual note #cc, p. 172.

Following the body of the satire, we return to the
second half of the outer envelope in vv. 21-22, 23, a
reaffirmation of Israel's vocation as Yahweh's servant
and reassurance of her salvation. Yahweh encourages
Israel to remember "these things," which in this context must be the impotence of idols as human creations
and the delusions of their worshippers as argued in the
preceding satire.[69] We may compare zikrû zō't in 46:8
which also recalls the immediately preceding polemic
against idolatry and calls to remembrance those "transgressors" who have been attracted to pagan religion.
The stanza itself is structured by chiasms between the
opening zĕkor 'ēlleh... kî and šûbâ 'ēlay kî concluding
v. 22, and between zĕkor and tinnāśēnî concluding
v. 21. This confirmation of Israel's vocation as
Yahweh's servant forms a suitable conclusion to a compositional unit begun by a trial speech and a satire of
idolatry. Clifford has pointed out certain verbal
contacts with vv. 9-20:[70] In contrast to those who
fashion (yāṣar) idols in vv. 9,10, Yahweh in v. 21
declares to Israel "I have formed you (yĕṣartîkā)."
The confession of the idol maker kî 'ēlî 'attâ in v. 17
contrasts with Yahweh's declaration kî Cabdî 'attâ.
The arrangement of this compostional unit is comparable
to the arrangement of Isa 41:1-20 with its opening
trial speech (vv. 1-4), ridicule of the nations' dependence upon idols (vv. 5-7), and stanzas affirming
Israel as Yahweh's servant (vv. 8ff.). In fact, the
first colon of the word of affirmation in 41:8, 'attâ

---

[69]On the discussion of to what 'ēlleh might refer,
see Spykerboer, 127; Muilenburg, IB 5, 505; Westermann,
142.

[70]Clifford, CBQ 42 (1980) 463.

yiśrā'ēl ᶜabdî, is nearly identical with the second
colon in 44:21, yiśrā'ēl kî ᶜabdî 'attâ. In this
pattern, the polemic against idolatry along with judgment of the gods in the trial speech serve as foils to
the proclamation of Israel as Yahweh's servant. The
ridicule of idol worship can give despondent Israel
additional confidence in her vocation and election. In
Isa 44:6-23 this pattern is reproduced, but the polemic
against idolatry is greatly expanded.

On the other hand, we have noted that the satire in
vv. 9-20 stands on its own and has in vv. 18-20 a
suitable conclusion. Were it not for the verbal and
rhetorical connections to v. 9 and the backward reference zĕkor 'ēlleh in v. 21, there would be little
relationship at all between the satire in vv. 9-20 and
both the opening trial speech (vv. 6-8) and concluding
oracle of assurance (vv. 21-22). This relative silence
is all the more striking when contrasted with the
profusion of structural and verbal connections which,
as we have seen, bind the other idol polemics 40:18-20,
41:6-7 and 46:5-7 to their compositional contexts. The
theme of the satire, to ridicule the idol worshippers,
is only loosely connected to the preceding trial speech
where the deities themselves are at court and where the
contested ground for belief is the deity's ability to
declare the future.[71] Hence the satire may well have
been inserted into the present text. At the time of
insertion, the texts could have been modified at the
seams (i.e. at vv. 9 or 21) to give a smooth transition
and an appearance of unity.

But was the insertion of the satire a later expansion to the book, as understood by Westermann and

---

[71]Melugin, Formation, 120.

Muilenberg? Or rather was the satire a preexisting text taken up into the book and given a suitable framework? This question hinges upon whether vv. 6-8 and 21-22, taken together, form a satisfactory unit. Westermann[72] wishes to see continuity between these verses on the basis of their common theme of Yahweh as redeemer (gō'ēl) of Israel. He must omit the first bicolon of v. 21, whose imperative zĕkor 'ēlleh would disrupt the unity and would appear to be an adjustment to accomodate the inserted satire. But this adjustment leaves only a torso on vv. 21-22, tinnāśēnî is left without a parallel, and the chiasm between zĕkōr 'ēlleh... kî and śûbâ 'ēlay kî is destroyed. In rejecting this theory, Schoors points out that it must also contend with a change of persons from the plural in v. 8 to the singular in v. 21.[73] Furthermore, compared to other trial speeches which introduce extended compositional units, the hypothetical unit 44:6-7,20-21 lacks substance. In v. 7 the gods of the nations are challenged twice, mî kāmōnî and mî yaśmîᶜ, but from then on the challenge is dropped--compare the sustained berating of the nations or their gods in 41:1ff. and 41:21-29, or their submission in 45:20-25. In 43:8-13, the trial speech most similar to this one, the challenge to the gods is only briefly brought in order to introduce an extended rîb directed at Israel. The brief challenges to the gods in 44:7 also appear to imply a further argument, which the ensuing satire would supply.

---

[72]Westermann, 142.

[73]Schoors, 232f.

Hence it is far more probable that Deutero-Isaiah composed vv. 6-8 and 21-22 around the preexisting satire on idolatry as its frame. As written they assume the satire; to alter them so as to remove all traces of the satire's influence--i.e. remove v. 21a which is integral to the chiasm of that stanza--is to destroy their integrity. On the other hand, the satire remains intact if v. 9 were to be removed or altered as a joint composed to fit the trial framework.[74] In its present redactional shape, 44:6-23 evinces a chiastic structure typical of Deutero-Isaiah (cf. 52:13-53:12; 45:24-45:13; 45:14-20).

A possible reason for the distinctive style of Deutero-Isaiah's idol polemics is that they represent a satirical genre which the prophet had honed in an earlier stage in his career. While we have demonstrated that Deutero-Isaiah's other idol polemics were written as parts of larger compositions for the book of consolation, they too show marks of a well-developed satirical style. Perhaps in the case of 44:9-20 Deutero-Isaiah took what he considered to be a masterful example of his earlier work and included it whole. The rhetoric of the concluding v. 20 may reflect the brash exuberance of the prophet in his youth. The prophet selected this earlier satire and framed it with a trial scene and a closing oracle of assurance in order to create a compositional unit suitable for the book of consolation.

---

[74]Verse 10, **mî yāṣar 'ēl**... could form a natural beginning to the satire. The satire's conclusion may have also been altered by additions at v. 18, put in the plural to fit with v. 9. If the original satire began with verse 10, it would have been entirely in the singular.

This reconstruction of the compositional history of Isa 44:6-23 also explains why vv. 21-22,23 have been noted to serve a larger function in the composition of the book, forming the conclusion of a large chapter up to the commencement of the Cyrus oracle.[75] The hymnic v. 23 also appears to have been inserted as an endpiece in the overall arrangement of the book and would not form an appropriate conclusion to 44:6-22 or 44:6-8,21-22 taken by itself. But if vv. 6-8 and 21-23 were composed as redactional endpieces to accomodate the satire, then the latter verses could serve a double purpose, to conclude both vv. 6-20 and a large chapter of the overall work.

4. The Prohibition of Idolatry as a Universal Claim

Our treatment of three disputed polemics against idolatry in this chapter (40:18-20, 44:9-20, 46:5-7) has investigated text, prosodic form, rhetoric and theme for each in the context of its respective compositional unit. A fourth polemic, Isa 41:5-7, has been discussed in the context of its unit 41:1-42:17.[76] We agree with recent critics[77] that evidence for Deutero-Isaianic authorship of these passages is overwhelming.

---

[75]Melugin (Formation, 90) identifies this unit as 42:14-44:23 and 42:10-13 as a simiar hymnic conclusion to the previous subsection 41:1-42:13. As an epilogue, 44:21-22 has specific verbal and thematic connections with 43:18,25 and 44:1-2. In our view, this endpiece serves as a transition between 41:1-44:23 and the following Cyrus oracle.

[76]See pp. 39-46, 150.

[77]See p. 129 n. 2.

We have noted that the prosody of these idol polemics is consistent with Deutero-Isaiah's style. Also,
throughout these passages run three themes that are
common to Deutero-Isaiah's attacks on idolatry in un-
disputed passages such as 42:17; 45:16,20,24; 46:1-2
and 48:5-8. First is the repeated refrain that idolators do not know (lōʾ yādĕᶜû).[78] Even where this verb
is not explicitly stated, it is implied by adjacent
passages contrasting idolatry with the true knowledge
that comes from Yahweh.[79] Second, the idolators will
be ashamed (yēbōšû)[80] because the idols cannot save.[81]
Third, there are repeated comparisons between God and
the idols. To make this comparison, the prophet does a
subject-object reversal: what God does for Israel, men
(or beasts) do for their idols. While Yahweh is the
creator of the universe, the idols are described as
human artifacts--hence the elaborate descriptions of
their manufacture.[82] While Yahweh is the sole actor
and savior in history, the idols are described as
fastened down so they cannot move (40:20, 41:7, 46:7)
or as carried about by men and beasts (45:20, 46:1-2,
7). While Yahweh proclaims his effective word, the
idols are dumb objects (41:26, 28), unable to answer
the pleas of their worshippers (42:17, 45:20, 46:7) and
to which men falsely attribute oracles coming from
Yahweh (48:5-8). While Yahweh gives strength to his

---

[78]Isa 44:9,18-20; 45:20.

[79]Isa 40:21; 44:8; 48:5-8.

[80]Isa 42:17; 44:9,11; 45:16,24.

[81]Isa 45:20; 44:17,20; 46:2,7; cf. 41:23-24 and by
implication, 41:5-7.

[82]Isa 40:18-20; 41:6-7; 44:9-14; 46:5-6.

people, the idol makers themselves grow weary (44:12) and must encourage each other (41:6-7).

Besides stylistic and thematic evidence for Deutero-Isaianic authorship of the disputed polemics against idolatry, three of these four passages fulfill specific rhetorical purposes in their respective compositional units, are necessary for their structural integrity, and therefore were composed as constituent parts of the whole. Thus the comparison of Yahweh with inanimate idols in Isa 40:18-20 corresponds to a parallel affirmation of Yahweh's power over the astral deities in vv. 25-26 and forms an essential part of the carefully crafted composition Isa 40:12-31, a sustained argument for Yahweh's incomparability and sovereignty in history. The description of the pagans scurrying about to build idols in Isa 41:6-7 does not similarly argue for Yahweh's incomparability, but rather points up the frenetic activity of the idolators in the face of a recognized menace, the advent of Cyrus, at which both the nations (41:5) and Israel (41:10) tremble in fear. The work of building idols, described in these verses as merely human striving, is helpless to avert a conqueror who comes as Yahweh's agent, while Israel can be reassured because it is Yahweh, the author of his conquests, who helps her. We have also noted, in view of the traditions lying behind Isa 41:1-20, that the nations' scurrying to build idols is formally related to the raging of the nations in the Zion psalms. Each of these idol polemics has its specific function in context, and Isa 41:6-7 cannot be moved to a position after 40:18-20 without violently disrupting the structure and argument of both compositions.[83]

---

[83]Against Schoors, 252-3; Westermann, 61.

Similarly, we have detailed the structural features which bind chapter 46 into a unity. There the polemic in 46:5-7, with its mention of the idol being carried on men's shoulders, parallels the opening mocking song of the idols carried off as booty by the conquering armies--an undisputedly authentic passage--and also sets up the grounds for the diputations with those Israelites enamored of idolatry in vv. 8-11 and 12-13.

On the other hand, the long satire Isa 44:9-20, while composed by Deutero-Isaiah, is only loosely linked to its context. It appears that its framework (vv. 6-8, 21-23) was added in order to fit a preexisting composition into the book of consolation. This finding, along with the apparent stereotypical character of all the idol polemics, suggests that the prophet was quite familiar with this genre and may have even been an accomplished satirist of idolatry before he composed the bulk of the poems found in Isa 40-55.

Like the trial speeches, some of these polemics against idolatry argue a universal claim binding upon all peoples. Granted, Isa 40:12-31 and 46:1-13 dispute specifically with Israel. Jacob/Israel is identified as the audience of 40:12-31 in v. 27, and chapter 46 is addressed to Israel (46:3,13), particularly those "transgressors" with "stubborn hearts" (46:8,12) who had become enamored of Mesopotamian religion. Isa 41:1-20, however, begins with Yahweh summoning the nations (v. 1). In this context, the nations and all assembled at the trial are also the literary audience of the remarks in vv. 5-7.[84] Yahweh questions them as to the cause of Cyrus's advances (vv. 2,4); even while in the midst of this direct address he describes the

---

[84]See above, pp. 113-119.

coming of Cyrus in the third person (vv. 2b-3).
Yahweh's speech in the third person continues in his
mocking description of the nations' idolatrous response
in vv. 5-7. The nations have been called, yet they
have turned elsewhere for help. In v. 8 Yahweh then
turns to Israel, with **wĕ-'attā** expressing and emphasizing an adversative relationship to what preceded: "the
coastlands saw and feared... but you, Israel... do not
fear..."; "the nations... encouraged each other [to
build idols]... but you, Israel, are my servant..."
Prior to this adversative, Yahweh's speech is addressed
to all the parties assembled before him in court,
Israel and the nations. The polemic against idolatry
ridicules the nations themselves for their folly. The
lengthy satire 44:9-20 is also set within a trial scene
challenging the idolators to come forward as "witnesses" to answer the challenge of Israel as Yahweh's
witnesses (vv. 8-9). While the conclusion of the
framework clearly indicates that this trial is to be a
demonstration for Israel's behalf ("remember these,
Jacob"), the actual satire convicts the idolators of
ignorance and stupidity ("they do not see, they do not
know," v. 9; "they do not know, they do not understand..." v. 18). Deutero-Isaiah is here not limiting
his attacks to Israelites enamored with idolatry, but
brands all idolators, Israelite and pagan alike, as in
the wrong. Similar claims upon the idolatrous gentiles
are found in other trial contexts (45:16,20,24).

Israelite prophets from Hosea and Jeremiah had consistently attacked idolatry when it became a snare for
Israel, but Deutero-Isaiah may be the first Israelite
prophet to attack a pagan religion as wrong in itself.
Such a move came easily. Living in exile among polytheistic cults which exalted the worship of images, the

Israelites had to be convinced that idolatry was wrong
in and of itself and not merely to be avoided because
of some peculiar tradition from the old country. One
should not overlook the profound universalism implicit
in this claim. While these polemics were for Israelite
consumption, and Deutero-Isaiah probably expected few
foreigners to be persuaded by them, nevertheless they
could at a later time become the basis for missionary
apologetics.

Briefly we will trace a trajectory from the native
Israelite aniconic tradition with its roots in the
specific covenant between Yahweh and Israel to Deutero-
Isaiah's universal disapprobation of idolatry in principle.   On the one hand, Deutero-Isaiah's view was
continuous with Israel's aniconic tradition. Preuss,
in his extensive study of mockery in polemics against
foreign religions,[85] has noted the distinctive role of
Israel's aniconic tradition in shaping the Hebrew
Bible's attacks on foreign gods. While most cultures
in the ancient Near East had literature attacking the
gods of rival lands, they did not aim to show that the
rival god was not in fact a deity. Rather the gods
contested with one another their claims for superiority. But the derision of the gods in Israel was, from
earliest times, bound up with scoffing at images.
Instead of polemics against what were perceived as
actual gods, Israelite polemics often targeted their
images to which were denied any divine power. This
mockery of images begins very early; it is already
implicit in such narratives as Rachel's theft of
Laban's household gods and her sitting on them while

---

[85]Horst Dietrich Preuss, Verspottung fremder
Religionen im Alten Testament, BWANT 92 (Stuttgart:
Kohlhammer, 1971).

alleging that she is menstruating (Gen 31:19-35),
Michal's use of a teraphim as a dummy to disguise
David's flight (1 Sam 19:10-17), and the polemic
against the Danite sanctuary (Judg 17-18). It is also
implicit in the derisive vocabulary which Israel
applied to idols: tĕrapîm, "rotting things" or "old
rags;" gillûlîm, "lumps of manure;" šiqqûṣîm, "vermin"
or "rubbish" (see Nah 3:6); and 'elîlîm, "flimsy,
insignificant things." Preuss correctly regards the
view of idols as artifacts lacking any numinous quality
as firmly established by the preexilic prophets, particularly Hosea.[86]

On the basis of such a tradition, Deutero-Isaiah and
his contemporaries had no qualms about satirizing the
Babylonian manufacture and reverence of idols as foolish worship of inanimate objects, although, as many
commentators have remarked, he ignored the evident
sensibilities of the polytheist. The pious Babylonian
might reply that an idol was no ordinary object, but a
sacred object which, through the proper rituals, had
been "transubstantiated" into the body of the god and
was henceforth infused with the god's presence and
power.[87] He would not have thought of the idol as the
total being of the god, but as rather its earthly
embodiment representing but never exhausting its cosmic

---

[86]Hos 8:4-6, 13:1-3, 14:3. Hosea also adds to the
vocabulary belittling images as contemptible natural
objects: the altar/image at Bethel is a "calf" (8:5;
10:5; 13:2); the image of Asherah is "a piece of wood"
(4:12); the idol is a "no god" (8:6). He terms Baal
"shame" and "rubbish" (9:10). Cf. Preuss, 120-131.

[87]Thorkild Jacobsen, in an article for the forth-
coming F. M. Cross festschrift (eds. P. D. Miller, S.
D. McBride, and P. D. Hanson, [Philadelphia: Fortress,
1986]) treats the question of how the Babylonians might
have viewed their cult-statues as embodying the being

reality.   Israel's aniconic tradition did not permit
Deutero-Isaiah to give credence to such subtleties.   He
saw the Babylonians lavishing attention on their idols
and concluded that they were worshipping inanimate
objects as gods.

On the other hand, despite continuity with the preexilic aniconic tradition, two features distinguish
Deutero-Isaiah's satires on idolatry from his preexilic
forebears.   He separates his polemics against idolatry
from the demands of covenant, and he then sets them in
the context of a universal judgment of the nations.

In preexilic Israel, image worship was recognized as
expressing allegiance to foreign deities, even while at
the same time those images were ridiculed as mere human
handiwork.   The decalogue's placement of Yahweh's
"jealousy" in the second commandment prohibiting images
(Exod 20:5; Deut 5:9) is an indication of this linkage.
Hosea and Jeremiah branded their worship as forni-
cation--a metaphor for violating the sanctity of the
covenant with Yahweh as Israel's "spouse" (Hos 1-3, Jer
3).   In the passages where Hosea attacks idolatry, he
does so with the understanding that such worship is a
deliberate spurning of Yahweh and a violation of covenant.   Hos 8:1-6 goes on to link idols with the Canaan-
izing practices of royalty,[88] and in a similar vein,
Isa 2:6-21 (cf. Mic 5:12-15) lists idolatry with other
foreign institutions--Philistine diviners, foreign

---

of the gods.   He describes the Babylonian ceremony for
the installation of an idol as a series of rituals
precisely to nullify its apparent origin as a human
creation.   The wooden statue is transubstantiated into
the body of a god, and its birth in heaven is symboli-
cally reenacted.

[88]Note parallels between Hos 8:4-6 and 1 Sam 8:7,
10-20; Deut 17:14-17.

alliances and chariotry--each of which had led the nation to exalt human works and ignore Yahweh.[89] Jeremiah (2:1-32) states, under the influence of Hosea, that the images are human creations without value or divinity, but he is equally insistent that idolatry is a rejection of God and a transgression of covenant. Jer 10:1-16 stands out as a pure satire on idolatry free from any notion of Yahweh's covenant jealousy. It expresses a perspective identical to that of Deutero-Isaiah but inconsistent with Jeremiah's other attacks on idolatry, and its authenticity has long been contested.[90] Jer 44:8 is a more typical expression of his linkage: "Why do you provoke me to anger with the works of your hands...?" Thus in preexilic Israel ridicule of idols as human works was linked to condemnation of their worship as a violation of the covenantal demand for exclusive allegiance to Yahweh.

---

[89]Here Isaiah, like Hosea before him, scoffs at images as the work of men's hands (2:8-9). While this passage expresses a thought found nowhere else in Isaiah, appears to have suffered considerable reworking and may be in part (notably v. 20) the work of a glossator, there is little reason to doubt the authenticity of v. 2:8b, which adds to the fine irony of man's self-humiliation in v. 9. See Preuss, 136-7; Wildberger, Jesaja 1-12, BKAT X/1 (Neukirchen-Vluyn: Neukirchener Verlag, 1972), 100, 113.

[90]Preuss (pp. 166ff) argues that Jer 10:1-16 is genuine to Jeremiah, in spite of the fact that most would regard it as the work of an editor and its verses appear to be in disorder. See, for example, John Bright, Jeremiah, AB 21 (Garden City: Doubleday, 1965), 79. If Preuss is correct, then Jeremiah, rather than Deutero-Isaiah, would mark the maturation of the satire on idolatry, and indeed it is on the basis of this oracle that Preuss assigns to Jeremiah a status alongside Hosea and Deutero-Isaiah as one of the three summits in the development of this tradition.

Deutero-Isaiah certainly recognized that one reason
to condemn idolatry is its violation of Yahweh's demand
of exclusive allegiance. Yahweh's sole sovereignty is
a frequent theme in Isa 40-55. However, the specific
polemics against idolatry discussed above avoid any
mention of Yahweh's demands and instead ridicule
idolatry as foolish in itself. There is no profit in
idolatry (**bal yôᶜîlû**, 44:9) because idols are lifeless
statues that cannot save (44:17; 46:7). Deutero-Isaiah
did not link his specific polemic against idolatry to
Israel's covenant with Yahweh, for that would miss the
point in an exilic atmosphere when Yahweh's very existence was in question. Jeremiah's appeals to the Mosaic
covenant and further threats of Yahweh's wrath were
ineffective for a people who had already experienced
the worst. Some among the exiles could and did choose
to abandon their allegiance to the Mosaic covenant in
preference for the seemingly more powerful Babylonian
deities, as did their brethren in Egypt (cf. Jer 44).
Therefore, Deutero-Isaiah stressed Israel's established
aniconic tradition, a view no doubt still widely held
among many of his fellow-exiles. He lifted it from the
demands of Israel's covenant and made it an independent
criterion upon which to judge idolatry. In this way he
could set up a more convincing contrast between the
impotence of the idol-gods and Yahweh's absolute power
and divinity, between the folly of those who worship
human artifacts and the confidence which Israel could
have as the servant of a faithful God.

Second, where Deutero-Isaiah did link the prohibition of idolatry to the demands of allegiance to
Yahweh, his ground was not Israel's particular covenant
with Yahweh, but rather the universal claims for monotheism set forth in the trial speeches. We noted that

the trial speech is the immediate context for both Isa 41:5-7 and 44:9-20. There the polemics against idolatry both have a supporting role as evidence for Yahweh's contentions at the trial and are in turn universalized by virtue of the trial's literary setting in the mythological gathering of all the gods and the nations at the place of judgment--the divine council. Since the trial speeches set up a contest between Yahweh and the gods on an international stage, their outcome was a universal decision binding on Israelite and gentile alike.[91] By extension, Deutero-Isaiah also enlarged the scope of Yahweh's judgment upon idolatry. He declared that the nations, and all who followed their example, would be put to shame for their idolatry (41:5-7; 44:9-11; 45:16,20,24).

As long as the prohibition of idolatry was bound up with Israelite covenant traditions, it was directed at Israel alone. Jeremiah even holds up the practices of the nations, though wrong, as examples of better faith (Jer 2:10-11).[92] As prophets representing Yahweh the covenant lord to those living within Israel, they were not concerned with foreign religions per se except to the extent that they encroached upon Israel. But the trial setting in Deutero-Isaiah called into judgment the religions of the nations outside the purview of the traditional Mosaic covenant. We have noted that the mythological setting of the trial speeches set up the grounds for a new covenant, universal and binding upon the nations. Those among the nations who witness

---

[91]See pp. 127-28.

[92]Again Jer 10:1-16, not to be ascribed to Jeremiah and sharing the same exilic perspective as Deutero-Isaiah, speaks of the wise and foolish among the nations and passes judgment upon their idolatry.

Yahweh's forensic triumph in the trial with the idol
gods--and in the mythological setting of the trial
speech this includes every person and every god in the
universe--become parties to this covenant (Isa 45:22-
25). Similarly, prohibition of idolatry, the second
commandment of the Mosaic law, is universalized and
thereby made binding upon the nations.

We have shown that with Deutero-Isaiah the traditional covenantal claims upon Israel, both the positive
demand for allegience to Yahweh alone as God and the
negative prohibition of idolatry, were made universal
and binding upon the nations. Paradoxically, by advan-
cing universal claims, the prophet now required the
assent of the nations in order that these claims be
confirmed. The recognition of Yahweh as God by the
nations became for the first time a sign and a proof
that Yahweh is God. Israel henceforth would come to
expect and even to need the nations' response in order
to vindicate its faith in Yahweh as Lord of all the
earth. We will consider this theme in the following
chapter.

CHAPTER 3
THE NATIONS IN DEUTERO-ISAIAH'S ESCHATOLOGY

It is now well established that Deutero-Isaiah expressed the wonderous nature and cosmic expanse of Yahweh's eschatological deeds with imagery drawn from the royal cult and the exodus traditions which it had assimilated. In this he followed the cult's ritual interpretation of history which linked Yahweh's act of redemption, the exodus, to the primordial act of creation.[1] Isaiah of Jerusalem or a Josianic redactor had used the ritual motif of the defeat of the raging nations against Zion to embellish and give religious significance to the Assyrian withdrawal from Jerusalem in the days of Hezekiah.[2] The royal cult and its associated prophets typically portrayed events of salvation history with a mythological dimension, seeing in history the hand of Yahweh who smites his historical foes just as he slew the primaeval dragon. Deutero-Isaiah similarly understood the depth dimension of history to extend to Yahweh's imminent acts restoring

---

[1]E.g., Pss 74:11-20; 114; Isa 51:9-11. See Cross, Canaanite Myth, 106-11; B. W. Anderson, "Exodus Typology in Second Isaiah," in Israel's Prophetic Heritage, Essays in Honor of James Muilenberg, ed. B. W. Anderson and W. Harrelson (New York: Harper, 1962), 177-95.

[2]Isa 14:24-27; 17:12-14; 29:1-8. See Brevard Childs, Isaiah and the Assyrian Crisis, SBT 3 (Napierville, Ill.: Allenson, 1967); R. E. Clements, Isaiah and the Deliverance of Jerusalem, JSOTS 13 (Sheffield: JSOT, 1980). Childs attributes these passages to Isaiah, Clements to a Josianic redactor.

the exiles to Zion following the defeat of the historical foe Babylon. His eschatology did not represent a
novel historicizing of the timeless events of myth, for
myth and history had mutually informed each other in
the royal cult and in hymns as old as Exod 15.[3]
Creation was viewed as both primordial and eternally
present in Yahweh's activity in nature and in history.
Hence Deutero-Isaiah had ample precedent for projecting
motifs from the myth of creation onto the plane of
historical time to depict his eschatology. He portrayed
this imminent act of Yahweh with the last movement of
the mythic pattern when, subsequent to vanquishing the
raging foe, the deity returns in a victory procession
to take up residence in his temple, restore fertility
to the earth, and manifest his universal sovereignty.

Because of its rootedness in the cosmic setting of
myth, Deutero-Isaiah's eschatology was essentially
universal in scope. It incorporated the nations of the
world as participants in the cosmic drama. In the
Canaanite mythic pattern the victory of the storm god
established him as king to the acclamation of all the
gods of the divine council; likewise in its Israelite
expression the nations of the world gave homage to
Yahweh the universal sovereign.[4] In Deutero-Isaiah's

---

[3]This is Cross's advance over Mowinckel's conception
which distinguished the historical faith of the preexilic prophets from the timeless world of myth as
celebrated in the cult. For Mowinckel, Deutero-Isaiah's
eschatology was a novel historicizing of atemporal
cultic reality. Cross recognized that Yahweh's historical victories and the mythological triumphs of the
storm god had been partially conflated from earliest
times, and that Deutero-Isaiah was heir to a tradition
in which myth and history informed each other. Cf.
CMHE, 79-144; Mowinckel, He That Cometh, 125-154.

[4]On the nations as representing the members of the
divine council, see p. 113, n. 133.

eschatological vision informed by this cultic pattern,
the nations had a dual role. On the one hand they were
Yahweh's enemies who would feel the wrath of Yahweh's
theophany, now mediated through his lieutenant Cyrus
(41:1-5,25; 45:1-6; 47; 49:24-26). But in addition,
the nations were to join the processional throngs and
give homage and offer tribute to the divine king at his
temple (45:14-17,22-25; 49:7;22-23; 55:1-5). We will
consider these latter passages, and also examine the
Cyrus oracle, which is a special case of a gentile
ruler serving Yahweh's purposes and assisting in the
restoration of Zion.

1. Isa 44:24-45:13: The Cyrus Oracle

The Cyrus oracle, Isa 44:24-45:13, is a unified
triptych with three large sections: 44:24-28, 45:1-7,8
and 45:9-13.[5] The first and last sections are evenly
balanced, each containing 20 cola, and they form an
envelope construction framing the longer middle section.[6] The three sections are connected by features of
prosody, vocabulary and content, forming one of the
finest examples of a well-crafted literary unity in the
book of Isaiah.

---

[5]So it is understood by Muilenberg, IB 5, 516;
Clifford, Fair Spoken, 114-21. Westermann (Isaiah 40-
66, 154) sees Isa 44:24-45:7 as a unit. Most form-
critics divide 44:24-45:19 it into three or four units
and delimit the Cyrus oracle to 45:1-7. On the other
hand, Torrey (The Second Isaiah, 354-55) and Bonnard
(Le Second Isaïe, 163-69) perceive the unit as encom-
passing 44:24-45:25.

[6]Of 34 cola, or of 40 cola if (bb):(bb) bicola are
counted as quatrains, (bb):l bicola as tricola, etc.

Isa 44:24-28

```
Thus says Yahweh, your redeemer,                        9
    who formed you from the womb:                       6
                                                      1:b

I am Yahweh, who makes all things,                     8
    who stretched out the heavens by myself,           7
    who spread out the earth--Who was with me?a        7
Who frustrates the omens of extispices,b               6
    makes foolsc of diviners;                          6
Who turns wise men back,                               7
    their knowledge he makes foolish;d                 5
Who confirms the word of his servants,e                7
    fulfills the counsel of his messengers;            7
                       1:1:1::1:b::1:b::1:1

Who says of Jerusalem, "It shall be inhabited,f        10
    of the cities of Judah, "they shall be rebuilt,"g  10
    I will raise up its ruins."                        7
Who says to the Deep, "Be dry,                         8
    I will dry up your rivers."                         6
Who says to Cyrus, "My shepherd,h                      8
    he shall fulfill all my purpose:                   5
To command concerning Jerusalem, 'It shall be
    rebuilt;i                                          10
    <my>j temple shall be refounded.'"                 6
                       1:1:b::1:b::1:b::1:b
```

Isa 45:1-7

```
Thus says Yahweh:                                   rubric
To my anointed,k to Cyrus,                             7
    [ ] hisl right hand I have grasped;               7
To subduem nations before him,                         7
    the loins of kings I have loosed;                  8
To open doors before him,                              8
    the gates will not be shut.                        8
                       1:1::1:1::1:1

I myself will go before you,                           8
    the mountains I will level;n                       6
Doors of bronze I will smash,                          8
    bars of iron I will cut in pieces;                 8
I will give you the treasures of darkness,            9
    hoards in secret places;                           6
In order that you may knowo that I am Yahweh,          9
    he who calls your name                             7
    is the God of Israel.                              6
                       1:b::1:b::1:b::1:b:b
```

For the sake of my servant Jacob,   6
  and Israel, my chosen,   6
I call you by your name,[p]   8
  I betitle you,[q] though you do not know me.   10
I am Yahweh, and there is no other;   7
  besides me there are no gods.   7
  I gird you with authority, though you do
  not know me.   11
In order that it may be known from the rising
  of the sun   9
  to its[r] setting that there is nothing besides me. 10
          b:b::1:(b:b)::1:1:(b:b)::1:1

I am Yahweh, and there is none other;   7
  forming the light, and creating the darkness;   7
  maker of weal,[s] and creator of woe;   8
I am Yahweh, maker of all things.   9
          1:1:1:1:1

Shower,[t] O heavens, from above,   7
  let the skies rain down righteousness;   7
Let the earth open[u] and salvation bloss<om>,[v]   7
  and righteousness sprout forth together;   7
  I, Yahweh, have created it.   7
          1:1::1:1:1

45:9-13

Does the pot quarrel[w] with its potter,   8
  the mud with its craftsman?   7
Does the clay say [   ],[x] "What are you doing?"   7
  the work claim, "Y<ou>[y] have no ability?"   7
Does one say to a father, "What are you begetting?"   8
  to the wife, "With what do you labor?"   8
          1:1::1:1::1:1

Thus says Yahweh,
  the Holy One of Israel and its Maker: rubric
How do you question me[z] concerning my children,   10
  or command me concerning the work of my hands?   8
I myself made the earth;   7
  humanity I created upon it;   8
My own hands stretched out the heavens;   8
  and all their host I command.   8
          1:1::1:1::1:1

I myself aroused him for victory,   10
  all his ways I make level;   7
He is the one who shall build my city,   5
  and send forth my exiles,[aa]   7
Not for a price, nor for a bribe,   9
  says Yahweh of hosts.   7
          1:b::b:1::1:b

TEXTUAL NOTES

[a]Read the k͟e͟t͟î͟b with 1QIsa[a] **my' 'ty** and G. The q͟e͟r͟ē͟' **mē'-'ittî**, "from myself," reflects a later theological sensitivity but ignores Deutero-Isaiah's rhetorical style.

[b]MT and all versions read **baddîm**, a noun from the root **bdd** meaning "idle talk" in Job 11:3, Isa 16:8. The word is suspect; we would expect a particple **bōdēd** or an adjectival form **badîd**. Here and in Jer 50:36 the word refers to a class of Babylonian diviners, and with North and Westermann we emend to **bārîm**, the **bāru** priests who performed extispicy.

[c]G ἀπὸ καρδίας < *mēl-lēb < *mĕhōlēl?

[d]Reading **yĕsakkēl** with a **sāmek** with 1QIsa[a] and 1QIsa[b]; MT has an aural confusion of **śîn** and **sāmek**. G reads βουλὴν αὐτῶν for **da[c]tām** by an inner Greek anticipatory dittography from the next bicolon.

[e]The plural, supported by some G mss, Targ., is called for by context. In MT it could easily have been confused with the following initial **waw**.

[f]Where MT reads **tûšab**, 1QIsa[a] and 1QIsa[b] read **tšb**. Rather than make the common emendation to a metrically inferior niphal **tiwwāšēb**, I prefer to see MT **tûšāb** as a vestige of an old Qal passive form. In MT the verb with a medio-passive meaning is 15 times pointed as a Qal **tēšēb**.

[g]Kohler, North and others consider this colon to be an expansion. Yet such 1:1:b tricola are common in Deutero-Isaiah, and the feminine singular suffix in the third colon referring back to Jerusalem can stand as an example of chiasm.

[h]G φρονεῖν < *da[c], a **dālet/rēš** confusion.

[i]See discussion.

[j]Adding a first person pronominal suffix with 1QIsa[a] and G.

[k]Reading with G τῷ χριστῷ μου, a more difficult reading than MT **li-mšîḥô**. We take this line to be the first colon in a divine speech of three bicola, and not part of the formula of address. See the discussion.

[l]G lacks the suffix. Omit the relative pronoun as a prosaizing expansion.

[m]MT reads **lě-rad**; we render it **lā-rōd**, the Qal infinitive of **rdd**. Cf. 41:26.

[n]MT reads **wa-hădûrîm**, "honorable ones," which is forced in this context. 1QIsa[a] **whrrym y'wšr**, 1QIsa[b] **hrwrym 'wš[** and G all support emendation to **hărarîm**, "mountains." The **qerē'** piel verb is preferable to the hiphil **ketîb** for reasons of prosody.

[o]Many exegetes remove **lěma[c]an tēda[c]** because it conflicts with the repeated assertion that in fact Cyrus does not know Yahweh. But such an argument is self-defeating, since any later conscious alteration of the text would tend to clean up what appears to be a failed prophecy rather than exaggerate Cyrus's piety in the teeth of his embrace of the Marduk cult. The text as it stands parallels v. 4b with repetition of verbs **yd[c]**, **qr'**, and **šiměkā**.

[p]Where MT reads **bi-šmekā**, 1QIsa[a] has **bšm** and G reads τῷ ὀνόματί μου.

[q]1QIsa[a] reads **hkynkh** from **kwn**; the Qumran scribe did not understand MT's rare verb **knn**, and neither does G.

ʳ1QIsaᵃ **wmmᶜrb** agrees with G δυσμῶν; but Gᴸ, Sym., Thdt. add αὐτὸν reflecting the MT consonantal text with a mappîq.

ˢ1QIsaᵃ reads **ṭwb**, the ordinary antonym of **raᶜ**.

ᵗWhere MT has **harᶜîpû**, G εὐφρανθήτω is reading a defective vorlage *ʰryᶜw.

ᵘ1QIsaᵃ reads **h'mr l'rṣ**, an anticipatory dittography from v. 10 (*h'mr l'[b]). This is additional evidence that an interrogative **hă** and not **hôy** stands behind the text of that verse; see below pp. 210-12. G reads ἀνατειλάτω, but it lacks the second half of the colon and may be reading the second verb as either **yipraḥ** or **yipreh**.

ᵛRead with 1QIsaᵃ **wĕ-yipraḥ**, a synonym of **tiṣmāḥ**, emended as a Qal (cf. Isa 35:1,2) because **'ereṣ** is their subject. MT has **wĕ-yiprû**, and according to Torrey MT takes the clouds (**šĕḥāqîm**) as the subject of both this verb and of **taṣmîḥ** pointed as a causative.

ʷSee discussion on pp. 210-12.

ˣOmit MT **lĕ-yōṣĕrô** metri causa; it is an expansion from the previous bicolon.

ʸSee the discussion on pp. 213-14.

ᶻhă-'ōtî tiš'alûnî is the standard emendation of MT hā-'ōtiyyôt šĕ'ālûnî. 1QIsaᵃ **h'wtwt š'lwny** follows MT.

ᵃᵃThere is no need to emend **gālûtî** to **gālût ᶜammî** with G; the meter is better with MT.

The structure of the Cyrus oracle features a large chiasm formed by the two outer sections 44:24-28 and 45:9-13 which both stress Yahweh's word over the

pratings of men. Yahweh refutes the supposed wisdom of
the Babylonian diviners and wisemen while confirming
the words of his servant in 44:25-26a, and similarly in
45:9-11 Yahweh disputes those who would question his
work. In 44:26b-27 the focus on Yahweh's speaking is
stressed by the threefold repetition of the participle
with definite article hā-'ōmēr; 45:9-10 has three corresponding interrogative particles (hǎ-) and a double
yō'mar in the rhetorical questions ridiculing those who
question Yahweh, answered by a third (kōh 'āmar) in
Yahweh's speech opening v. 11. In 44:24 Yahweh's power
to perform his word in history is prefaced by assertions that he created all things, heaven and earth;
45:12 has similar assertions prefacing Yahweh's stirring up Cyrus. Finally, both outer sections conclude
with the efficacy of Yahweh's word substantiated in
Cyrus, who, as Yahweh's "shepherd" and deputy, will
perform his purposes, specifically to rebuild Jerusalem
and its temple and return the exiles (44:28; 45:13).
The central section Isa 45:1-8 has a reverse progression from Yahweh's deeds on earth to his work in creation and a parallel progression from Cyrus's general
conquests to that act which will be done specifically
for Israel and Yahweh. Repeated participial phrases
including the phrase 'ǎni yhwh ᶜōśeh kol (44:24; 45:7)
form an inclusio around the first two sections. The
second and third sections are linked by repeated piel
verbs and initial first person pronouns. This structure is summarized in Table 6.

Westermann rightly views 44:24-28 as incomplete in
itself. It is grammatically a long series of participial phrases, a single lengthy sentence built upon the
initial noun clause "I am Yahweh." From a form-critical
standpoint such self-identifications, while descriptive

TABLE 6: The Structure of the Cyrus Oracle

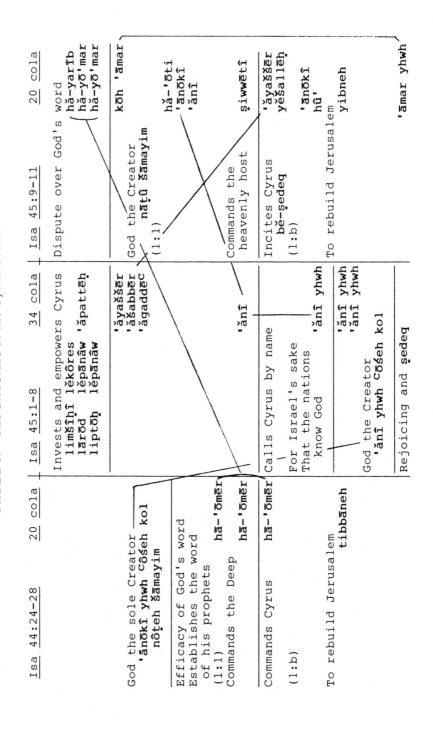

of Yahweh's creatorship and sovereignty in history, normally introduce a word of salvation, but that word does not come until the following commissioning of Cyrus in 45:1-7,8.[7] 44:24-28 is composed of three strophes, each in turn built up with three similar bicola.[8] The first strophe describes Yahweh's creation of heaven and earth with three Qal participles. The second strophe affirms the efficacy of Yahweh's word against the oracles of Babylonian diviners with three bicola each beginning with hiphil participles. The third strophe describes Yahweh's providential activity on behalf of Israel with the participle **hā-'ōmēr** repeated three times, which, as was noted, connects to the three-fold use of this verb in the final section of the oracle (45:9-11). This prediliction for structures in threes continues throughout the oracle.[9]

The chief difficulties for interpretation of this section lie in the concluding two verses. Mention of the rebuilding of Jerusalem and the temple in v. 28b appears to repeat v. 26b; hence Westermann emends the text by rearranging the lines and Muilenberg deletes the last half-verse. The reference to the deep in v. 27 also appears out of context; as an act of creation its mention would be expected prior to the rebuilding of Jerusalem in v. 26b. In examining v. 28b, we note that while MT **lē'mōr** may possibly be a prosaizing expansion, G ὁ λέγων is even more questionable since it appears to

---

[7]Westermann, 154.

[8]Muilenberg, 516.

[9]A similar three-fold repetition of the particles **kî** and **hinnēh** in 40:2 and 40:9-10 defines the chiastic structure of 40:1-11. This is described by David Noel Freedman, "The Structure of Isaiah 40:1-11," to appear in a festschrift honoring Francis I. Andersen.

be reinterpreting MT by attraction to the preceding hā-'ōmēr; it would also violate the pattern of three-fold repetition noted above. The infinitival clause beginning lē'mōr can be understood according to the structure of Isa 49:6,8-9 as describing the consequent action of Cyrus as Yahweh's agent. In accordance with Yahweh's decree, he will command Jerusalem's rebuild-ing: "to command concerning Jerusalem, 'let it be rebuilt.'"[10] This second call for the rebuilding of Jerusalem thus differs from the first in specifying Yahweh's agent and commanding him to that purpose.

The command drying up the Deep in v. 27 properly precedes the act of founding the temple, according to the traditional mythic pattern of creation.[11] But its unusual placement following the initial promise that Jerusalem will be rebuilt in v. 26b points to an ano-ther purpose, as Deutero-Isaiah draws an analogy with the command to Cyrus. Yahweh commands the Deep with an imperative "be dry," and then dries up its waters; similarly Yahweh commands Cyrus to rebuild Jerusalem and the temple. Cyrus is a pagan ruler; similarly the Deep, an enemy of God in the traditional myth of crea-tion, had been taken up by the royal cult and the classical prophets as a symbol for Israel's enemies Assyria and Egypt.[12] Yet for Deutero-Isaiah, as for

---

[10]Clifford, Fair Spoken, 114. Alternatively, lē'mōr could introduce a direct quotation of a divine command to Cyrus. The consonantal MT tbnh could be repointed as a Qal imperfect and tiwwāsed likewise repointed to tĕyassēd, but then the le- prefix on Jerusalem must be omitted: "saying, 'You shall rebuild Jerusalem, you shall refound my temple.'"

[11]See Carroll Stuhlmueller, "The Theology of Crea-tion in Second Isaias," CBQ 21 (1959) 447-51.

[12]Isa 17:12-14; 5:30; 8:7-8; 30:7; Ezek 29:3-5; Pss 46; 89:10-11.

Isaiah before him, the hostile powers of nature and political rulers are under Yahweh's sovereignty. Yahweh himself brings the waters of Sea and River (Assyria) against Jerusalem;[13] Yahweh dries up the waters of the Nile.[14] Implicit in this collocation of images is a reply to those who find it implausible that God should call a pagan ruler to rebuild Jerusalem: Just as Yahweh can command the hostile powers, so Cyrus can be Yahweh's chosen instrument who is called and empowered to perform his purposes. This controversy over Cyrus re-emerges in explicit form in 45:9-13.

The tradition of viewing foreign kings as instruments of the divine will was hardly new; prophets as early as Elijah had discerned the will of Yahweh in their actions against Israel.[15] Westermann discerns behind the phrase that Yahweh "stirs up" Cyrus (41:2,25; 45:13) passages in Jeremiah which speak of Yahweh "stirring up" the Medes against Babylon and the older tradition of the foe from the north, the direction from which God unleashed invading armies against Israel.[16] Clifford sees in the background of Deutero-Isaiah's depiction of Cyrus Isaiah's oracle commissioning Assyria as "the rod of my wrath" to chastize Judah (Isa 10:5-11,13-15).[17] While there is no direct liter-

---

[13]Isa 5:18-30; 8:17.

[14]Isa 19:5-7.

[15]Cf. 1 Kgs 19:15-18. On the root conception of the universal divine imperium behind this tradition, see G.E. Wright, "The Nations in Hebrew Prophecy," Encounter 26 (1965), 225-37.

[16]Jer 1:13-16; 13:17; 50:9; 51:1,11. See Westermann, 88.

[17]Clifford, 117-20.

ary dependence upon that oracle, the Cyrus oracle does
contain motifs similar to the latter's description of
Assyria's role in God's plan: he is sent by Yahweh
(10:6), he plunders the nations' treasures (10:6b,13b),
he destroys the enemy (10:7, cf. 41:2), and he tramples
the foe in the street (10:6b, cf. 41:25). Like the
Assyrian, Cyrus is ignorant of the fact that Yahweh has
been the cause of his success (45:3-4); compare, "He
does not so intend, and his mind does not so think..."
(10:7). Finally the oracle's rejoinder, "Shall the axe
vaunt itself over him who hews with it, or the saw
magnify itself against him who wields it" (10:15), is
reutilized in the third section of the Cyrus oracle to
dispute with those Israelites who cannot believe God
can act in such a way (45:9-10): "Does the pot quarrel
with its maker, the mud with its potter...?"

While previously the prophets had seen world rulers
as Yahweh's instruments to chastize Israel; Deutero-
Isaiah also saw in Cyrus one chosen for the work of
redemption, particularly for the task of rebuilding
Jerusalem. Various commentators have described how
Cyrus, though a gentile ruler, is invested with all the
symbols and authority of a Davidid.[18] As Isaiah before
him had invested the Davidic king (Isa 9:1-6; 11:1-9),
Deutero-Isaiah similarly applies the traditions of the
Judean royal cult to Cyrus. Like David, Yahweh anoints
Cyrus and grasps his right hand (45:1),[19] gives him a
name and girds him with strength (45:4-5),[20] in order

---

[18]See Westermann, 157-61. He discusses the form of
this oracle in relation to royal coronation texts both
in Israel and in Mesopotamia, noting especially parallels with the Cyrus Cylinder.

[19]Cf. 1 Sam 10:1; Ps 89:21,22,26.

[20]Cf. Isa 9:5;11:5; 2 Sam 7:9.

that he may do righteousness on the earth   (45:8,13).[21]
Cyrus is betitled rōᶜî,   "my [Yahweh's] shepherd"
(44:21);[22] he gets his power from Yahweh who conquers
the unruly Sea (44:27-8);[23] and through him the entire
earth is to witness the victory of Yahweh and the
vindication of his people (45:6).[24] Most importantly
Cyrus, like the Davidic kings Solomon and Ahaz, is to
build or repair the temple of Yahweh (44:28).[25]

     The second movement of the Cyrus oracle, the commis-
sioning oracle proper, is constructed in five strophes
including the hymnic refrain in v. 8.   The first
strophe, like the second strophe of the first section
(44:25-26a), is built with three balanced 1:1 bicola.
After the opening rubric of address kōh 'āmar yhwh, the
three bicola evince a parallel structure: each A colon
begins with two words prefixed by the preposition le--
first a prepositional phrase or infinitive (limšîḥî,
lārōd, liptoḥ) then a prepositional phrase (lĕ-kôreš,
lĕpānāw, lĕpānāw)--and each B colon contains the finite
verb, twice in the first person and the third a niphal
passive. This striking parallelism directs us away
from placing the words limšîḥî lĕ-kôreš in the formula
of address as it is usually translated.   The effect of
this construction is to emphasize Yahweh's action in
directing Cyrus's advance, as the finite verb denoting
divine activity in the B colon governs the infinitive
phrase or prepositional phrase describing Cyrus and his

---

[21]Cf. Ps 72:2,12-14, Isa 9:6; 11:4.

[22]Cf. Ezek 34; Zech 10:2-3; 11:4-16; 13:7.

[23]Cf. Ps 89.

[24]Cf. Isa 11:9; Ps 2:8-12.

[25]Cf. 2 Sam 7:13; Isa 9:6; 11:6-9.

conquests in the A colon. The passive verb yissāgerû
should also be rendered as expressing divine intention-
ality   and   activity   as with   similar   verbs   denoting
Yahweh's will in 44:26.

The second strophe (vv. 2-3) begins with 'ănî and,
like the   parallel third strophe of the first   section
(44:26b-28),   is built of three parallel 1:b bicola and
an unbalanced tricolon.   Here Yahweh addresses Cyrus in
the second person.   Piel imperfects in the first person
singular are in the final position of three   successive
cola: 'ăyaššer, 'ăšabbēr, and 'ăgaddēc, which may be
connected with a similar series of three first   person
piel   verbs   at   the conclusion of   the   third   section
(45:12d,13).   The three bicola describe Yahweh's aid to
Cyrus   during his march,   his sieges at city gates   and
his   plundering   of temple treasures.   The   concluding
tricolon   states God's purpose,   that Cyrus might   know
that He is the source of his victories.

The third strophe (vv. 4-6a) has a chiastic   structure   in   four bicola and tricola.   An   outer   chiasm
formed by balanced b:b and 1:1 bicola each   introduced
by lĕmacan, frames   a   pair of unbalanced   units--an
1:(b:b) bicolon and an 1:1:(b:b) tricolon--which   each
describe   the   irony that Yahweh calls and   empowers   a
king who is not his worshipper: "I betitle you/ I gird
you with authority, though you do not know me."   In the
outer bicola there is a progression in Yahweh's purpose
from   Israel (v. 4a) to all the world (v. 6a).   The
fourth strophe (vv. 6b-7) is a quatrain in which a pair
of   statements of self identification 'ănî yhwh... form
a   chiasm around pairs of participial clauses in   short
meter describing Yahweh's creation of all   things   by
merisms: light and darkness, weal and woe.

Note that there is nothing in Cyrus's conquests per
se that would unequivocally manifest Cyrus's (45:3b),
Israel's (45:4) or international (45:6) recognition
that Yahweh is behind him. Rather, the purposes expressed in these verses of the Cyrus oracle must refer
to a further act on his part. This no doubt is the
same act as depicted in 44:28 and 45:13: to return the
exiles to their homeland and rebuild the temple. By
this act alone can both the hope of Israel be realized
and the reputation of Yahweh be vindicated before the
nations. The God of Israel in exile was scorned because
he had not protected his people from exile and because
his sanctuary was in ruins and therefore ritually profaned.[26] By Israel's return to Zion and its rebuilding,
Yahweh would vindicate his name before the eyes of the
nations (cf. Ezek 36:8-25).[27] Even the prophecy that
Cyrus will know that Yahweh has called him would be
realized in his decree to rebuild the temple, for in
such decrees the king typically attributes his work of
temple rebuilding as obedience to a command of the
deity who has favored him.[28] Such is the case in the
decree of Cyrus recorded in 2 Chr 36:23, Ezra 1:2:
"Yahweh, the god of heaven, has given me all the kingdoms of the earth, and he has charged me to build him a
house at Jerusalem." The Cyrus oracle was in fact
regarded as largely fulfilled by the Chronicler who, in

---

[26]Note that Deutero-Isaiah consistently identifies
the temple with Jerusalem; the entire city is holy; it
shall no longer be profaned (52:1); it is the dwelling-
place of Yahweh (52:8); built of precious stones
(54:11-12) and the locus of pilgrimage (49:22-23).

[27]Cf. Blank, Prophetic Faith, 117-26.

[28]E.g. Akkadian temple inscriptions Samsuiluna C and
Yahdun-Lim.

the words of Deutero-Isaiah, describes how Yahweh had
stirred up (hēᶜîr) Cyrus to make this decree.

The fifth and final strophe of this section (v. 8)
is a short hymnic passage connected to the preceding
strophe again by repetition of 'ănî yhwh [bĕrā'tîw],
this time at its conclusion. As Yahweh had created all
things, so now ṣedeq, yešaᶜ and ṣĕdāqâ would come forth
in heaven and earth. This is Yahweh's new creation, the
fructification of the desert. In the underlying ritual
pattern nature's sprouting forth is associated with the
return of the Divine warrior from his conquests to take
his place in the temple; in Deutero-Isaiah the motif is
associated with the return of the exiles and the
rebuilding of Zion.[29] At the culmination of the first
movement (44:28) Cyrus was commanded to rebuild Jerusalem and the temple; now at the culmination of the
second movement (45:6-8) that one all-significant deed
will bring forth rejoicing of nature, justice on earth,
and international recognition of Yahweh's divinity.

The third section of the Cyrus oracle (45:9-13) has
three strophes: vv. 9-10, 11-12 and 13. The first
strophe is plagued with corruptions. MT and the versions show confusion as to whether in this series of
three bicola they begin with hôy and a participle or
hă- and an active verb. MT has hôy alternating with
hă-, 1QIsaᵃ is conflate, reading hwy rb, hwy h'wmr and
hwy h'wmr, and G appears to be reading hă-. We regard
the introduction of hôy to be secondary because it
confuses the scansion of the first bicolon. Acting as
a verbal element, hôy makes rāb one of the nominal elements joined by 'et. But this leaves the second colon
unintelligible as it stands: ḥereś 'et ḥarśê 'ădāmā, "a

---

[29]cf. 41:18-19; 43:18-20; 49:9-13; 51:9-11; ch. 35.

pot with potsherds of earth." G "ploughland with ploughers of the soil" unacceptably shifts the point of comparison. Torrey's emendation to ḥāraš 'ădāmâ "a pot with a craftsman of earth," is still strained--there is no biblical attestation of this appellation for a potter as, for example, the term ḥāraš ᶜēṣîm for wood carver. Volz moves in the right direction and reads hă-yārîb as an interrogative particle on a verb, but under influence of G he goes on to assume a haplography of ḥrś: "Streitet der Ton mit dem Töpfer, mit seinem Meister der Ton von Erde?"[30] The extra hereś is unwarranted, since G is simply reading MT in this colon. With hă-yārîb as the verb, the bicolon is best redivided giving balanced comparisons between the nouns: the pot with its maker, the earth with its craftsman (or with its ploughman according to G). We read harāšô as craftsman to be consistent with the metaphor developed in these verses; the third person pronominal suffix differs from the consonantal MT ḥrśy only by wāw/yôd interchange. Hôy arose by a simple metathesis of wāw and yôd in the second and third bicola: *hyw'mr < hwy 'mr, which then by analogy contaminated the first colon: *hyrb < hwy rb. The construction by rhetorical questions should be carried through consistently in all three bicola--it is certainly so required in the second bicolon, and the third bicolon carries on the same figure of a product questioning its maker: mah taᶜăśeh, mah tôlîd, mah tĕḥîlîn. Finally, one would like to continue Deutero-Isaiah's consistent style of building stanzas with the repetition of three similar verbal elements, and the threefold repetition of the interro-

---

[30]Volz, *Jesaja II*, 65-66; cf. C.F. Whitely, "Textual Notes on Deutero-Isaiah," *VT* 11 (1961) 458.

gative **hă-** at the initial position of three successive
bicola forms a chiasm with the corresponding threefold
repetition of the definite article **ha-** with initial
participles in the first section (44:26b-28a).

Classifying Isa 45:9-13 as a woe-oracle with **hôy**
would also be unusual from a form-critical standpoint.
Woe oracles begin with an invocation with **hôy** followed
by a specific group of evildoers.[31]   But here the
invocation with **hôy** lacks a concrete referent. The woe
oracle is a form of extreme invective originating in
funerary laments; it is followed by an indictment and
sentence.[32]   But Isa 45:9-13 is rather a dispute with
those who do not believe the good which Yahweh is about
to do for them, and the dispute is followed by words of
salvation. The figure of a pot quarreling with its
maker is a rhetorical device which may occur in the
indictment section of a woe-oracle (Isa 10:15, 29:16),
but not in the inital invocation. In those contexts it
has the subsidiary function of setting forth in meta-
phorical language Yahweh's dispute with those who would
question his authority.[33]   If the word **hôy** in this

---

[31]E.g. Isa 5:8,11,18; 29:15; 30:1; 31:1; Am 5:18;
6:1

[32]Cf. Waldemar Janzen, Mourning Cry and Woe Oracle,
BZAW 125 (Berlin: de Gruyter, 1972).

[33]Isa 29:15-21 is the closest merging of **hôy** with
the figure of the pot questioning its maker, but the
two devices are not thereby confused. The **hôy** (v. 15)
is directed against "those who hide from Yahweh...
whose deeds are in darkness," who turn things upside
down. After they are compared to a pot questioning the
potter in v. 16, Yahweh announces his judgment in terms
of his own divinely ordained reversal of nature
(vv. 17-21) when the blind shall see, the deaf shall
hear, the meek and the poor will be vindicated, while
they, the "scoffers" and "ruthless" will be destroyed.

passage were retained, it would be so merged with the
rhetorical figure as to be directed against the metaphor rather than a concrete object; the invocation and
its following indictment would become confused.

Recognizing the inconsistency between the supposed
woe invective in vv. 9-10 and the disputation in vv.
11-13, and since the woe-oracle is found nowhere else
in Deutero-Isaiah, Elliger and Westermann have even
concluded that the vv. 9-10 are secondary.[34] But their
secondary attribution is tenuous when the formal marker
hôy rests upon such an uncertain text. On the other
hand, rhetorical questions are Deutero-Isaiah's stock
in trade, and our emended text with a triplet of questions introduced with the interrogative hă- is carried
over into the rhetorical question in v. 11b as it is
usually emended. The unity of vv. 9-10 with 11-13 is
easily established by the threefold repetition of
yăday(im) as the hands of the potter (vv. 9bb) and of
the Creator (v. 11bb, 12ba), the pairs tôlîd / bⁿnay
(vv. 10a, 11ba) and poᶜal (vv. 9bb, 11bb), and the
repeated rubric (kōh) 'āmar yhwh (vv. 11aa, 13cb) which
directly answers the purported speech (yō'mar) of the
creation to its creator (vv. 9ba, 10a).

Another difficulty with this stanza is the B colon
of the second bicolon: poᶜolĕkā 'ên yādayim lô. There
have been two main lines of interpretation. The RSV
reads from MT a continuation of the question begun in
the previous colon: "What are you doing? Your work has
no handles," to which the objection is often raised

---

[34]Westermann, 165; K. Elliger, Jesaja II, 179-82.
Westermann's hypothetical trial speech with the idol
gods in vv. 11-13 cannot be accepted; the idol gods in
the trial speeches are human creations, and the point
there is precisely that they do not speak.

that **yād** used of inanimate objects normally takes the
feminine plural rather than the dual.[35] Otherwise
po^colĕkā is to be understood as a subject of yô'mar,
and the **yādayim** are those of the craftsman, meaning his
ability or strength.[36] For this rendering **lô** is usually
emended to **lekā** on the basis of G οὐδὲ ἔχεις χεῖρας and
the Peshitta,[37] and North further emends po^colĕkā to
po^cal kî: "does the work [say] that you [the craftsman]
have no ability?"[38] This approach to the text is to be
preferred: it better fits the prosodic structure, and
the term **yādayim** is a key word twice repeated in vv. 9-
13 to refer to the "hands" or power of the Creator.
Isa 29:16 may lie in the background: "Does the pot say
to its potter, 'he has no understanding?'"

The second and third strophes, vv. 11-12,13, begin
and end with rubrics which do not mark out a new oracle
but rather answer the questioning of vv. 9-10. The two
strophes may be distinguished by their meter--vv. 11-12
form a strophe in balanced 1:1 meter and v. 13 is in
1:b meter--and by the thematic shift from the general
acts of God to the specific deed to be performed on
behalf of Jerusalem. In these features they parallel
the second and third strophes of the first section
(44:25-26a and 26b-28). Yet together they form an
elaborate chiasm: the rubrics in vv. 11a and 13c frame
a series of bicola each beginning with a pronoun in the
chiastic sequence 'ōtî, 'ānōkî, 'ănî, 'ānōkî, hû'--

---

[35]Cf. GK #87o.

[36]cf. Ps 76:6, Deut 32:36, Jos 8:20, 2 Kgs 19:26.

[37]1QIsa^a reads wpw^clkh 'yn 'dm ydym lw, "and your
work is not a human which has hands."

[38]North, The Second Isaiah, 153.

recalling the several first person colon-initial pronouns in the central section (vv. 2a, 5a, 6c and 7c).
Yahweh's speaking ('āmar) answers the people's questioning (tĕṣawwūnî) with assertions that he creates,
commands (ṣiwwêtî) his creation, and stirs up Cyrus to
build his city and release his exiled people. The
sequential devolution of Yahweh's power from creation
to the rebuilding of Jerusalem parallels that in the
first section 44:24-28, even to the repetition of the
phrase naṭû šāmayim (44:24b,45:12b).

Cyrus, here identified only as "he" but who is
understood by its antecedent in 45:1,[39] is also the
focus of this section. The issue in dispute being how
a foreign ruler can be the instrument of Israel's
salvation, Yahweh asks "will you question me concerning
my children?" and identifies "his children" as all
humanity: "I created humankind upon it [the earth]."
The prophet here implies that everyone, Israelite and
gentile alike, is created by Yahweh, and hence Yahweh
can as easily perform his purposes with a gentile ruler
as with an Israelite. Furthermore, just as Yahweh,
here called by his title "Yahweh of hosts," commands
all (kol) the hosts of heaven, so he can stir up a
human lieutenant such as Cyrus and level all (kol) his
ways. The comparison of Cyrus, an earthly ruler, to
the ṣābā' of heaven who were worshipped as gods in
Mesopotamia (cf. Isa 40:25-26), yet both of whom are
under God's command, is parallel to Yahweh's earlier
commands first to the Deep and then to Cyrus in 44:27-
28. If Yahweh can command even the forces of nature,

---

[39]Melugin (p. 125) cites this as evidence that 45:9-
13 belong with the oracle investing Cyrus, but he
supposes that these verses were composed later, "after
the preceding two poems had been joined."

even the so-called gods of the nations, he can certainly command Cyrus. Cyrus will fulfill God's purpose
without the need for a bribe or special influence in
the court on the part of the exiles because Yahweh has
stirred him up bĕ-ṣedeq (cf. 45:8)--the repetition of
the preposition bĕ- before ṣedeq, māhîr and šōḥad suggests that they should be understood in parallel. This
section ends at the same point as 44:28, with Cyrus
rebuilding Zion.

Did Cyrus's activity as a world conqueror, coupled
with his tolerant policies towards his subjects, contribute to the universal scope of Deutero-Isaiah's
vision of Yahweh's new act of redemption? Certainly
from a practical standpoint the exiles needed the help
of powerful gentiles in order to be restored to their
homeland. One could argue that Deutero-Isaiah hoped in
advance of Cyrus's arrival for a benevolent policy
towards Babylon's subject peoples. It was customary
for a challenger to the prevailing empire to ally
himself with restive vassals as Babylon once sought out
Hezekiah's support against Assyria (2 Kgs 20:12-13);
such a lenient policy was an effective instrument of
diplomacy. Cyrus's own propaganda[40] proclaimed the
king's compassion and justice as extending to all the
earth. It has been argued that subsequently Deutero-
Isaiah became critical of Cyrus for his embrace of the
Marduk cult and his leniency towards Babylon,[41] yet
such suppositions cannot be confirmed, since the prophecies concerning Cyrus were made prior to Babylon's

---

[40]The "Cyrus Cylinder" and the "Verse Account of
Nabonidus," ANET, 315a,f.

[41]North, Suffering Servant, 75ff., Lindblom, Servant
Songs, 71.

downfall. The Cyrus prophecies correctly predicted a central moment in Yahweh's new redemption of Israel, when Cyrus afforded the exiles a possibility to return to Zion and decreed the temple's reconstruction.

Yet the Cyrus oracle does not recognize Israel to be a small speck of a nation that could find deliverance if it positioned itself to take pragmatic advantage of the larger tide of history. The center of the world order does not shift to Cyrus and his political capital, but to Yahweh and to Zion his central sanctuary. Deutero-Isaiah's conception of Cyrus's work was primarily shaped by his utilization of the Israelite traditions of the royal cult and Yahweh's universal sovereignty. These traditions understood Yahweh, the universal creator and sovereign over all the hostile powers of heaven and earth, to be in control of all history and to employ foreign rulers as his instruments. Cyrus in Isa 44:24-45:13 is deemed to conquer for the very purpose of vindicating Yahweh's cause by liberating the exiles and specifically by restoring his temple in Jerusalem, the seat of his world dominion.

Cyrus also provided the model for a gentile ruler exalting Zion. By extension, all the gentile rulers were to serve Yahweh's will by bringing the exiles back from the nations and contributing their wealth to the restoration of the temple. This is in fact the subject of the verses which immediately follow the Cyrus oracle (45:14-25).[42]

---

[42]See pp. 93-94, 243.

2. Isa 55:1-13: The Nations Serve Israel, Recipient of the Davidic Covenant

The royal traditions which inform the eschatological vision of the nations exalting Zion are most clearly illuminated in Isa 55:1-13. In this concluding unit to the book of consolation, Yahweh invites his people to feast at a messianic banquet on Mount Zion and disputes with those who would doubt whether he can deliver on such a promise. Israel in vv. 3-5 is invested with the eternal Davidic covenant which specifically empowers her to command the nations, who come running to serve and to glorify her.

55:1-5

Lo! All who thirst, come to the water,	8
and [ ] those without money, come <and buy>![a]	8
Buy and eat [ ] without money,	8
without price, wine and milk!	8
Why do you spend money for what is not bread,	9
your labor for what does not satisfy?	9
Listen [ ][b] to me that you may eat what is good,	8
and delight yourselves in rich fare;	9
Incline your ear and come here [ ];[c]	8
listen, that you may live.	8

1:1::1:1::1:1::1:1::1:1

I will make[d] with you an everlasting covenant,	8
the enduring graces to David.	8
As I appointed him[e] a witness to the nations,[f]	9
a leader and commander of nations;	9
So you shall summon peoples who know you not,	9
peoples that you do not know[g] shall run[h] to you;	9
Because of Yahweh your God,	8
the Holy One[i] of Israel, for he has glorified you.	9

1:1::1:1::1:1::1:1

55:6-11

```
Seek Yahweh where he may be found;                          10
   approach him where he is near.                           10
Let the wicked man abandon his ways,ʲ                        7
   and the evil man his thoughts;                            7
Let him return to Yahweh, that he may be merciful
      to him,                                               11
   to our God, for he will abundantly pardon.ᵏ             11
                                        1:1::1:1::1:1
```

```
For my thoughts are not your thoughts,ˡ                     11
   and your ways are not my ways, says Yahweh.             11
For as the heavens are higherᵐ than the earth,              8
   so are my ways higher than your ways,                   11
   and my thoughts than your thoughts.                     11
                                          1:1::1:1:1
```

```
For just as rain comes down,                                7
   and snow to the sky [    ]ⁿ does not return,             7
Until it waters the earth, fertilizes it and causes
      it to sprout,                                        13
   giving seed to the sower and bread to the eater;ᵒ      12
So [ ]ᵖ my decree [ ] goes forth from my mouth,            8
   and does not return to me empty,ᑫ                        7
Until it does [ ] what I purpose,                           7
   prospers that for which I send it.ʳ                      7
                                  1:1::1:1::1:1::1:1
```

55:12-13

```
For you shall go forth in joy,                              7
   and be led forthˢ in peace.                              7
Mountains and hills will break forth [    ]ᵗ into
      singing,                                             11
   All the trees of the steppe will applaud.              10
Instead of thorns shall come up cypress,                    7
   instead of briars shall come up myrtle.                  7
It shall display the Nameᵘ of Yahweh,                       7
   an everlasting sign that shall not be cut off.           8
                                  1:1::1:1::1:1::1:1
```

TEXTUAL NOTES

ᵃMT is a conflate text as compared with G (πίετε is
a paraphrastic translation of *'ĕkōlû to agree with
"wine"; Gᴮᴼᴸ read φάγετε) and 1QIsaᵃ. We reconstruct
*'ēn lō kesep lĕkû šibrû / šibrû wĕ'ĕkōlû bĕlô' kesep,
omitting the initial relative particle as prosaizing

and positing an additional **šibrû** to fill out the
colon.[43] This text can generate G by haplography, and
an additional dittography of **lĕkû šibrû** yields MT.
1QIsa[a] can be generated from MT by haplography, a
parablepsis from the first to the second **šibrû**. Thus:

```
    *lĕkû šibrû šibrû wĕ'ĕkōlû                  bĕlô' kesep
G:  *lĕkû  [   ] šibrû wĕ'ĕkōlû                  bĕlô' kesep
MT: lĕkû        šibrû wĕ'ĕkōlû <ûlĕkû šibrû> bĕlô' kesep
1Q: lĕkû        [                    ] šibōrû bĕlô' kesep
```

Note the several chiasms formed by **sibrû, 'ên lô kesep,
bĕlô' kesep** and **bĕlô' maḥîr**.

[b]MT **šimᶜû šāmôᶜ**; we omit the infinitive absolute as
a scribal dittography.

[c]MT **'êlay** is metrically excessive and may be a
dittography from v. 2b. G inserts **'êlay** twice.

[d]MT reads a cohortative **wĕ'ekrĕtâ** which is grammatically incorrect in a passage which requires a preterite. It is a late expansion when long endings were
used indiscriminately. 1QIsa[a], which ordinarily has
longer endings, reads **'ekrōt**.

[e]With 1QIsa[a], we read the long suffix **nĕtattîhû**.
Syr. reads a second person suffix, a harmonization to
v. 5.

[f]Torrey suggests that Deutero-Isaiah is engaged in
wordplay, first reading **lĕ'ummîm** as the plural of
lĕ'ōm, then as **lĕ-** and the plural of **'ummâ**. But just
as **gôy** is twice repeated in v. 5a, so it is more probable that **lĕ'ummîm** is twice repeated here in v. 4. G
distinguishes each of the words for nations which MT
places in pairs: ἔθνεσι and ἄρχοντα, ἔθνη and λαοί;
this is probably paraphrastic and not good evidence
against MT.

---

[43]As suggested by Cross, personal communication.

gThe unbalanced 7-13 bicolon of MT suggests some disorder, which can be corrected by reversing the verbs **yĕdā°ūkā** and **tēda°**, as supported in part by G which renders the first verb ἃ οὐκ ᾔδεισάν σε.

hWith 1QIsaᵃ **yrwṣ** we read the singular against MT **yārûṣû**

iOmit the inital **lāmed** of MT **liqdôš** as does 1QIsaᵇ; in 1QIsaᵃ it is written <u>supra lineam</u>. Cf. Isa 49:7.

jReading the plural with G; MT has a singular **darkô**.

kG omits **ʼel ʼĕlōhênû** and adds *****ḥattĕʼōtêkem** after **li-sĕlōḥ**.

l1QIsaᵇ transposes the nouns "my thoughts" and "your thoughts."

mReading a verb **gābĕhû** with MT and G (although the latter has a singular). 1QIsaᵃ **kî kĕ-gōbah** has dittography of **kāp**.

nMT **šammâ**, lacking in G, is a dittography of the preceding **šāmayim**.

oReading with MT **lā-ʼōkēl**; 1QIsaᵃ reads an infinitive **le-ʼĕkōl** and G reads a noun **ʼokel**.

pMT **yihyeh**, **ʼăšer** and **ʼet ʼăšer** are prosaizing expansions, due in part to the original **ʼăšer** in the final colon of v. 11.

qG lacks **ʼēlay rêqām**

r1QIsaᵇ reads **ʼt ʼšr šlḥty**

s1QIsaᵃ **tklw** is modernizing.

tOmit MT **lipnêkem** as an expansion disrupting the meter.

u1QIsaᵃ transposes **lĕ-šēm** and **lĕ-ʼôt**.

Clifford has identified the form of the opening
verses of Isa 55:1-13 as an invitation to a cultic
feast, specifically a messianic banquet on Mount
Zion.[44] As in the invitation of lady wisdom in
Prov 9:1-6,11 that "your days may be multiplied,"
Anat's invitation to Aqhat to join the gods and live
forever, (CTA 17.6.2-5, 17-33), and the invitation to
the vintage festival with its attendant hieros gamos in
CTA 23.6-7, the invited guests are offered "food" and
"wine" that they might "live," meaning in all three
parallel texts to dwell in proximity to the deity. The
abundance of "the waters," "wine and milk," draws upon
images of the mountain of God as the source of the
cosmic waters and garden of God.[45] Cross sees here a
development from the royal festival of the Jerusalem

---

[44]See Richard Clifford, "Isaiah 55: Invitation to a
Feast," in The Word of the Lord shall Go Forth: Essays
in Honor of David Noel Freedman in Celebration of his
Sixtieth Birthday, ed. C.L. Meyers and M. O'Connor
(Winona Lake, Eisenbrauns, 1983) 27-35. Other relevant
Ugaritic texts with invitations to feasts not mentioned
by Clifford include Ug V 1.1.3-4, a banquet of the gods
in which El becomes inebriated, and CTA 4.4.27-39,
where El invites his consort to eat and drink and share
his bed. The call to eat and drink in Cant 5:1 has a
similar background, a feast originally connected to a
hieros gamos; see M. Pope, Song of Songs, AB 7C (Garden
City: Doubleday, 1980) 504-9.

[45]Compare Isa 33:20-24 where Zion is a place of
broad streams, Ezek 47:1-12 where from the temple flows
a river which irrigates the desert, and especially Joel
4:17-18 where streams of wine and milk flow on her
hills. This point has been noted by Spykerboer (Structure, 180-1) who correctly interprets the import of
these verses without understanding their form. On the
tradition of fresh-water streams flowing from the temple, Cf. Jon Levenson, The Theology of the Program of
Restoration of Ezekiel 40-48, HSM 10 (Missoula, MT:
Scholars Press, 1976), 11-15; Richard J. Clifford, The
Cosmic Mountain in Canaan and the Old Testament, HSM 4
(Cambridge: Harvard, 1972) 131-60.

cult.[46] The stipulation that Yahweh will provide abundant provisions for his temple without need for payment
has been noted in the Cyrus oracle (45:13) where the
restoration of Jerusalem will also be without price,
and the democratized Davidic covenant announced in
vv. 3-5 similarly bespeaks royal traditions. However
this oracle, like the Cyrus oracle, is not exhausted by
a programmatic political interpretation. Yahweh's
sovereign purpose unfolds in historical events, yet
breaks out of history into a new creation, here a
messianic banquet described in mythic terms.

Once the form of the opening verses has been established as an invitation to celebrate on Yahweh's mountain, and the conventional hypotheses that they are
either imitations of market crys[47] or a wisdom genre[48]
have been laid to rest, there remains little reason to
subdivide Isa 55 into shorter units. Clifford has
posited a unified structure for this chapter as built
from two parallel stanzas of equal length, vv. 1-5 of
18 cola and vv. 6-11 of 19 cola, followed by a shorter
concluding section, vv. 12-13 of 8 cola.[49] Verses 6-11
open with a second summons to come into Yahweh's cultic
presence in parallel with the invitation in v. 1: "Seek

---

[46]Cross, Canaanite Myth, 144, 263.

[47]E.g. von Waldow, "Anlass und Hintergrund," 22;
Westermann, Isaiah 40-66, 281-81.

[48]Begrich, Studien, 39-61. His view is more defens-
ible; the prominence of the form of the invitation to a
feast in wisdom traditions (i.e. Prov 9:1-11, Sirach
24:19ff.) is due to wisdom circles having taken up this
form from older Canaanite sources.

[49]Clifford, Fair Spoken, 190f. Because he mistakenly renders the scansion of v. 10 in 6 cola instead of
4, his count is less symmetrical: 18, 21 and 9 [sic]
cola respectively.

Yahweh where he may be found, call upon him where he is
present."[50] The opening invitations are each linked to
exhortations to repentance aimed at those who have
adopted a worldly view of life. Verse 2 chastizes those
who labor for proximate goods instead of devoting themselves to God the source of lasting benefit, and v. 7,
which has been termed a "torah liturgy,"[51] introduces
an argument about the transcendent value of God's purposes compared with the ordinary purposes of men. Both
stanzas conclude with substantiations composed of
several assertions of increasing complexity which support the initial invitations' promises of the abundance
to be found at Yahweh's sanctuary.[52] After these two
parallel exhortations to pilgrimage, the chapter closes
fittingly in vv. 12-13 with a description of Israel's
actual return to mount Zion on a processional way. Its
description of God's presence as an eternal sign forms
a chiasm with the eternal covenant proclaimed in v. 3.
This structure is diagramed in Table 7.

The invitation in vv. 1-3a has an opening quatrain
with a chiastic structure formed by the repeated imperative šibrû and the price: bĕlô' kesep and bĕlô' meḥîr.
The following bicolon (v. 2a) disputes with those
faithless or recalcitrant people who will not come.
The next quatrain (vv. 2b-3a) resumes the repeated

[50]Clifford (Fair Spoken, 192-3) has noted parallels
to similar invitations to worship at the shrine of the
deity in Amos 5:4 and Jer 29:10-14.

[51]Clifford, "Invitation to a Feast," 31; Melugin,
Formation, 86; cf. Begrich, Studien, 58.

[52]Melugin (Formation, 86) correctly terms vv. 8-11 a
substantiation of the exhortation in vv. 6-7; his analysis can be extended to vv. 1-5 once vv. 1-2 are also
recognized as an exhortation to worship.

TABLE 7: The Structure of Isa 55

	vv. 1-5	vv. 6-11	vv. 12-13
Invitation:			
to the feast/ temple	Come to the waters lĕkû šibrû leḥem 'ĕkōlû	Seek God where He is near dĕrōšû qĕrā'ūhû	
admoni-tion to repent	Why labor for nought? šimᶜû 'ēlay 'iklû lĕkû Listen, that you may live	Forsake your evil ways dĕrākâw maḥšĕbōtâw yaśōb Return, that He may be merciful	
God's purpose		kî He will pardon	kî Exiles leave Babylon tēṣē'û
Substantiation:			
1st asser-tion	New covenant 'ekrōt ᶜôlām	kî my ways are not your ways maḥšĕbōtay dĕrākay	Sign of the covenant ᶜôlām lō' yikkārēt
2nd asser-tion	hēn David's authority as commander of nations hēn Zion will command the nations	kî heaven is higher than earth kēn my ways are higher than your ways	
3rd asser-tion		kî rain fertilizes the earth lō' yāšûb leḥem lĕ-'ōkēl kēn God's word ful-fills its purpose lō' yāšûb	Nature rejoices
God's purpose	kî He will glorify Israel	yēṣē'	

imperatives **šim^cû, 'iklû, haṭṭû, lěkû** and concludes
with an exhortation to repentance and renewal: "listen,
that you may live." A two-part substantiation begins
with v. 3b. Yahweh declares first a renewal of the
blessings of the Davidic covenant, now democratized to
all Israel (v. 3b), and second that Israel will have
authority, like David of old, to command the nations.
The second assertion makes a comparison by means of a
compound sentence in which each clause is marked by the
particle **hēn:** first the subordinate clause[53] recalling
David's authority of old (v. 4), then the statement of
Israel's new authority (v. 5). The stanza ends with a
purpose clause containing **kî** and elaborating upon the
last assertion: "because of Yahweh your God... for he
wills to glorify you."

Eissfeldt, Westermann and others have compared
vv. 3b-5 with the Davidic psalms 89 and 18.[54] Breach
of the eternal Davidic covenant, the basis of the
preexilic monarchy (Ps 89:20-38; 2 Sam 7:8-16), had
constituted a major theological crisis for the exiles.
Deutero-Isaiah here announces the restoration of a
portion of that covenant. While there is no restored
dynasty or promise of its eternal sway over Israel, now
the eternal promises of divine support and the international stature of the Davidid as the earthly representative of Yahweh are bestowed upon Israel. In Deutero-
Isaiah **ḥesed** and **běrît** are synonymous terms, used in

---

[53]On the syntax of **hinnēh/hēn** in subordinate
clauses, see T.O. Lambdin, _Introduction to Biblical
Hebrew_, (New York: Scribners, 1971) 169.

[54]O. Eissfeldt, "The Promises of Grace to David in
Isa 55:1-5," in _Israel's Prophetic Heritage_, ed. B.W.
Anderson and W. Harrelson (London: 1962) 196-207; Wes-
termann, 283-86.

parallel both here and in 54:10 to mean the covenanted
and gracious commitment of the divine suzerain to his
vassals. It is consistently described as eternal:
here, in 54:10, and in 54:8 (ḥesed cōlām).[55] Ḥesed in
this sense is a technical term for the Davidic covenant
in 2 Sam 7:15 and Ps 89:2-5,29, and the language in Isa
55:3b refers specifically to Ps 89: ḥasdê cōlām (v. 2),
bĕrîtî ne'ĕmenet lô (v. 29). In that psalm Yahweh's
cosmic victories (vv. 6-19) are the basis for the
earthly exaltation of David (vv. 20-38), whose hand
Yahweh places on Sea and River (v. 26) and who as
Yahweh's "first-born" is "the highest of the kings of
the earth" (v. 28).

Vv. 4-5 is a paraphrase of Ps 18:44-45 (2 Sam 22:44-
45), which reads:

> 44. You rescued me from the strife of peoples,[56]
>   you set me[57] as the head of nations;
>   peoples whom I did not know served me;
> 45. Foreigners come fawning[58] to me,[59]
>   as soon as they hear they submit to me.

The psalm ascribes David's military victories and the
consequent submission of the surrounding nations to his

---

[55]ḥasdô in 40:6 is probably a textual corruption
from ḥamdô, "its attractiveness," by confusion of mēm
and sāmek.

[56]Read with Ps 18:44 cām, a collective; 2 Sam 22:44
reads cāmmî in MT, but G[L], Syr., Targ. read cām.

[57]Read with Ps 18:44 tĕśîmēnî; 2 Sam 22:44 reads
tiśmĕrēnî in MT, but G[L], Syr., Targ. of 2 Sam 22:44
read with Ps 18:44, while the Targ. of Ps 18 reads with
2 Sam 22:44.

[58]Ps 18:45 reads yĕkaḥḥăśû; 2 Sam 22:45 yitkaḥḥăśû.
The reflexive sense of a hithpael is preferable, although the consonantal text of Ps 18:45 may be reading
a niphal yikkāḥiśû.

[59]Transposing the cola with 2 Sam 22:45.

rule to the power of Yahweh his God. Deutero-Isaiah's
interpretive paraphrase of the psalm describes David
not only as a "leader and commander of nations," a
position he attains through conquest, but also as a
"witness" to God's sovereignty. This is a retrojection
of Israel's vocation as a witness to Yahweh's divinity,
as set forth in the trial scenes in 43:8-13 and 44:6-8.
For Deutero-Isaiah, David as military victor recedes
before David whose earthly exaltation is a witness to
Yahweh's sovereignty.   While the nations come cringing
and fawning to meet the victorious conqueror in
Ps 18:45, in v. 5 the nations come running out of
respect for Yahweh's awesome power "because of Yahweh
your God, the Holy One of Israel, for he has glorified
you." They come in submission to Israel as vassals of
her reconstituted Davidic sovereignty and to partake of
the "messianic banquet."[60]

The structure of vv. 6-11 parallels that of vv. 1-5:
an opening invitation, an admonition to repentance, and
a series of substantiations.   Its invitation begins
with imperatives as in v. 1, and the admonition in v. 7
shares with its counterpart of v. 2b similar condition-
al-purpose constructions--imperative and imperative in
v. 2b, jussive and jussive in v. 7b. Verbal repetition
(dĕrākâw, maḥšĕbôtâw and yāšōb) and a causal clause
introduced by kî provide linkage to the following substantiation (vv. 8-11) which progresses in three assertions of progressively increasing length (vv. 8, 9 and
10-11), each introduced by kî. The first assertion "my
thoughts are not your thoughts, and your ways are not
my ways" identifies the audience's sin as worldliness
and distance from God. It reinforces the preceding

_____

[60]Cf. Isa 25:6.

admonition (v. 7) that "the wicked man abandon his ways
and the evil man his thoughts." The second and third
assertions, like the second assertion in vv. 4-5, are
analogies. While vv. 4-5 compare two clauses each
introduced by **hēn**, these assertions are built with a
parallel syntax "just as (**kî**)... so (**kēn**)..." and "just
as (**kî**)... [until (**kî 'im**)...] so (**kēn**)... [until (**kî
'im**)...]." While the analogy in vv. 4-5 describes
Israel's new covenant in terms of the old Davidic
covenant, here claims for the incomparability and certainty of Yahweh's thoughts and purposes are made as
analogies first to the vast expanse of creation and
then to the reliability of natural phenomena. Yet the
figure of the regularity of nature and its provision of
bread in v. 10 may also be a traditional metaphor of
royal theology, as it is often used in preexilic texts
to depict the unconditional nature of God's decree and
blessing in the Davidic covenant.[61] It also recalls
the initial invitation to come to the waters and eat in
vv. 1-2.

The short concluding section is one of several passages in Deutero-Isaiah describing a ritual procession
returning to the temple, with life-giving waters making
the desert bloom along the processional way.[62] This
manifestation of God's blessing corresponds to the
messianic banquet of the chapter's opening verses. It
also opens with the particle **kî** in continuity with the
substantiating assertions of vv. 8-11 and is further
linked by repetition of the verb **yṣ'**. As God's word
goes forth from his mouth (v. 11), so Israel will go
forth from Babylon (v. 12), and as the going forth of

---

[61]Cf. 2 Sam 23:4; Pss 89:35,38; 132:15.

[62]Cf. Isa 35; 41:17-20, 49:9-11.

Yahweh's word is compared to the rain and snow coming
down from heaven (v. 10), so Israel's going forth will
be accompanied by the fructification of nature (v. 13).

Verse 13 ends with this new fertility described as
becoming la-yhwh lĕ-šēm, the "Name of Yahweh," the
manifestation of God's presence.[63] It is also "an
eternal sign ('ôt ᶜôlām) which will not be cut off."
While the "signs and wonders" performed in Egypt at the
Exodus had been frequently recalled in the cult,[64] they
were over and gone and had little meaning for the
exiles (cf. 43:16-21). In contrast, this sign, and
God's gracious presence, is to be permanent. God's
manifestation in nature is called a sign in Ps 65:9,
and more specifically P calls the rainbow the sign
('ôt) of the eternal covenant made with Noah (Gen 9:12-
13).[65] Note that in 54:9-10 Deutero-Isaiah uses similar language to invoke the covenant of Noah: as God

---

[63]The theology of Yahweh's "Name" is a found especially in D and Dtr, where Yahweh is said to place his
name in the Temple. In Exod 23:21 Yahweh invests an
angel with his name; in Isa 30:27 the Name is a hypo-
stasis which "comes, burning in anger." See S. Dean
McBride, "The Deuteronomic Name Theology," Harvard
dissertation, 1969. Reference in this chapter to the
Davidic covenant (2 Sam 7) is another connection with
Deuteronomic circles. On other Deuteronomic connections to this chapter, see W. Brueggemann, "Isaiah 55
and Deuteronomic Theology," ZAW 80 (1968) 191-203.

[64]Ps 78:43; Jos 4:6-7.

[65]P shares with Deutero-Isaiah a concern to broaden
the notion of an eternal covenant--in preexilic times
only a characteristic of the Davidic covenant--to apply
to all Israel. For P Israel's other constitutive covenants are eternal covenants providing a secure basis
for a reconstituted Israel. Hence the "signs" ('ôt) of
P's covenants are also eternally present: the rainbow
(Gen 9:12-13), circumcision (Gen 17:11), and the
Sabbath (Exod 31:13,17).

swore that the waters would never again cover the
earth, so now God swears he will never again give vent
to his wrath against Jerusalem, and as God's promise to
Noah is forever, so his new ḥesed will not be moved
(lō' yāmūš) and his běrît cannot be shaken (lō' tāmûṭ).
Here also the fertility of the land is a sign that will
not be cut off (lō' yikkārēt), a sign of the the
renewed Davidic eternal covenant (běrît ʿôlām) which
Yahweh has cut ('ekrot) with Israel (55:3). The link
between the covenant and its sign forms an inclusio
which binds the entire chapter together.

Chapter 55 is thus a model of elegant structure.
The unity of this chapter does not support Westermann's
view that 55:6-13 form the epilogue of the book,[66] but
the chapter as a whole may well serve that purpose.
Its depiction of the messianic banquet on mount Zion, a
motif with roots in the concluding movement of the
underlying myth of creation, forms a fitting conclusion
to Deutero-Isaiah's prophecies. After the prologue
(40:1-11) and chapter 40's praise of God's incomparable
power as Creator, the remainder of the prophet's corpus
depicts God's new act of redemption as a re-creation,
an historical reenactment of the mythic pattern of
God's creation of the cosmos. Yahweh announces his
judgment upon the gods, wages his war of vindication
through Cyrus, and calls upon Israel to return to Zion.
Now in chapter 55, with the created order set aright,
Israel may rejoice in the abundance and prosperity
flowing from the restored sanctuary.

---

[66]Westermann, Sprache und Struktur, 81; followed by
Melugin, Formation, 86-7; Spykerboer, Structure, 184.
Cf. E. Hessler, "Gott der Schöpfer: Ein Beitrag zur
Komposition und Theologie Deuterojesajas," diss.,
Greifswald, 1961, 98, 102, 253ff.

3. The Procession of the Nations to Zion in Deutero-Isaiah and in the Royal Cult

The passages in Deutero-Isaiah which portray a procession of the nations to glorify Zion and bring the exiles home include Isa 45:14, 49:22-23, and related notices affirming the international glorification of the servant (49:7; 42:1-4,6; 52:13; 53:12). They enunciate a theme which became a general expectation within the restoration community. Except for a brief period during the glory days of the Solomonic empire, there is little evidence of significant participation of the nations in the cult of pre-exilic Israel. But at the time of the restoration, the pilgrimage of the nations to Zion became an important expectation to reify the salvation of Yahweh.[67] Deutero-Isaiah was pivotal in the development of this expectation.

The background for these passages lies in processions of the royal cult which celebrated God's universal rule. God's sovereignty established Zion as a shrine to be honored by all nations and the Davidic king as preeminent among the kings of the earth. The concluding verses of Isa 55 form one of several passages in Deutero-Isaiah describing an anticipated ritual procession to Zion,[68] and this one is specifically enabled by God's renewed grant of the Davidic covenant, the ḥasdê dāwîd han-ne'ĕmānîm, to Israel. In the preexilic cult, temple processions were headed by

---

[67]Isa 60-62; Hag 2:6-8; Zech 8:20-22; Isa 14:1-2.

[68]Cf. Isa 35; 40:3-5,9-11; 41:17-20; 49:9-11; 51:9-11; 52:11-12.

the Davidid, who at the New Year's festival[69] led the ark into the temple.[70] These processions,[71] accompanied by the clapping of hands and shouts of joy (rinnâ),[72] celebrated the victory of Yahweh as divine warrior over Sea,[73] Yahweh's sovereignty over the nations of the world,[74] the concommittant victory of the king,[75] the election of Israel and Zion as Yahweh's abode,[76] and the autumn rains renewing the land.[77] According to the Chronicler, when the ark entered the sanctuary the congregation sang "Give thanks to Yahweh for he is good, for his fidelity is forever" lĕ-ᶜôlām ḥasdô (2 Chr 5:13),[78] praising the enduring ḥesed of

---

[69]See S. Mowinckel, Psalmen II, 3-4; The Psalms in Israel's Worship, tr. D.R. Ap-Thomas (Nashville: Abingdon, 1962), 106-7. He first called Pss 47, 93, 96-99 enthronement psalms and argued that their Sitz im Leben was the processions of the autumn New Year's festival, when the ark was carried about in procession in a manner analagous to the cultic drama of the Babylonian Akītu festival. His basic position has been widely accepted. For a recent discussion of these processions, see Choon-Leong Seow, "Ark Processions in the Politics of the Monarchy," Ph.D. dissertation, Harvard University, 1984.

[70]2 Sam 6:12-19; 1 Kgs 8:5-6; Pss 24; 47; 68; 96; 97; 98; 132.

[71]Pss 68:25-28; 132:8.

[72]Pss 47:1; 98:7-9.

[73]Pss 24:1-2,7-8; 68:1-3.

[74]Pss 47:2,7-9; 68:29-33; 96; 97; 98.

[75]Ps 132:11-12,17-18.

[76]Pss 47:5,10; 68:16-19; 96:5; 97:8; 98:3, 132:13-14.

[77]Pss 68:8-10; 96:11-12; 98:7-9; 132:15.

[78]1 Chr 16:34; Ezr 3:10; Cf. Jer 33:11; Pss 100:5; 106:1; 107:1; etc.

Yahweh to his temple and dynasty in the language of the
Davidic covenant (cf. Isa 55:3). While most of the
liturgical contexts of this expression are post-exilic,
Jer 33:11 confirms that this song of praise accompanied
thank-offerings in the preexilic temple. Deutero-
Isaiah in turn draws upon these motifs from the royal
cult to describe a new procession to Zion led by
Israel, the democratized recipient of God's běrît and
ḥesed. At this procession the nations were to be in
attendance.

Such a procession in which the nations come to
Jerusalem bearing tribute is described in Isa 49:22-
23.[79] Commanded to release the imprisoned exiles (cf.
43:5-7), the kings and queens of the nations also aid
in their return, marching in the procession as atten-
dants to the exiles and carrying them to Zion as though
they were tribute in a royal procession:

> For thus says Yahweh:
> Now, when I will lift my hand to the nations,
>   and raise my signal to the peoples;
> They will bring your sons in their bosom,
>   bear your daughters on their shoulder.
> Kings will be your foster fathers,
>   and their princesses your nursing mothers.
> With faces to the ground they will bow to you,
>   they will lick the dust of your feet,
> That you may know that I am Yahweh,
>   none will be shamed who wait for me.

This image of foreign rulers bowing down and licking
the dust is taken directly from a tradition which is
also expressed by Ps 72, which had exalted the international sovereignty of the Davidid:

---

[79]The text of this unit will be discussed below in
conjunction with its compositional unit, Isa 49:1-26.

Ps 72:8-11

May he have dominion from sea to sea,   6
    from the River to the ends of the earth;   7
May his f<oe>s[80] kneel down before him,   8
    his enemies lick the dust,   9
May the kings of Tarshish [ ][81] render tribute;   9
    the kings of [ ][82] Seba bring gifts.   9
May [ ][83] kings bow down before him,   7
    all nations serve him.   7

In Psalm 68, from the Solomonic period, a procession of
the nations accompanies the processions of the tribes
of Israel (vv. 25-28) celebrating the victorious entry
of God the Divine Warrior into his sanctuary.[84] In vv.
18-19 Yahweh marches from Sinai leading captives in
train and receiving gifts, and in vv. 30-34 (which

---

[80]MT ṣiyyîm, "dwellers of the wastelands" is a corruption of ṣārâw due to misreading the adjacent rēš wāw
as a mem and reinforced by the parallel word 'iyyîm of
the following verse; cf. Isa 34:14; 13:21-22.

[81]MT 'iyyîm is an ancient variant and synonym of
taršîš; the conflation here was no doubt influenced by
the following colon. Nevertheless the resulting 1:b
meter is out of place in this psalm.

[82]MT šĕbā' û-sĕbā' is a clear case of a conflate
text preserving alternate readings. The original is
sĕbā' which, after a common sāmek/śîn confusion, was
reinterpreted as šĕbā' (with a šîn).

[83]One of the two instances of kol in this bicolon is
an expansion; the first is metrically excessive.

[84]Two rival understandings of Ps 68 have been put
forward. Albright ("A Catalogue of Early Hebrew Lyric
Poems (Psalm LXVIII)," HUCA 23 [1950] 1-39) proposed
that the psalm was a collection of 30 incipits of old
independent psalms composed from the 13th to 10th cen-
turies b.c.e. and brought together in the Solomonic
period. Mowinckel (Der achundsechzigste Psalm, Avhand-
linger utgitt av Det Norske Videnskaps-Akademi [Oslo:
Dybwad, 1953]) has argued for the psalm as a unified
liturgy of the enthronement festival. The latter position has won the widest support.

appear be in disorder) delegates from Ethiopia and
Egypt come bearing tribute:

Ps 68:18-19

    The chariotry of God were two myriads,   7
      thousands the archers[85] of Yahweh,   7
      when <he came>[86] from Sinai to the temple.   7
    You went up to the heights,   6
      you took your captives,   5
      you received gifts from their hands.[87]   8

Ps 68:30-34

    [][88] Your temple towers over Jerusalem,   9
      to you kings bring tribute.   9
  . . . .[89]

    Let them bring[90] bronze[91] from Egypt,   10

---

[85]This standard emendation of MT šin'ān to šannānê
based on Ugaritic tann, the composite bow, was first
noted by W.F. Albright, "Notes on Psalm 68 and 134,"
Norsk teologisk tidsskrift 56 (1955) 2-4. Cf. Cross,
102 n. 39. The following 'ădōnay of MT is simply an
aural confusion for yhwh.

[86]Emending MT bām to be-bā'; see Deut 33:2.

[87]MT bā-'ādām may be a corruption of bādām, "from
their hands," based on the frequent contraction bdm,
badēm for "in/from their hands" in Ugaritic.

[88]With Dahood (Psalms II, AB [Garden City: Doubleday, 1968] 149) we take the prefixed min on MT
mēhêkālekā as an enclitic mem attached to the preceding
suffix lānû-m. For other reconstructions, see
Albright, HUCA 23 (1950) 31; A.R. Johnson, Sacral
Kingship in Ancient Israel (Cardiff: University of
Wales, 1967) 84 n. 6.; Seow, 214.

[89]On the translation of the intervening lines,
apparently directed against Egypt and her vassals, see
Albright, 32-33; Dahood, 149-150; Seow, 214-15.

[90]Repointing as ya'ătîyû, a hiphil jussive.

[91]This hapax legomenon is related to Egyptian ḫšmn,
"bronze," or Akk. ḫašmānu, a type of blue cloth. See
Gunkel, Die Psalmen, 292; Dahood, 150; Albright, Norsk
teologisk tidsskrift 56 (1955) 5.

```
    let Cush hasten its wares⁹² to God.            9
  O Kings of the earth,                            5
    sing to God,                                   6
  raise a song to Yahweh!                          6
```

Roberts has identified Ps 47 as another psalm from the
Solomonic period celebrating God's imperial rule over
Israel's vassals.[93] When the Ark as Yahweh's emblem
goes up (ᶜālâ) to take his place in the temple, both
the gods of the heavens and the rulers of the earth
gather to sing his praises:

Ps 47:2-10

```
  Clap your hands, all you peoples!                 6
    shout [    ]⁹⁴ with the sound of rejoicing!     7
  For Yahweh is the awesome Elyon,                  7
    the great king over all the earth.             7
  He subdues peoples beneath us,                    7
    nations under our feet.                         8
  He has chosen us for his⁹⁵ possession;            8
    the pride of Jacob which he loves.             8
  [Yahweh]⁹⁶ goes up with a shout,                  7
    [God] with the sound of the shophar.
```

---

⁹²Reading a hiphil jussive and taking **yād** as connoting resources or wares; see Dahood, 151.

⁹³J.J.M. Roberts, "The Religio-Political Setting of
Psalm 47," <u>BASOR</u> 221 (1976) 129-132.

⁹⁴Delete MT **lē-'ĕlōhîm** as an expansion <u>metri causa</u>.

⁹⁵While G, Syr read the third person singular suffix
on **nahălâ,** recent commentators have noted the awkward
construction of **lānû** as the direct object of **yibḥar.**
Roberts (<u>BASOR</u> 221 (1976), 130) corrects with G, emending **nahǎlātēnû** to **nahǎlātô** and **lānû 'et** to **'ōtānû.**
Cf. Seow, 181-2; Dahood, 285.

⁹⁶Throughout most of the psalter where **yhwh** and
'ĕlōhîm are in parallel cola **yhwh** is preferred in the A
colon while **'ĕlōhîm** is found in the B colon. But in
the Elohistic psalter the terms are reversed. This
probably reflects regional preferences in the oral
recitation of songs known throughout Israel. The earliest form of any particular psalm must be determined

Sing, O gods,[97] sing!   9
  sing to our king, sing!   10
Indeed, he reigns <over>[98] all the earth,   7
  O gods, sing a psalm!   8
Yahweh reigns over the nations,   7
  [   ][99] he sits on his holy throne;   7
The princes of the peoples have gathered   8
  to[100] the God of Abraham.   7
Surely Yahweh is Suzerain[101] of the earth,   6
  he is greatly exalted.   4

These psalms preserve memories of Jerusalem's preemi-
nence in the days of David and Solomon, when the actual
tribute brought by vassals to Jerusalem confirmed
Yahweh's substantial victory over the nations and his

---

by individual analysis of text and meter. Here the
meter is improved if **yhwh** is made the A word in accordance with an origin outside of the Elohistic psalter;
note also **yhwh** in the A colon of v. 2. See R.G.
Boling, "Synonymous Parallelism in the Psalms," JSS 5
(1960) 221-55; and the discussion of the identical Pss
40:14-18 and 70 by J.S. Ackermann, "An Exegetical Study
of Psalm 82," Harvard dissertation, 1966, 169-71, 275-6.

[97]On taking the heathen gods as the subject, see
Roberts, 130; Seow, 186-7; Dahood, 285f.

[98]MT has a short colon; adding ^cal with some mss.
(cf. vv. 3b, 9a) and vocalizing MT **melek** as a verb
yields better meter and prosody. Alternatively, a word
may be missing here; compare v. 3.

[99]MT **'ĕlōhîm** is an expansion that fills the meter.

[100]MT reads ^cam, but most read ^cim with G, Syr. ^cim
with the meaning "to" is an early usage found in Ugari-
tic, and ^cim is parallel to the preposition **lĕ-** in
4QDeut 32:43; Ps 18:28; Job 11:5. See Roberts, 131 n.
12; F.M. Cross, The Ancient Library of Qumran and
Modern Biblical Studies (Grand Rapids: Baker, 1961)
183.

[101]On **māgān** as "suzerain" as attested in Punic and
Ugaritic, see Dahood, Psalms I, 16-17. The **lāmed** is
emphatic; see Ps 89:19.

status as the highest God.[102] In David's reign his
Syrian vassals brought a **minḥâ** to Israel which he
dedicated to the temple (2 Sam 8:6-12), and during the
heady early years of king Solomon all the kingdoms from
Egypt to the Euphrates brought offerings on a regular
basis (1 Kgs 5:1; 10:25). At the temple's consecration
a great assembly of people gathered from all over the
empire (1 Kgs 8:65).

The processional background of Isa 49:22-23 illuminates its puzzling image of the nations coming when God
raises his banner (**nēs**), when he lifts his hand (**'eśśa'
yād**). Westermann and Orlinsky are of the opinion that
here God is declaring holy war against the nations.[103]
The **nēs** was indeed commonly set up to signal a military
attack[104] or to signal people to flee to a defensive
stronghold.[105] The figure of God lifting his hand
usually signifies an oath;[106] but in Ps 10:12 a suppli-
cant calls on God to raise his hand to bring retribu-
tion upon the wicked.[107] We would add that the closest
relation of lifting a hand to lifting a **nēs** is found in
Exod 17:8-16, where Moses lifts his hand (v. 11) in
order that Israel might prevail over the Amalekites.

---

[102]J. J. M. Roberts, "The Davidic Origin of the Zion
Tradition," JBL 92 (1976) 392-44.

[103]Westermann, Isaiah 40-66, 221; Orlinsky, "The So-
called 'Servant of the Lord'," 47.

[104]Exod 17:15; Isa 5:26; 13:2; 18:3; 31:9; Jer 4:21;
51:12,27.

[105]Jer 4:6, Num 21:8; cf. Isa 30:17, Ps 60:6.

[106]Deut 32:40; Ezek 20; 36:7; 44:12; 47:14;
Ps 106:26.

[107]Cf. Isa 10:32 and 2 Sam 20:21 on lifting the hand
as a belligerent human gesture.

Exod 17:16 preserves an archaic fragment (emended):

> Yea, a hand on the banner of Yah!
> The battle belongs to Yahweh!

However, neither the context of Isa 49:22-23 or its
background in processions of the royal cult will
sustain the view that God here raises his banner to
declare holy war. Although in the following verses
(49:25-26) God indeed fights against Israel's foes,
that stanza functions as a disputation asserting God's
power to liberate the exiles and does not continue the
image of the procession in vv. 22-23. In v. 22 the nēs
is raised to ('el) the nations beckoning them to come
and bring the exiles with them; it is not a banner
raised against them using the adversative prepositions
ᶜal or bĕ-. In this passage, as in later post-exilic
passages perhaps derivative of it (Isa 62:10; 66:19;
11:10,12), the nēs is rather the signal for a procession.[108]

Battle and procession are closely related, correlated by the underlying myth of creation where Yahweh
the divine warrior first goes out to battle the foe and
then returns in a victory procession to his temple.[109]
As two complementary movements in a single mythic pattern, battle and procession necessarily partake of the
same symbols. Processional psalms such as Ps 68 celebrate God's victories over his foes. In Ps 47, quoted
above, the notice that Yahweh subdues Israel's enemies
(v. 4) is followed by the word that God "goes up" to

---

[108]See Schoors, I am God your Savior, 108-9. He
also discusses the probable dependence of Isa 11:10,12
on Deutero-Isaiah. There Yahweh lifts his hand
"again," a second aliyah perhaps with the first return
of Isa 49:22 in mind.

[109]Cross, Canaanite Myth, 162-63.

his throne with shouting and singing by the assembled
nations (vv. 6-10). A comparable symbol is the Ark of
the Covenant, which served as both a battle palladium
and as the standard in cultic procession.110 Yahweh's
nēs, the Ark, and indeed flags of the modern era serve
both as battle standards and as banners in the following victory parade.

In other contexts where Deutero-Isaiah depicts a
procession to Zion, it is often accompanied by a signal
from Yahweh. Isa 49:11 and 22a both describe Yahweh's
direct action as lifting up (rwm) an object to facilitate the exiles' return to Zion; while in v. 22a he
lifts up a banner, in v. 11 God turns mountains into a
road and lifts up a highway (cf. 40:3-5). The procession to Zion is accompanied by a new creation where
nature rejoices, which in Isa 55:13 is called an
"eternal sign" and "the Name (presence) of Yahweh."111
The highway, the blooming of the desert, and Yahweh's
"sign" or "banner" all mark the great procession of the
returning exiles who celebrate the advent of God's
sovereignty in the sight of the entire world. These
various symbols of divine refulgence will be conflated
in Isa 60-62112: Zion displays "light," "the glory of
Yahweh," "vindication" (ṣĕdāqâ), "praise," and a
"banner" (nēs) before the nations.113

110Num 10:35; 1 Sam 4; 2 Sam 6; Ps 132.

111See above, pp. 222f.

112See Schoors, 108-11 on the anteriority of Isa
49:22-23 to Isa 60-62.

113In this regard, Weinfeld notes Sumerian hymns
where the pilgrimage of kings bearing gifts is sig-
nalled by the temple's refulgence reaching out over the
nations. Thus a hymn to Enlil depicts his temple:

Besides these parallels with the procession of the
rulers in Isa 49:22-23, Deutero-Isaiah also draws upon
these royal and specifically Solomonic traditions for
the names of the typical tribute-bearing nations: Egypt
(Ps 68:32), Ethiopia (Ps 68:32) and Seba (Ps 72:10),[114]
which will again serve Zion by contributing to her
restoration. If we are correct that the distinction
between Seba and Sheba is artificial,[115] then Seba is
also the fabled land whose queen came with gold and
spices for King Solomon (1 Kgs 10:1-13) pursuant to an
extensive trading relationship (1 Kgs 9:26-28).

> Its awe and splendor reach unto the heavens;
> Its shade is spread across all the lands,
> Its front stretches away to the center of heaven;
> All the lords, all the princes,
> Bring hither their holy offerings,
> Offer prayers and orisons to you...
> Their offerings and heavy tribute,
> They brought into the storehouse,
> Into the main courtyard they conducted their gifts,
> Into the Ekur, the lapis-lazuli house, they brought
>   them in homage.

Similarly, a hymn to the temple of Ningirsu reads:

> Its splendor and refulgence reach to the heavens,
> The awe of the temple lies over all foreign lands;
> To its name gather strangers from all the ends of
>   the heavens...

See Moshe Weinfeld, "Zion and Jerusalem as Religious
and Political Capital: Ideology and Utopia," in Richard
Elliott Friedman, ed., The Poet and the Historian:
Essays in Literary and Historical Biblical Criticism,
HSS 26 (Chico: Scholars Press, 1983) 104-11.

[114]The location of Seba is disputed. North (The
Second Isaiah, 120) distinguishes Seba in the Sudan
from Sheba on the Arabian penninsula; he locates Seba
in Africa on the basis of Gen 10:6, where he is a son
of Kush (Ethiopia). Schoors (p. 73n.) argues that Seba
is in northern Arabia since Havilah, another son of
Kush, is mentioned in connection with the sons of
Ishmael in Gen 25:18.

[115]See above, p. 235 n. 82.

Solomon's rule was celebrated for Israel's parity with Egypt, by which Solomon could gain the hand of an Egyptian princess in marriage (1 Kgs 3:1). These are the very nations which, in Deutero-Isaiah's eschatology, will bear tribute to Zion and confess Yahweh's sovereignty. Thus Isa 45:14:[116]

> Thus says Yahweh:
> Workers from Egypt and traders from Ethiopia,
>   Sabeans bearing tribute,
> Will come over to you and become yours,
>   they will follow after you;
> In chains they will come over and fall prostrate,
>   they will petition you:
> "Surely in your midst is God, and there is none other,
>   nothing else is God..."

They are also the nations which Yahweh trades as ransom for Israel in Isa 43:3-4:

> I give Egypt as your ransom,
>   Ethiopia and Seba in exchange for you.
> More precious than they are you in my sight,
>   more valuable, for I love you.
> I give land<s>[117] in place of you,
>   nations in exchange for your life.

In both passages these nations have the rank of vassals, from whom the sovereign Yahweh can demand tribute or whom he can cede to others as a ransom (cf. 1 Kgs 9:11-13). As these are typical nations drawn from reminiscence of Solomon's empire in the royal cult, no gepolitical import should be read into the latter prophecy.[118]

---

[116]For a discussion of the text, see pp. 88, 96-98.

[117]We adopt the ususal emendation of MT 'ādām to 'ădāmôt, presuming a haplography. In Deutero-Isaiah 'ādām refers to generic man and never to the nations.

[118]Therefore fact that Cyrus never conquered these lands is no argument against him as their intended recipient, as supposed by Simon, **A** **Theology** **of** **Salvation**, 99-100.

The context of Isa 45:14 in the unit 45:14-25
further specifies the terms of the nations' vassal
status. There, as we saw, it introduces a pair of
confessions of the nations and a trial speech exhorting
the nations to turn to Yahweh and accept his sovereignty. In connection with this eschatological vision of
the nations bearing tribute to Jerusalem, the irresistible oath (v. 23) of Yahweh becomes the basis for the
assurance that this vision will indeed come to pass;
indeed the portrayal of the nations as enchained captives affirms Yahweh's power to enforce his oath. But
since the trial speech and its accompanying exhortation
contains an attempt to persuade the nations, and since
the fate of those nations who turn to Yahweh is salvation (v. 22) rather than the humiliation of slavery,
the depiction of prisoners coming in chains in v. 14
must be qualified. Torrey apologetically points out
that the figure of foreign kings prostrating themselves
is not in itself indicative of slave status, as
prostration was the customary greeting of a vassal of
any rank to his lord.[119] But that is inadequate to
explain the chains. Perhaps the solution lies in the
distinction implicit in the nations' confessions that
idolators will be shamed (vv. 16,24), while those who
have accepted Yahweh as God are by implication deemed
righteous. Yahweh as sovereign has the irresistible
power to compel all to submit to his rule, and while
some will come willingly and offer tribute, others, as
idolators and rebels, will be compelled to come in
chains.

---

[119]Torrey, The Second Isaiah, 387; Schoors, 112.

4. Conclusion: The Nations under the Eschatological Reign of God

Preparatory to the eschatological reign of God, Deutero-Isaiah expected God to do battle with the idolatrous nations and to establish his sovereignty. God's conquests, continuous with the traditions of the Jerusalem cult and its antecedent mythology of the cosmic victories of God in the activity of creation, are universal in scope (e.g., 42:10-13). In the Cyrus oracle and in the trial speeches in Isa 41-42, Cyrus is identified as God's protagonist and God as Cyrus's commander and patron who has assured his victory. This portrayal of Cyrus as God's agent for world conquest, though based upon native Israelite traditions, matched the Cyrus of history who was in fact a world conqueror.

Furthermore, as we have noted in discussing the Cyrus oracle, Cyrus's historical conquests, attributed to God's grant, are but the prelude to a further act on Cyrus's part which would clearly manifest Yahweh's world sovereignty, namely the rebuilding of the temple in Jerusalem. Through this one act, Israel and the nations will recognize that Yahweh is God (45:4-5), and the eschatological reign of God will begin as nature rejoices and righteousness sprouts forth (45:8). This role for Cyrus as God's anointed is also derived from the theology of the royal cult where the climax of God's act of creation is the founding of his temple. Thus Deutero-Isaiah does not laud Cyrus based upon a realistic appraisal of his political ambitions. Beyond any of Cyrus's own historical purposes, Deutero-Isaiah views him as the instrument of God's greater purpose. Cyrus is to be the first gentile ruler to liberate the

exiles and to exalt Zion, the navel of the earth and
dwelling place of the one God. The restoration of Zion
is likewise imbued with universal significance as the
capital of God's realm established through the international conquests of Cyrus.

Once the temple at Zion had been restored, it would
become the locus of God's sovereignty and the place to
which the nations of the world would come, bearing
tribute and offering homage. Isa 55:1-13, considered
above, demonstrates the traditions of Judean royal
theology which lie behind the motif of the nations
attending and aiding the glorification of Zion. We
have noted that this chapter is an invitation to a
feast at Yahweh's mountain sanctuary. There God invests
Israel with the eternal Davidic covenant, by which she
will command the nations to come running and to serve
her. It is significant that the specific feature of
the Davidic covenant which Deutero-Isaiah lifts up is
David's international sovereignty. But the historical
conquests of David by which he could demand submission
of the nations--who in Ps 18:45 come trembling out of
their hiding places to meet the conqueror--had been
subsumed into the cultic traditions through which the
Davidic covenant had come to be represented. For
Deutero-Isaiah, David's glory is termed a "witness" to
Yahweh's mythological victories, and likewise Israel's
new glory will be a manifestation of Yahweh's own
decree (vv. 10-11) as a renewed royal grant (ḥesed)
bestowed upon Israel. Israel's royal splendor will be
so awe-inspiring that the nations will come running.

We cannot tell from this text whether the nations
come to partake of the bounties of the messianic banquet or to contribute their wealth to make it possible.
But behind the motif of the messianic banquet is the

mythology of the temple as the source of the cosmic "waters" and the garden of God.[120] Yahweh himself is the source of the abundance at his temple. Hence while the nations are to submit to Israel and perhaps to bring their riches to add to the feast, their coming to Zion may include the right to partake of God's bounty. They come "because of Yahweh your God, the Holy One of Israel, for he has glorified you."

The preexilic royal and processional psalms depicting the tradition of God's international sovereignty from which the images in Isa 45:14, 43:3, 49:22-23 and 55:3-5 were drawn do not employ the motif of foreign rulers submitting to Yahweh and the Davidic king in Jerusalem as a negative judgment upon the nations; their purpose was rather to glorify the sovereignty of Yahweh by exalting his anointed. As depicted on Assyrian and Egyptian reliefs, it was general practice throughout the ancient Near East that vassal nations demonstrate their loyalty to their overlord by bearing tribute and paying homage to his gods. Thereby they received in return their sovereign's protection. The Davidic empire at its height had been the earthly counterpart to Yahweh's divine _imperium_; the nations bringing tribute to Jerusalem were acknowledging their proper place as Israel's and Yahweh's vassals.[121] By bringing tribute in submission to God, the nations were righteous and could be assured of their Lord's protection. If they asserted their independence and rebelled,

---

[120]See p. 222 n. 45.

[121]The classic statement on Yahweh's _imperium_ and the prophet's role as its spokesperson is by G. Ernest Wright, "The Nations in Hebrew Prophecy," _Encounter_ 26 (1965) 231.

they would incur God's wrath (cf. Ps 2).[122] Similarly, Deutero-Isaiah shows no mercy on Babylon or on idolators who offend God's sovereignty; his words of judgment upon Babylon, tyrants, and idolators[123] affirm God's sovereign power to punish the nations who would flaunt his authority. Yahweh's universal rule will be manifest to all peoples: for the benefit of those who are willing subjects and to the detriment of those who persist in their idolatry.

But as a monotheist, Deutero-Isaiah has altered the traditional demands upon a vassal in one key respect. The nations could not simply worship Yahweh as the imperial deity alongside their local gods. Allegiance to Yahweh differed from allegiance to the imperial cults of Asshur or Marduk in its total rejection of idolatry and the demand for the worship of Yahweh alone. These twin claims were asserted to be universally binding.[124] In this sense Deutero-Isaiah demanded more than simple allegiance to a divine overlord; he demanded a conversion.

---

[122]See John Gray, The Biblical Doctrine of the Reign of God (Edinburgh: T & T Clark, 1979) 173-4. Solomon's prayer (1 Kgs 8:41-43) calls upon God to act on behalf of those foreigners who hear of God's might and come to pray towards the temple. The premier biblical example of the protection afforded a vassal by an imperial overlord is Ahaz's petition for Assyrian aid in the Syro-Ephraimite war (2 Kgs 16:7-9). For clauses of protection in Hittite vassal treaties, see ANET, 203f., 529.

[123]Cf. respectively, Isa 43:14-15 and ch. 47; Isa 41:11-12, 49:25-26, 51:22-23 and 54:11-17; Isa 44:9-20, 41:5-7, 42:17 and 45:16,24a.

[124]See above, pp. 113-128, 190-192.

Deutero-Isaiah is not a universalist in the modern sense, and his depiction of the nations as part of the economy of salvation is not out of an altruistic concern for their welfare. Any benefits offered to the nations are subordinate to Israel's redemption, and the primary role of those nations obedient to the divine will is to support Israel's restoration by transporting her exiles and giving financial support to rebuild Jerusalem. Reflecting the preexilic tradition of God's choice of foreign rulers as his instruments, Deutero-Isaiah assigned the task of prosecuting Yahweh's war to the gentile Cyrus, and in return Cyrus received the right to conquer nations and plunder their "treasures of darkness." The nations' subsequent participation in the processions of the renewed cult on mount Zion are to give greater glory to Yahweh as their sovereign, to Israel as the chosen nation with the exalted status of Yahweh's servant, and to the restored Jerusalem as the imperial capital of Yahweh's realm.

On the other hand, we must reject the view put forward by Snaith and others that Deutero-Isaiah had nothing but contempt for the nations as idolators who would be excluded from salvation.[125] The prophet did not draw a complete disjunction between righteous Israel and the idolatrous nations, and given the preexilic traditions of the royal cult behind Deutero-Isaiah's conception of divine activity which were them-

---

[125]N.H. Snaith, "Teaching... Consequences," 160-5, 185; H. Orlinsky, "The So-called 'Servant of the Lord,'" 47-48; P.A.H. de Boer, Second Isaiah's Message, 80-101; D. Hollenberg, "Nationalism and 'The Nations'," 23-26; F. Holmgren, With Wings as Eagles, 26-48; Martin-Achard, A Light to the Nations, 16-17; Schoors, 119, 236.

selves universal in scope, such a disjunction is not even to be expected. In prophesying the eschatological renewal of the idealized glory of the royal cult with its international acclamation of Yahweh's rule, Deutero-Isaiah expected God's benevolent and righteous sovereignty to extend to the entire world. The nations too could be beneficiaries of Yahweh's victory. And, as we saw in discussing the trial speeches and the polemics against idolatry, the nations were also expected to stand alongside Israel as worshippers of the one God.

CHAPTER 4
THE SERVANT AND THE NATIONS

1. General Remarks

This is not the place for a rehearsal of the manifold controversies surrounding the so-called "servant
songs." Questions as to whether they are secondary
insertions into the text of Isa 40-55,[1] what genres
they might represent, and above all, what is the identity of the servant[2] all remain in dispute. These
important questions will only be touched upon in this
chapter, which is concerned primarily with the servant's relation to the nations.

We assume with most recent scholarship that Deutero-
Isaiah was the author of all the servant passages.[3]

---

[1]This assumption, first advanced by Duhm, has been
accepted by most form critics including the recent
commentaries by Westermann, North and McKenzie. Yet it
has been questioned of late by rhetorical critics, and
for a recent refutation, see T.D.N. Mettinger, A Farewell to the Servant Songs: a Critical Examination of an
Exegetical Axiom, Regiae Societatis Humaniorum Litterarum Ludensis Scripta Minora (Lund: CWK Gleerup, 1983).

[2]See C.R. North, The Suffering Servant in Deutero-
Isaiah: An Historical and Exegetical Study (London:
Oxford, 1948); Colin G. Kruse, "The Servant Songs:
Interpretive trends since C.R. North," Studia Biblica
et Theologica (Fuller Theological Seminary) 8 (1978) 3-
27.

[3]North, Suffering Servant, 156-191 has effectively
refuted Elliger's linguistic arguments against Deutero-
Isaianic authorship. We also concur with his finding a
style of prosody identical with the rest of Isa 40-55.

The further firm implication of our compositional ana-
lysis--which places 42:1-4,5-9 and 49:1-6 in the context of larger poems[4]--is that the text in its present
form is the conscious work of Deutero-Isaiah. It is
conceivable that the servant songs reflect a late development in the prophet's thought,[5] but attempts to
isolate them as a distinct stratum are likely to fail.
Any such development would be obscured as the prophet
subsequently edited his own earlier work to reflect his
mature thought.[6]

     The finding that Deutero-Isaiah, and not some redac-
tor, is responsible for the present form of the large
compositional units in Isa 40-55 strongly supports a
collective interpretation of the servant. It is certainly more parsimonious to assume that the anonymous
servant in the songs was a refinement and idealization
of the prophet's conventional appellation of Israel as
the servant than to posit two different servants,
Israel and a particular individual, which he somehow
came to identify as one. Proposals for the Gattungen
of the various servant passages as a royal oracle

---

[4]See pp. 23-62, 262-288.

[5]Carroll Stuhlmueller, "Deutero-Isaiah: Major Tran-
sitions in the Prophet's Theology and in Contemporary
Scholarship," CBQ 42 (1980) 1-29; J. Lindblom, The
Servant Songs in Deutero-Isaiah (Lund, 1951) 26, 66ff.
See below, pp. 313-14.

[6]E.g., the early satire of idolatry in 44:9-20 was
edited and given a framework to fit with the succession
of trial speeches in chs. 41-45. The prophet may have
similarly revised an earlier version of his work to
accomodate his mature conception of the servant; i.e.
41:21-42:17 may have at one time contained stanzas
celebrating the servant-Israel's salvation similar to
those of 41:8-13 which were later replaced with the
anonymous servant of 42:1-9.

(42:1-4), an oracle upon the installation of a prophet (49:1-6), a psalm of confidence (50:4-9) and a psalm of thanksgiving (53:1-12)[7] are not of themselves sufficient to demonstrate that the servant was an individual in light of Deutero-Isaiah's penchant for personification (cf. 41:8-16; 42:19; ch. 47) and for democratization of preexilic offices to apply to all Israel (cf. 55:3-5). The prophet freely reutilized and subordinated traditional genres to the concerns of his message. Hence interpretation should begin with investigation of the literary compositions which contain the servant passages as contituent parts. Their arrangement in these larger compositions, rather than their formal antecedents, best reveals the conscious artifice of the prophet. The servant in 41:1-42:17 is juxtaposed with the servant-Israel; in 49:1-26 he is placed opposite Zion. These compositions intend the servant of Yahweh of the so-called "songs" to be construed as continuous with the servant-Israel. The reason for the servant's heightened anonymity may lie in the need to idealize "faithful Israel" as distinct from the whole body of exiles, many of whom may have rejected or ignored Deutero-Isaiah's message as suggested by the evident persecution of the "disciple" in 50:4-11.[8]

---

[7]Melugin, Formation, 64-74. The most recent attempt to deal with this vexing issue is by Klaus Baltzer, "Zur formgeschichtlichen Bestimmung der Texte vom Gottes-Knecht im Deuterojesaja-buch," in Probleme biblischer Theologie, Festschrift Gerhard von Rad, ed. H.W. Wolff (München: Kaiser, 1971) 27-43. He reads the four servant songs together as comprising a prophetic biography.

[8]E.g., Isa 54:13-17; cf. below, pp. 310-12.

The collective interpretation of the servant has been advocated by Blank; Cross similarly labels these passages "songs of the vocation of Israel," recognizing that they express a self-conscious wrestling with the question of Israel's vocation.[9]

North and Stuhlmueller have remarked that the servant songs show a universalistic hope for salvation of the gentiles that distinguishes them from the rest of Isa 40-55. North contrasts the "high idealism of the Servant Songs" which stands in "dissonant contrast" to the main body of Deutero-Isaiah;[10] Stuhlmueller highlights this contrast as a primary basis for separating out the servant songs, where "Dt-Isa made the colossal leap from an exclusive concern for Israel's salvation and its concommitant anti-gentile attitude to world salvation."[11] But our previous discussion of the vision of Yahweh's universal sovereignty which pervades the trial speeches, polemics against idolatry, and especially passages depicting the nations participating in the processions to Zion and contributing to the restoration of his temple belies this supposed distinction. The universal scope of Yahweh's dominion pervades the entire corpus of the Babylonian Isaiah, and hence any universalism to be found in the servant songs stands in continuity with, rather than in contrast to, the rest of his corpus.

---

[9]Blank, Prophetic Faith, 76-81. Cross, personal communication. Cf. Canaanite Myth, 346: "the old oracles of kingship and the inaugural oracles or 'confessions' (autobiographical oracles) of the prophet [were] proclaimed to the nation Israel. Israel herself was to be ambassador to the nations bearing the law to the peoples."

[10]North, 184.

[11]Stuhlmueller, 21-27.

2. Isa 42:1-9: The Servant as Mediator of God's Universal Sovereignty

We have noted that 42:1-4,5-9 is an integral part of the extended compositional unit 41:1-42:17[12] which begins with an an address to the assembled nations. Isa 42:1-4 continues the scene of the second trial speech 41:21-29; its opening hēn contrasts the negative judgment upon the gods of the nations with Yahweh's word confirming his servant as ambassador of tôrâ to the nations.[13] The representatives of the nations in audience at the preceding trial scene are likewise the audience which witnesses God's confirmation of the servant in 42:1-4, to whom God speaks about his servant in the third person. Commentators have recognized that audience to be God's retinue in the divine council.[14] As the divine speech about the servant is proclaimed in an international setting, so the servant's mission is likewise to be international in scope.

As inseparable parts of the single composition Isa 41:1-42:17, the trial speeches judging the nations (41:1-4; 41:21-29) lead into two parallel affirmations of the servant's international stature. The servant-Israel will be triumphant and secure in the midst of the general devastation of the nations (41:8-13), and correspondingly, the anonymous servant will be Yahweh's ambassador bringing mišpāṭ to the nations (42:1-4). These parallel passages share the motifs of God's support for the servant, the servant's justification in

---

[12]See above, pp. 23-62.

[13]See above, pp. 54-55.

[14]Cf. Baltzer, 30-38; North, 142.

the midst of universal judgment, and the release of the
prisoners and return of the scattered peoples.15   They
are in turn followed by the rejoicing of the nations as
Yahweh goes out to conquer (41:16,17-20; 42:10-13). We
noted that the composition as a whole is based upon a
ritual pattern derived from traditions of the royal
cult and antecedent patterns of Canaanite myth.16   As
portrayed in· such texts as Pss 2 and 89, God's judgment
against the raging nations and the forces of chaos is
prelude to his anointing the Davidic king who then
takes up universal sovereignty as God's "servant." The
same mythic pattern in miniature is found within 42:5-
6, where a hymnic apostrophe praising Yahweh as creator
of heaven and earth and all living creatures precedes
his designating the servant "a light to the nations"
and "covenant to the peoples." Here Deutero-Isaiah
applies to the servant the inherently universal tradition of Davidic royal theology, a tradition which he
also employs in both the Cyrus oracle and in depicting
the international primacy of Israel (55:3-5).17

15See above, pp. 41-43.

16See above, pp. 56-60.

17The royal motifs in this servant oracle are widely
acknowledged; see O. Kaiser, Der Königliche Knecht; Ein
traditionsgeschichtliche Studie über die Ebed-Jahwe
Lieder bei Deuterojesaja, FRLANT 70 (Göttingen, Vandenhoeck & Ruprecht, 1959). Mowinckel (He that Cometh,
190,   245 n. 15) and Schoors (ETL 40 [1964] 35-39) even
view Isa 42:5-9 as originally a Cyrus oracle reapplied
to the Servant. Baltzer (33-34) would reject the royal
background of this passage in favor of the judicial
function delegated to the prophet as Yahweh's "vizier"
on the basis of texts such as Ps 68:7 where Yahweh
himself liberates the prisoners. His analysis, based
upon a prior excision of the servant song from its
context, ignores the parallels to the ritual pattern of
the royal cult which are evident from our study of the
song in its compositional unit.

In 42:1-4 the **mišpāṭ** and **tôrâ** which the servant is
to bring forth to the nations refers to the manifestation of God's vindicating judgment in world history.[18]
This is the fulfillment of the **mišpāṭ** against the
nations in the trial scenes (41:1) and the answer to
Israel's complaint that it has no **mišpāṭ** in 40:27. But
for the nations this judgment is not entirely negative,
since "for his **tôrâ** the coastlands wait" (42:4). It
would be a mistake to render **mišpāṭ** abstractly as
"truth" or "true religion;"[19] this is not a missionary
theology. The parallel term **tôrâ** in other contexts in
Deutero-Isaiah similarly denotes God's covenant and
accompanying salvific judgments rather than a
"teaching."[20] Isa 51:4-5 in particular equates **tôrâ**,
mišpāṭ, **ṣedeq** and **yēšaᶜ** as the judgment of Yahweh's
"arm," and there also the nations hope for Yahweh's
rule.[21] Both Isa 42:1-4 and 51:4-5 reflect the motifs

---

[18]W.A.M. Beuken, "**Mišpāṭ**: The First Servant Song and
its Context," VT 22 (1972) 3-30.

[19]So Blank, 82-83; Volz, Jesaja II, 153.

[20]Cf. Isa 42:21, and the discussion of Schoors, I am
God your Savior, 157, 204-5.

[21]Isa 51:4-5 has often been regarded as secondary;
so most recently Schoors, 145-67; and Westermann Isaiah
40-66, 232-4. Other exegetes more sensitive to rhetoric and poetic sense have preserved vv. 4-5 as integral
to a larger unit of varying lengths: Muilenburg (IB 5,
588-89) and Torrey (The Second Isaiah, 394-5) see a
unit 51:1-16; Bonnard (Le Second Isaïe, 244-45) notes a
diverse unity in 51:1-52:12 of which 51:1-8 is a major
section; and Clifford (Fair Spoken, 156-64) sees a unit
in 50:1-51:8.
We recognize Isa 51:1-8 to be a single composition
in three stanzas, vv. 1-3, 4-6, and 7-8, each with a
parallel structure. Each begins with masculine plural
imperatives "listen to me" followed by a vocative noun
or noun clause naming the addressee. In vv. 1 and 7
the addressee is called by a participial phrase **rōdĕpê**

of the Zion tradition as expressed in the undated

ṣedeq, měbaqqěšê yhwh and yōděᶜê ṣedeq; in vv. 4 and 7
the addressee is a noun for people or nation: ᶜammî,
lě'ûmmî, and ᶜam tôrātî bě-libbām. A second type of
imperative clause follows in vv. 1b-2a,6a,7b which
lacks a specified addressee. Third, in each stanza
these imperatives are followed by clauses beginning
with kî (vv. 2b,3a,4b,6b,8a). Finally, the second and
third stanzas have similar conclusions which describe
the transitoriness of the world and human attitudes
which "wear out like a garment" or "dissolve like
smoke" in contrast to Yahweh's salvation which lasts
forever.
    The literary form in this unit, defined by several
stanzas repeating nearly identical opening phrases
and/or concluding refrains, is the song cycle. While
the individual stanzas of a cycle may contain oracles
in any of several Gattungen--woe oracles, judgment
oracles, oracles against the nations, etc.--the cycle
has its own formal characteristics to which the component stanzas are conformed. (e.g. Amos 4:4-13;
Isa 7:18-23; 9:7-10:4+5:24-25; Jer 50:35-38; Ezek 25:8-
17; Hab 4). In the song cycle Amos 1:3-2:16 each
oracle shares a common opening "for three transgressions of... and for four... I will not hold back" and a
similar conclusion "I will send fire upon... and it
will consume...." The cycle of woe oracles Isa 5:8-12,
18-23 compares to this unit in that each stanza opens
with an address to a certain group: "those who join
house to house," "those who rise early in the morning,"
"those who call evil good," etc. Perhaps the oracle
with the closest formal similarity to 51:1-8 is the
two-part judgment oracle in Isa 32:9-14, where each
stanza (vv. 9-10, 11-14) begins with imperatives
addressed to the "women at ease" followed by words of
judgment beginning with kî. Isa 51:1-8, with its
repeated openings and refrains, is in the form of such
a song cycle; Isa 51:9-52:12 may also show the influence of this form.
    Verses 4-5, with their resemblance to the servant
songs, cannot be distinguished from the unit 51:1-8 on
the basis of vocabulary; there is verbal repetition of
ᶜām (vv. 4,5,7), tôrâ (vv. 4,7), ṣedeq (vv. 1,5,7), and
yešaᶜ/yěšûᶜâ (vv. 5,6,8). The stanza vv. 4-6 has all
four structural features noted above: imperative
clauses, kî clause, and closing refrain. Removing vv.
4-5 is thus unwarranted and obscures the formal structure of the unit.

ISAIAH 42:1-9

259

oracle Isa 2:2-4.[22] There too **tôrâ** consists of the decree of God's righteous rule which goes forth (**tēṣē'**) to the nations, judges them, and brings to them the benefits of peace. In political terms, the nations would sign vassal treaties binding them to peaceful commerce under Israelite sovereignty. **Tôrâ** thus has the dimension of a universal covenant--a **běrît ᶜam**--binding all nations to honor God as their sovereign and to deal with each other according to its laws.

The coastlands who await this new government also rejoice at Yahweh's conquests in vv. 10-13. These are the provinces who presumably have also chafed under the Babylonian yoke, and who, like those "survivors" in 45:20-25, would find salvation in Yahweh's just order as his vassals. Many of them had once been Israelite vassals in the glorious days of the Davidic empire.[23]

---

[22]The dispute over the date of Isa 2:2-4/Mic 4:1-5, whether 8th century as argued by Wildberger ("Die Völkerwallfahrt zum Zion, Jes. II 1-5," VT 7 [1957] 76) or 6th century as preferred by von Rad (Old Testament Theology, II, 294) and Eissfeldt (The Old Testament: an Introduction, 318), among others, is beside the point. It expresses a Zion tradition which was alive in pre-exilic Israel in which Yahweh judges the nations (Pss 2; 48; Isa 17:12-14) and brings peace by destroying their weapons of war (Pss 46; 76; Isa 9:3-4).

[23]Mauchline and Christensen have suggested that throughout Israel's history the borders of the Davidic empire demarcated the proper sphere of Yahweh's and Israel's sovereignty, forming the basis for the prophets to invoke Yahweh's authority to judge the nations for treaty violations (Amos 1-2) and fuelling the irridentist activities of Jeroboam II and Josiah. See Duane Christensen, Transformations of the War Oracle in Old Testament Prophecy, HDR 3 (Missoula: Scholars Press, 1975) 55-7; John Mauchline, "Implicit Signs of a Persistent Belief in the Davidic Empire," VT 20 (1970) 289. Cf. Gen 15:18 [J]; Exod 23:31 [E or D]; Deut 1:7; 11:24; Josh 1:4; Amos 6:14; Ezek 47:13-23; Zech 9:1-9.

Recognition that royal and Zion traditions are antecedent to the first servant song and to its larger
compositional unit gives a basis for understanding the
problematic expression bĕrît ᶜām. Some have attempted
to render the phrase by giving an unusual meaning to
bĕrît; so Torczyner "vision of the people(s),[24]
E. Kutsch "obligation of the people,"[25] and D. Hillers
"emancipation of the people."[26] In criticizing Hillers,
Smith raises an objection which North had levelled
against Torczyner, that such an obscure meaning for the
common word bĕrît would presumably baffle the prophet's
audience accustomed to the common meaning "covenant."[27]
If bĕrît means covenant, then North has enumerated
three possible translations:[28] First, it could mean
Israel as a "covenant-people." This takes bĕrît ᶜām as
a subjective genitive, but then one might expect ᶜām
bĕrît. Westermann correctly objects that in the context of both 42:6-7 and 49:8-9 the phrase is one of a
list of tasks for an office through which God affects
others.[29] Second, the servant could be the "(mediator

---

[24]H. Torczyer, "Presidential Address," JPOS 16
(1936) 7. Torczyner's proposed Akkadian cognates have
been questioned; see J.J. Stamm, "Bĕrît ᶜām bei Deuterojesaja," in Probleme biblischer Theologie, ed. H.W.
Wolff (Munich: Kaiser, 1971) 510-24.

[25]He is criticized by M. Weinfeld, "Covenant vs.
Obligation," Bib 56 (1975) 124-5; and by Delbert
Hillers, "bĕrît ᶜām: Emancipation of the People," JBL
97 (1978), 175-6.

[26]Hillers, 175-82.

[27]Mark S. Smith, "bĕrît ᶜām / bĕrît ᶜôlām: A New
Proposal for the Crux of Isa 42:6," JBL 100 (1981),
241-3.

[28]North, The Second Isaiah, 112.

[29]Westermann, Isaiah 40-66, 100.

of my) covenant with the people," where ^{c}am in the singular refers to Israel. This is the position of Snaith[30] and de Boer[31] based upon the observation that elsewhere in Deutero-Isaiah the term ^{c}am in the singular refers consistently to Israel and not to the nations. Finally, the rendering "(mediator of my) covenant with the peoples," where ^{c}am is taken as a collective, best fits the parallelism with 'ôr gôyîm in Isa 42:6 and a collective noun ^{c}am in the immediately preceding verse.[32] A similar use of the collective gôy is found in Isa 55:5, and the collective ^{c}am in its antecedent Ps 18:44 refers to the nations which serve David and Israel as vassals.[33] Isa 51:4 offers another parallel, where Yahweh's mišpāṭ goes out as 'ôr ^{c}ammîm, a "light to the peoples."

We substantially follow Smith, who has given the best nuance of this crux to date not by seeking an odd translation that would be obscure to the prophet's audience, but by relating this term to the traditional běrît ^{c}ôlām of the Davidic covenant. "The obvious phonetic resemblance between běrît ^{c}ôlām and běrît ^{c}am suggests that Second Isaiah is playing upon the memory of the Davidic covenant theology."[34] Elsewhere the prophet reinterprets the covenants with Abraham (51:2), Noah (54:10) and David (55:3-5) to apply to Israel as a collective; in each case he understands their covenants according to Judean royal theology as an eternal divine

---

[30]Snaith, "Teaching... Consequences," 157-8.

[31]de Boer, Second Isaiah's Message, 94.

[32]Smith, 243; Muilenberg, 468-9.

[33]Isa 13:4; 25:3; cf. Hillers, 181.

[34]Smith, 242.

grant (běrît ᶜôlãm) rather than as a bond with obligations. Isa 55:3-5 specifically lifts up the international dimension of the Davidic covenant as God's grant authorizing Israel to command the nations. In Isa 42:1-9 God's sovereignty over the nations is expressed through the office of his servant who will bring forth mišpāṭ and tôrâ to the nations. Hence the parallel phrases běrît ᶜãm, "covenant to the peoples," and 'ôr gôyîm, "a light to the nations" both build upon the universalistic traits of preexilic royal theology to envision the servant-Israel's office as one mediating God's divine government to all nations.

3. Isa 49:1-26: The Servant's International Jurisdiction and the Restoration of Zion

Chapter 49 is of interest to a study on the place of the nations in Deutero-Isaiah both for its description of the servant's jurisdiction over the nations and for the images in vv. 7 and 22-23 of kings and queens prostrating themselves before Israel and coming to Zion carrying the exiles upon their shoulders.[35] Form critics have divided the chapter into from three (49:1-6, 7-13 and 14-26)[36] to as many as seven units (49:1-6, 7, 8-12, 13, 14-21, 22-23 and 24-26).[37] But if one is not prejudiced by the scholarly fashion since Duhm to separate out the servant songs as later additions,

---

[35]See above, pp. 234-241.

[36]Westermann (pp. 206-218) distinguishes v. 13 as an additional fragment; Westermann and Schoors (pp. 97-121) also transpose v. 7b after v. 12.

[37]Melugin, Formation, 142-152; Cf. Begrich, Studien, 14-16.

chapter 49 can be shown to be a single composition in
two movements, each with a chiastic structure. The
case for the unity of Chapter 49 depends upon a sensitivity to the way Deutero-Isaiah transforms traditional
forms and combines them into his compositions as well
as the elucidation of rhetorical connections that bind
the chapter into a whole. This unity was not the
result of a secondary arrangement, for the structures
of its subunits are to some extent influenced by their
role in the larger composition.[38]

49:1-6

Listen to me, O nations![a]	7
hearken, O distant coastlands!	8
Yahweh has called me from the womb;	8
from my mother's belly he mentioned my name.	9
He made my mouth like a sharp[b] sword,	7
in the shadow of his hand he concealed me.	8
He made me into a sharpened arrow,	8
in his quiver he hid me.	8
He said to me, "you are my servant,	7
Israel, [ ][c] in you I will be glorified."[d]	8

1:1::1:1::1:1::1:1::1:1

But I thought, "I have labored in vain;	11
for nought and for nothing I have spent my strength;	10
Nevertheless my case is with Yahweh,	8
and my wages are with my God.	8
‹I will be honored in the sight of Yahweh,	8
and my God will be my strength.›"[e]	8

1:1::1:1::1:1

And now says Yahweh:	rubric
"I formed ‹you›[f] in the womb to be my servant,	9
to restore Jacob to me,	7
and to gather[g] Israel together."	7
And he said:	rubric

---

[38]Muilenberg; Torrey, 384; Clifford, 146-55. Bonnard
(p. 217) cautiously notes their literary unity but
allows that vv. 1-6, 7-13 and 14-26 may have been
uttered separately.

```
"Is it too light a thingh that you have become
     my servant,                                            9
   to reconstitute the tribes of Israel,i                   8
   restore the survivorsj of Jacob?                         8
 I appoint you a light to the nations,                      8̄
     [   ]k that my salvation may reach to the ends
     of the earth."                                         8
                                     l:l:l::l:l:l::l:̄l
```

49:7

```
Thus says Yahweh,                                           5
   Redeemer of Israel, its Holy One;                        8
To one whose self is despised, an abhorred nation,l         9
   the servant of rulers:                                   5
Kings will see <and> arise,m                                9
   princes will prostrate themselves;                       5
Because of Yahweh, for he is faithful,                      6̄
   the Holy One of Israel, for he has chosen you.           9
                                     b:l::l:b::l:b::b:̄l
```

49:8-13

```
Thus says Yahweh:                                        rubric
In a time of favor I answer you;                           8
   in the day of salvation I help you.                     9
I formed youh and I appoint you                            9̄
   as a covenant to the peoples, to reestablish
     the earth,                                            8
   to reapportion the desolate ancestral lands,            9
To say to the prisoners, "go free!"                        8̄
   to those in darkness, "show yourselves!"                8
                                     l:l::l:l:l::l:̄l

By the side of <every> roado they will feed;               7
   on [   ] the barren heights will be their pasture.      7
They will neither hunger nor thirst,                       9
   the desert wind and the sun will not strike them.       8
For <on> broad pasturesp he will lead them;                8̄
   to springs of water he will guide them.                 9
I will make every mountainq into a road;                   6̄
   my highways will be built up.                           7
Lo! these come from afar,                                  10̄
   lo!r these from the north and from the west,            10
   and these from the land of Sewan.s                      8
                                     l:l:̄l

Rejoice, O heavens, and sing, O earth,                     8
   let the mountains break fortht with rejoicing;          7
For Yahweh has consoledu his people,                       7̄
   he has had compassion upon his afflicted ones.          7
                                     l:l::l:̄l
```

49:14-16

But Zion says:	rubric
"Yahweh has abandoned me,	6
my God^V has forgotten me."	7
Can a woman forget her suckling child,	7
lack compassion^W for the offspring of her womb?	6
Even if they would forget,^X	7
I will not forget you.	7
Lo, I have engraved you upon my hands,	7
your walls are before me always.	7
	b:b::b:b::b:b::b:b

49:17-18

Your builders^Y outstrip your destroyers,   9
   and those who laid you waste go forth from you.   9
Lift up your eyes and look around,   9
   all of them gather and come to you.   9
As I live--says Yahweh--   6
   you will wear them all like an ornament,   9
   you will bind them on like a bride.   8
                                           l:l::l:l::b:l:l

49:19-21

For I had <de>vasted you and laid you waste,^Z   8
   had razed you <to> the ground;   5
But now you will be too crowded for settlers;   8
   those who had devoured you will be far away.   6
                                              l:b::l:b

They will yet say in your ears,   7
   the children of your bereavement: 5
"The place is too narrow for me,   5
   make room for me, that I may dwell."   7
                                              l:b::b:l

And you will say in your heart,   7
   "who has borne me these?   6
I was bereaved and barren, [   ]^{aa}   9
   but these--who has reared them?   6
I was left completely alone,   9
   these--where are they from?"   5
                                           l:b::l:b::l:b

49:22-23

For thus says [   ] Yahweh:^{bb}   rubric
Now, when I will lift my hand to the nations,   8
   and raise my signal to the peoples;   8
They will bring your sons in their bosom,   7
   your daughters they will bear^{cc} on their shoulder.   9

```
Kings will be your foster fathers;                          8
    their princesses your nursing mothers.                  8
With faces to the ground they will bow to you,              8
    they will lick the dust of your feet;                   8
                                    1:1::1:1::1:1::1:1
That you may know that I am Yahweh,                          7
    [  ] none will be shamed who wait for me.               6
                                                          1:1
```

49:24-26

```
Can spoil be taken from a warrior,                          8
    can captives be rescued from a tyrant?dd               8
For thus says Yahweh:                                   rubric
Even captives of the warrior shall be taken,ee            7
    the spoil of the tyrant shall be rescued.              7
[ ] Your causeff I will defend;                            7
    [ ] your children I will rescue.                       7
I will make your oppressors eatgg their own flesh;         8
    they shall be drunk with their own blood as with
        wine.                                              8
That all flesh might know,                                 7
    that it is I Yahweh who vindicates you,                8
    the Mighty One of Jacob who redeems you.               7
                            1:1::x:1:1::1:1::1:1::1:1
```

TEXTUAL NOTES

aMT has an unbalanced 6/9 bicolon; we transpose **'iyyîm** and **lě'ummîm** for better meter.

bG is reading **baḥûr**.

cWe omit **'ăšer** as a prosaizing addition which is absent from G. There is no textual or metrical warrant for omitting "Israel."

d1QIsab reads **ht[   ]** (**hitpā''artî**)

eThis bicolon is transposed from v. 5c. It is a confession of the servant in the first person which does not fit the context of the divine speech begun in 5a. The servant's desire for honor fits with his expectations of justice and a reward in v. 4b. Questions remain, however. One might suspect that **kbd** with the sense "to be heavy" is meant to contrast to the following verb **nāqēl**. 1QIsaᵃ has ᶜ**ezrî** for MT ᶜ**uzzî**.

ᶠMT has a participial phrase descriptive of Yahweh similar to that in 44:2. However, it is attractive to emend **yōṣĕrî** to '**eṣṣārĕkā** on the basis of 1QIsaᵃ **ywṣrk** and to read the beginning of a direct quotation, a divine speech to the servant with a syntax similar to vv. 6 and 8. Our emendation also requires first person pronouns on the prepositions **lî** and '**elay**, easily explicable by **wāw/yōd** confusion.

ᵍ<u>Ketîb</u> **lōʼ yēʼʼāsēp**; <u>qerēʼ</u>, 1QIsaᵃ and G read **lô yēʼʼāsēp**. The negative particle is surely a corruption; yet it is intelligible with the sense "that Israel not pass away." But the preposition **lô** is also not to be expected with the verb '**sp**, which is normally followed by '**el** or ᶜ**al**. Read here a Qal infinitive **le-ʼĕsōp** in parallel with the infinitive of the transitive verb **lĕ-šôbēb**. Cf. pairs of infinitives in vv. 6a and 8b.

ʰ1QIsaᵇ adds an expansionary interrogative **hē**.

ⁱReversing **yaᶜăqōb** and **yiśrāʼēl** according to the order in 1QIsaᵃ to give metrical balance.

ʲReading the <u>ketîb</u> **nĕṣîrê** with 1QIsaᵃ, 1QIsaᵇ; it is presumably a **qatîl** form.

ᵏOmit **lihyôt** as a prozaising expansion triggered from v. 6a.

ˡThis colon is ambiguous, and a certain translation may be impossible. MT reads **li-bzōh nepeš** with an active infinitive that should be repointed as a participle **lĕ-bōzēh nepeš**, "to one despising <his> life." G τὸν φαυλίζοντα τὴν ψυχὴν αὐτοῦ also has an active verb and makes the pronominal suffix explicit. But we follow 1QIsaᵃ, which reads the passive participle lĕ-bāzûy, "to one whose self is despised," as do the later Greek versions. The second phrase may be read in any of five ways. MT reads a piel of t^cb whose subject is gôy "one whom the nations abhor." But following G the verb could be pointed as a pual, "one abhorred by the nations;" and if gôy is the subject of the passive verb it could be read "an abhorred nation"--our preference. Clifford and NJV emend gôy to gĕwîyâ forming a parallel with nepeš, and this too could be read with an active or passive verb "one who abhors his body" or "one whose body is abhorred." Any number of permutations of these readings can yield acceptable parallelism, meter, and sense consistent with Deutero-Isaiah's other descriptions of the servant.

^mReading an imperfect wĕ-yāqūmu with 1QIsa^b.

^nOn this tricolon, see comments. The verb 'eṣṣārĕkā is lacking in G. It was probably lost by oral haplography due to its similarity to the previous verb, particularly since ṣādē and zāyin were often confused in later Hebrew. Yet it is not to be omitted; cf. 42:6.

^OMT reads ^cal dĕrākîm; G was reading *^cal kol dĕrākîm; 1QIsa^a has ^cl kwl hrym. The adjective kol in the first colon helps the meter and probably was at some point transposed to the second colon, where it is excessive (G and 1QIsa^a being conflate). MT dĕrākîm is an adequate parallel to šĕpāyyîm (cf. Jer 3:2, Isa 41:18), and 1QIsa^a hārîm must be rejected as perhaps a correction of a text that had suffered haplography of kap. Several recent speculations seeking to reconcile these seemingly disparate words include Thomas's suggestion of an original dĕkākîm, a noun from the root dkk, "to crush" (often used of rock in Arabic), meaning desert wastes of dunes or crushed rock,[39] and Gelston's translation of šĕpāyyīm as "tracks."[40] G has τρίβοις reading šōpĕṭîm for šĕpāyyīm.

PMT and all versions read kî mĕraḥḥămām, an awkward piel participle. We would expect a parallel to mabbûᶜê mayim in the second colon. We suggest bĕ-merḥāb, which could have suffered confusion with bĕ-raḥămîm.

qMT has hāray by attraction to mĕsillōtay; G correctly has the bare singular.

rG omits the second hinneh, but for metrical balance one is tempted to add a third.

ssĕwen is a city in southern Egypt, etymologically related to modern Aswan. This reading is based upon 1QIsaᵃ swnyym, while MT has sînîm. See Ezek 29:10; 30:6 for the expression mim-migdōl sĕwēneh, "from Migdol to Syene;" there MT may be misreading a locative hē < *sĕwēnāh.

tG supports the jussive ketîb yipṣĕḥû, 1QIsaᵃ supports the imperative qerē' û-piṣḥû. The longer jussive is preferable for metrical balance.

uThe piel perfect niḥḥam of MT, supported by G, is to be preferred over 1QIsaᵃ mĕnaḥḥēm.

vMT reads 'ădōnāy. 1QIsaᵃ has a double reading w'dwny and, above the line, 'lwhy; this second tradition is supported by Gᴬ, Gᴸ, and some mss of Gᴼ. Other G mss read καὶ ὁ κύριος < *'dwny. Since 'ădōnāy is probably an oral transcription of yhwh, 'ĕlōhay is the more likely parallel to yhwh in the first colon.

---

[39]D. Winton Thomas, "A Note on derakim in Isa 49,9," JTS 19 (1968) 203-4.

[40]A. Gelston, "Some Notes on Second Isaiah," VT 21 (1971) 518-21.

wMT reads a piel infinitive prefixed by privative **min**, "from having compassion."

xRead an energic ending *metri causa*.

yMT reads **bānayik**, but 1QIsa[a] **bōnayik** is undoubtedly correct (cf. G). While MT reads a piel participle **mĕhārrĕsayik**, 1QIsa[a] correctly reads **mē-hōrĕsayik**, a Qal participle with comparative **min** (cf. G).

zFollowing Torrey, we read <he>ḥrabtîk wĕ-šōmamtîk as active verbs describing Yahweh's past destruction of Zion (cf. 47:6, 42:24). The consonantal MT, reading a series of nouns and lacking a verb, is an unintelligible fragment. This emendation requires the addition of a **hē** since **ḥrb** should be a hiphil. G lacks **'ereṣ**, but in the emended text it fits well as an accusative of location.

aaG lacks MT **gōlâ wĕ-sûrâ**, and it is evidently a dittography and corruption of the preceding **glmwdh** which yielded **gl swrh** by **sāmek/mēm** and **dālet/rēš** confusion.

bbMT **'ădōnāy** is an oral expansion not found in either G or 1QIsa[a]. 1QIsa[a] adds an inital **kî**.

ccMT **tinnāśe'nâ** is awkward and metrically excessive; an active verb **nāśĕ'û** is supported by G ἀροῦσι. This reconstruction could yield MT through a dittography of the last two consonants of **kātēp** with **pēh/nūn** confusion: *ktp nś'w < *ktp tp nś'w < *ktp tn nś'w < *ktp tnś'w. That reading, being perceived as a passive, would be corrected for person and gender to MT.

ddWe read **cārîṣ** with 1QIsa[a], cf. G and v. 25. MT has **ṣaddîq**.

---

eeWhere MT and G read **šĕbî gibbôr** and **malqôḥ ^cārîṣ**, 1QIsa^a has the terms reversed, **mlkqwḥ gbwr** and **šby ^cryṣ**, a secondary transposition by attraction to the order in v. 24. It also has the niphal **ylqḥ** in place of the Qal passive **yuqqaḥ** in MT.

ffMT **yĕrîbēk** is reading the noun **yārîb** (Ps 35:1, Jer 18:19) translated "adversary." Its attestation in Jer 18:19 is textually uncertain, and if it is read in Isa 51:22 it means "defender." Worse, it displays a unique and doubtful nominal pattern.[41] We accept the reading of 1QIsa^a **rybyk** (**rîbayik**) with the second **yōd** written <u>supra lineam</u>, which is supported by G κρίσιν σου, "your case." The reading in 1QIsa^a and G also gives better metrical balance.

ggThe hiphil **ha'ăkaltî** of MT, supported by G, is superior to 1QIsa^a which reads a Qal **w'wklty**.

*   *   *   *

Chapter 49 opens in vv. 1-6 with a song of the vocation of the servant-Israel, which is formally a prophetic call narrative dependent upon Jer 1:4-10. Prophetic call narratives, as well as the calls of

---

[41]Cf. <u>GK</u> #85d. The few other **yōd**-preformative nouns from other ^cayin-weak verbs (**yĕqûm**, **yĕtûr**), while a different verbal pattern, are equally uncertain and may be misunderstood verbal forms.

Moses and Gideon (Exod 3-4; Judg 6:11-17; Isa 6:1-13;
Jer 1:4-10; Ezek 1-3) form a single genre and follow a
common pattern which Habel has analyzed into six
parts.[42] (1) An initial theophany or divine confronta-
tion--Exod 3:2-6 (the bush); Isa 6:1-4 (the cherubim of
the divine council), Ezek 1:4-28 (the chariot)--is
present by implication in the setting of the nations
assembled at the divine council in Isa 49:1. (2) There
follows an introductory word of preparation for the
prophet's mission: God identifies himself to Moses
(Exod 3:6); Isaiah's mouth and sin is cleansed (Isa
6:3-7). The servant's call from the womb (Isa 49:1b)
is derived from Jeremiah's similar preparation: "Before
I formed you in the womb ('essārĕkā bab-beṭen) I knew
you," (Jer 1:5). (3) The actual commission delineates
the specific task to which the prophet is assigned.
Thus Exod 3:10, "Now go, I send you to Pharaoh to lead
out my people Israel from Egypt;" Isa 6:8-10, "Go, and
say to this people...." cf. Jer 1:7 and Ezek 2:1-8).
The servant's commission briefly stated in Isa 49:3,
but as with Isaiah's and Jeremiah's call, it will be
restated with more precision in the fifth section.
(4) The prophet typically objects, reluctant to take on
such a difficult task: Exod 4:1, "They will not believe
me," Exod 4:10, "I am not eloquent," Isa 6:5, "I am
unclean, and a man of unclean lips," Jer 1:6, "I am but
a youth and don't know how to speak." Isaiah's second
objection "How long, O Lord?" (6:11a) comes upon reali-
zing the dimensions of his task. Similarly, the servant complains in Isa 49:4, "I have labored in vain...
my strength is spent." This verse is influenced by the

---

[42]N. Habel, "The Form and Significance of the Call
Narratives," ZAW 77 (1965) 297-323.

style of personal laments in Jeremiah and in the psalms
where the complaint is followed by affirmations of
confidence in God's goodness and power.[43] (5) Then God
reassures the prophet: Exod 3:12, "I am with you,"
Jer 1:7-8, "do not say 'I am only a youth'... be not
afraid," and similarly in Isa 49:6 "Is it too light a
thing?..." In Isa 6, Jer 1 and Isa 49 this reassurance
is joined to a reaffirmation of the commission. The
statement of the servant's mission in Isa 49:5-6, "I
appoint you a light to the nations (nĕttatîkā lĕ-'ôr
gôyîm)" followed by the series of infinitive clauses
"to restore... to gather up... to establish..." particularly resembles the restatement of Jeremiah's mission
in Jer 1:10: "I appoint you a prophet to the nations
(nābî' lag-gôyîm nĕttatîkā)... to pluck up and to break
down, to destroy and to overthrow, to build and to
plant."[44] (6) The final characteristic of the call

---

[43]cf. Ps 31:23, Jer 20:9-11, 11:20, 15:19-20.

[44]This formal dependence on Jeremiah's commission
makes unlikely the interpretation of the infinitives
lĕ-hāqîm, lĕ-hāšîb, etc. in Isa 49:5 as denoting God's
actions accompanying his calling the servant. That
view has been proposed most recently by Mettinger, A
Farewell to the Servant Songs, 35-37. In order to
support his view that the collective servant-Israel did
not have a mission to Israel, he uses Isa 51:16 where a
series of infinitives following the finite verb describe Yahweh's consecutive actions:

    I have put my words in your mouth, and hid you in
    the shadow of my hand, stretching out (linṭōᶜ) the
    heavens, laying the foundations (wĕ-liysōd) of the
    earth, and saying to Zion (wĕ-lē'mōr lĕ-ṣiyyôn),
    "You are my people."

to make a case that the infinitives in 49:5-6 be understood similarly:

    And now says Yahweh,
      who formed me in the womb to be his servant,
    While restoring Jacob to himself,
      and gathering Israel together,

narrative is one or more signs, always related to the
prophetic word and serving to strengthen the prophet in
his mission. God provides Moses with a rod and other
signs and promises "I will be with your mouth." The
sign as empowering the word is explicit in Jer 1:9
where Yahweh touches his mouth and puts his words in
it (cf. Isa 6:6-7 and Ezek 2:8-3:3) and similarly in
Isa 49:2 where the servant is equipped with a mouth
like a sharp sword. The equipping of the prophet as
with military equipment, also characteristic of royal
oracles,[45] is a feature of Jeremiah's and Ezekiel's
call: "I will make you this day into a fortified city,
an iron pillar and walls of bronze" (Jer 1:18, cf.
Ezek 3:8-9). Similar expressions spice Jeremiah's
confessions: "If you utter what is precious, you will
be as my mouth... and I will make you a wall of bronze"
(Jer 15:19-20, cf. 23:29). Westermann recognizes the
hiding of the servant in a quiver (Isa 49:2b) to be
another part of the servant's equipment.[46]

But Isa 49:1-6 is not a pure prophetic commission,
although that is the Gattung upon which it is based.
For one thing, Deutero-Isaiah is overstocked with com-
missionings, from the prophet's call in 40:1-11 to the
first and second servant songs. Therefore Cross des-

Is it too light a thing, considering you are my servant,
  that I shall only raise up the tribes of Jacob,
  and restore the survivors of Israel?

This proposal appears to be special pleading unless all
the infinitive clauses describing the servant's mission
(42:6-7; 49:8-9) are also taken as describing Yahweh's
activity. The formal dependence of Isa 49:1-6 on
Jeremiah's call makes such tortured exegesis unlikely.

[45]Ps 2:9, Isa 11:4.

[46]Cf. Pss 31:21; 61:5; Westermann, Isaiah 40-55, 209.

cribes the servant songs as "songs of the vocation of Israel" to emphasize that they deal with Israel's vocation as a repeated issue, much as Jeremiah's confessions repeatedly reaffirm his call and mission.[47]

The address to the nations in v. 1 also suggests that the call narrative is being interpreted in a larger context.[48] This opening address to the nations, together with the servant's mission to "the ends of the earth" in v. 6, form an inclusio around the call narrative. Similar statements describing the attitude of the nations demarcate the conclusions of every subunit of ch. 49 that begins with an address formula **kōh 'āmar yhwh:** in v. 7 the nations bow down before the servant, at the conclusion of vv. 8-13 peoples come from the world's extremities accompanied by the rejoicing of nature, in vv. 22-23 the nations bow down before Zion, and at the end of vv. 24-26 "all flesh" recognize Yahweh. The entire chapter is thus framed by successive references to the nations, who are called to recognize the servant, for whom the servant is to be a light, who are to do obeisance, to make pilgrimage, to bring the exiles to Zion, and to exalt Yahweh.

Attempts to isolate vv. 1-6 from vv. 7-13 on the basis of its recognizable form as a call narrative have not been convincing. That approach has often led to questionable emendations, such as Westermann's deletion of "I form you and appoint you as a covenant to the peoples" from v. 8 in order to divine in vv. 7-13 an address to Israel rather than to the servant as in vv.

---

[47]Personal communication.

[48]Cf. Amos 7:10-17, where an abbreviated call narrative (v. 15) is set in the context of polemics against Amaziah the high priest.

1-6.[49]   His argument is somewhat self-contradictory,
since he considers 49:7-12 to be of the same stratum--
an expansion on the servant songs--as 42:5-9 wherein
this phrase figures prominently. In addition, his
emended text of v. 8 is, as he admits, metrically
incomplete:

> bĕ-ᶜēt rāṣôn ᶜănîtîkā   8
> bĕ-yôm yĕšûᶜâ ᶜăzartîkā [   ]   9
> lĕ-hāqîm 'ereṣ   4
> lĕ-hanḥîl nĕḥālôt šômēmôt   9

Without this emendation, the verse in question scans
well as a bicolon followed by a balanced tricolon.

Connections between vv. 1-6 and 8-13 are numerous.
There is verbal repetition of lĕ-hāqîm and mērāḥôq used
in similar contexts. The pair 'ôr gôyim (v. 6) and
bĕrît ᶜām (v. 8), found joined together in 42:6, are
similarly preceded by the verbs 'eṣṣārĕkā (vv. 5 and 8)
and nĕtattîkā (vv. 6 and 8) denoting God's appointment
and are likewise followed by a series of infinitival
clauses depicting the work of the servant. As was
noted above, much of this vocabulary and syntax, including the expression lĕ-'ôr gôyîm and the series of
infinitival clauses, may be derived from a single
source in Jeremiah's call.

We will put aside v. 7 for the moment, which comes
at the center of the chiasm formed by vv. 1-6 and 8-13.
The key phrase bĕrît ᶜām is found in v. 8b, and it
stands chiastically opposite its counterpart 'ôr gôyîm
of v. 6. This prosodic structure, characterized by one
or two indicative verbs governing consecutive construct
chains or infinitival clauses introduced by le-, is the
same structure as found in 42:6 and 49:5,6a,6b.

---

[49]Westermann, 213-14.

At first glance, however, this prosody appears to
require the collocation of the universal term bĕrît cām
and the apparently specific task of restoring the land
denoted by the parallel infinitival clauses lĕ-hāqîm
'ereṣ and lĕ-hanḥîl nĕḥālôt šōmēmôt. This would con-
tradict the universal scope of the bĕrît cām as has
been surmised from the context of 42:6 and its antecedent traditions[50] and would rather support a nationalistic interpretation of bĕrît cām as "covenant to the
people [Israel]."

Nevertheless Torrey, who also sees a universal scope
for bĕrît cam, has no qualms about the parallelism
between li-brît cām and lĕ-hāqîm 'ereṣ, which he translates "to uplift the world."[52] He recognizes that the
parallel terms lĕ-hāqîm 'ereṣ and lĕ-hanḥîl nĕḥālôt
šōmēmôt also have universal connotations and should not
be restricted to the specific restoration of Israel's
land. 'ereṣ is nowhere used of the land of Israel in
Deutero-Isaiah. It most often signifies the entire
earth as Yahweh's creation;[53] elsewhere it denotes the
domain of God's conquests,[54] the international sphere
of God's dominion,[55] or most interestingly, the inter-

---

[50]See above, pp. 256-262.

[52]Torrey, The Second Isaiah, 383-84. Yet his emendation, omitting 'eṣṣārĕkā on the basis of G as an
expansion based upon 42:6 (which he renders as a tricolon) leaves a bicolon that is metrically unbalanced.

[53]Isa 40:12,21,22,23,28; 42:5; 44:23,24; 45:8,12,18,
19; 48:13; 49:13; 51:13,16.

[54]Isa 41:5,9; 42:10; 43:6; 46:11; 48:20 (also qĕṣôt
'ereṣ).

[55]Isa 45:8,22; 52:10; 54:5.

national jurisdiction of God's servant.[56] The infinitive lě-hāqîm refers to the reestablishment of Israel
in 49:6, but it may also refer to the creation of the
earth as in Prov 30:40.   The parallel term něḫālôt is
significantly a plural.   The singular nǎḫalā is almost
always a designation for Israel as Yahweh's heritage;
this is its meaning in Isa 47:6.   But the plural is
very rare,[57] and here it could well refer to a plurality of nations.   The verb hanḫîl is used of God appor-
tioning the nations in Deut 32:8, and in Ps 2:8 the
Davidid is given authority to possess the heritage
(nǎḫalā) of the nations.   Thus the collocation of
li-brît ᶜām with parallel infinitival phrases denoting
the restoration of the lands need be no impediment to
an exegesis that is universal throughout.   Verse   8b
first characterizes the servant's appointment as a
"covenant to the peoples" and then specifies his
mission to restore the entire earth, specifically the
hereditary lands of all the nations that had been left
desolate since Nebuchadnezzar's conquests.

Clifford is but the most recent exegete to prefer a
narrower nationalistic scope for the mission of the
servant.   He notes that the tasks for which the servant
is commissioned in 49:8-12--apportioning the lands,
liberating the prisoners, and leading the exiles home
to Zion--correspond to the work of Moses, who also
receives a covenant.[58] This is consistent with the

---

[56]Isa 42:4; 49:6. Cf. Torrey, 384.

[57]Cf. Josh 19:51 where the plural něḫālōt summarizes
a list of hereditary lands of the several tribes.

[58]Clifford, Fair Spoken, 150-54. Moses is responsible for restoring the tribes to their ancestral lands:
see Num 32:33-42; 33:50-35:16; Ps 78:55 and Isa 43:16-
20.

Gattung of Isa 49:1-6 as a prophetic commissioning
which, as we saw, was employed for the Elohistic description of Moses' call in Exod 3. However, prophecy
in preexilic Israel had come to be envisioned as international in scope; the prophet was conceived of as
Yahweh's emissary and representative responsible to
administer God's divine government over the nations.[59]
Furthermore, the preexilic cult had conflated the
Mosaic tradition with royal ideology, likening the king
to Moses as the new "shepherd of Jacob" who guides
Israel his flock (Ps 78:71-72).[60] To the king was
attributed international jurisdiction with the nations
as his **nǎḥalâ** (Ps 2:8); he also receives a covenant;
and he vindicates the downtrodden (Ps 72). The servant is thus an amalgam of both royal and prophetic
features, conflated in an office with a universal
jurisdiction common to both antecedents. As representative of Yahweh's sovereignty, he is the mediator of a
"covenant to the peoples."

The person of the servant is also recognizable in
v. 7, at the center of the chiasm formed by the
parallel descriptions of the servant's mission in
vv. 5-6 and v. 8. The one whose form is disfigured,
who is enslaved, yet at the sight of whom kings will
rise in astonishment, is congruent with the despised
servant in 50:4-9 and 52:13-53:12. Regardless of how
the difficult third colon is rendered,[61] there are

---

[59]Jer 1:5,10. See K. Baltzer, "Considerations
Regarding the Office and Calling of the Prophet," HTR
61 (1968), 567-81.

[60]Compare the language in Ps 78:52-55.

[61]See above textual note #1, pp. 267-8. The possible
emendation of **gôy** to **gěwîyâ** in NJV is, of course,
suggested by the servant passage Isa 50:6.

verbal parallels: The verb **bzh** in the passive sense is
used of the servant in Isa 53:3, and if rendered as an
active verb **bōzēh napšô** it is congruent with the
servant's exposing himself to death in 53:12. Evidently the servant is the subject of both the commissioning
in vv. 1-6 and the words of salvation in vv. 7, 8-13.

Westermann proposes transposing v. 7b to the end of
v. 12 in order to restore a single form-critically
complete "proclamation of salvation." This is a form
which often concludes with a clause beginning with
lĕmaᶜan and stating purpose or import of God's saving
act.[62] Westermann's emendation is unacceptable on
grounds of prosody: v. 7 is distinguished by 1:b meter
while vv. 8-12 are in balanced 1:1 meter throughout.
Furthermore, the last clause of v. 7b, the one which
begins with **lĕmaᶜan**, need not be at the conclusion of
the prophet's compositional units as they have been
defined here.   Such clauses can also occur in the
middle of several units, e.g. the Cyrus oracle.   We
note that the form of v. 7 is consciously constructed
to match that of vv. 22-23 which describes with much
the same vocabulary kings and princes coming to honor
Zion.   Both v. 7 and vv. 22-23 end with parallel recognition formulae which declare that through the nations'
homage Israel will come to recognize Yahweh's gracious
favor, yet neither of these sections comes at the
conclusion of its respective movement in what we consider to be a diptych.   If the structure of vv. 7-12(13)
deviates from the ideal expected by the form critic,
this may be due to its participation in the larger
rhetorical structure of the chapter.

---

[62]Westermann, 213-14.

Taking vv. 1-13 as a unity, we notice that v. 7
marks the center of a chiastic structure. It is framed
by side-panels of equal length, 25 and 24 cola respectively. The distant (mē-rāḥôq) coastlands (v. 1) form
an inclusio with the distant (mē-rāḥôq) lands from
which the exiles return in v. 12 accompanied by the
rejoicing of all creation in v. 13. Verses 6 and 8a
immediately adjacent to v. 7 frame it in a chiasm by
repetition of yĕšûʿātî/yĕšûʿâ and the pair lĕ-'ôr gôyîm
and li-bĕrît ʿām; they both refer to the international
scope of Yahweh's salvation. These are in turn sur-
rounded by infinitival clauses describing the recon-
stitution of Israel in vv. 5 and 9-10. Thus verse 7 is
purposely highlighted as the centerpiece of vv. 1-13,
and the image of kings bowing down to the servant/
Israel is the climax of both the servant's mission in
vv. 1-6 and the repatriation of the exiles in vv. 8-12.
Recognition of this chiastic structure obviates the
need to rearrange and transpose these verses as has
been the practice of so many exegetes.

The structure of 49:1-13 thus highlights the nations
as the context for the servant's mission. The logic of
the chiastic structure calls for interpretation not by
a sequential reading of the text, but rather by a
chiastic reading from the outside to the center. The
nations or their representatives first witness the
announcement of the servant's vocation in the divine
council (vv. 1-6), and then they hear God tell his
servant that his mission is to reestablish Israel on
its land (v. 5) and to administer his salvation to the
ends of the earth (v. 6). In the corresponding second
half God also helps the servant (v. 8a) and appoints
him to the mission of gathering the exiles of Israel
from the distant nations (v. 12). He will likewise

reestablish all the nations in their lands as a
"covenant to the peoples." Through all this God's
promise to the servant in v. 7 will be fulfilled: kings
and princes will prostrate themselves before one who
had once been a lowly slave.

Corresponding to 49:1-13 is the second half of the
chapter, a large chiastic construction in five symmetrical subunits,63 which gives comfort to Zion. Zion's
restoration in vv. 19-21 is at the center of the
chiasm; it contrasts Zion's former bereavement
(sikkulâ) with her new-found prosperity and describes
Zion's astonishment at the reunion with her children.
It is framed by outer stanzas which are each disputations: the first disputing with the lament that God has
forgotten Zion (vv. 14-16), the last disputing the
proverb that captives cannot be taken from the mighty
(vv. 24-26). Inside these disputations are parallel
depictions of the exiles returning to Zion: the first
as a consequence of God's remembrance (vv. 17-18), the
second supported by a pilgrimage of the nations
(vv. 22-23). They each use familial terms, images of
clothing or carrying, and the verb nś'. In the first
(vv. 17-18) Zion lifts up (śě'î) her eyes and is
depicted as a bride adorning herself with exiles as
ornaments. In the second (vv. 22-23) Yahweh lifts
('eśśa') his hand and the exiles come, carried
(nāśě'û) by kings and princesses who are called
"foster fathers" and "wet nurses." In this half of
chapter 49, Zion, the place of Yahweh's sanctuary,
stands at the center. The actions of Yahweh to remember and restore the exiles in the first half of the
chiasm are matched by the actions of the nations who

63Of 9, 7, 14, 11, and 12 cola, respectively.

release their captives and carry the exiles on their
shoulders in the second half. The nations are serve
Yahweh's sovereign will by restoring the exiles to
Zion.[64]

These two chiastic structures in vv. 1-13 and 14-26
are related in structure and theme. The naked opening
lament in v. 14 does not open a new compositional unit,
but presumes the prior words of promise. Clifford has
noted this abrupt opening, and also the balance between
49:1-13 and 49:14-26 as complementary halves of equal
length, of 57 and 53 cola respectively.[65] To further
establish the chapter's unity we shall adduce other
connections and parallels between vv. 1-13 and 14-26.

We have already noted that the view outward towards
the nations forms an inclusio between vv. 1 and 26b.
Besides verbal repetition of be*ṭen*, '*ēlleh*, *šōmēmôt*/
šōmamtîk, *ṣē'û*/*yēṣē'û*, *mĕlākîm*, *śārîm*/*śārôtêhem* and
yištaḥăwû, the two halves evince a parallel rhetorical
development. Indeed, the career of the servant from
the womb to his leading the exiles home and the career
of Zion from the womb to the ingathering of her children are remarkably parallel; the servant and Zion may
be likened to the <u>yang</u> and <u>yin</u>, masculine and feminine
aspects of a single redemptive plan. The careers of
both begin in the womb (vv. 1, 15); they both complain
that they are weak or abandoned (vv. 4,14); in response
Yahweh gives one the vocation of the servant who will
gather and reestablish the tribes of Israel on their
land (v. 5-6), and the other is reassured that her
walls will be rebuilt (vv. 16-17) and that the exiles

[64]Cf. God's command of the divine council and Cyrus
to restore Israel in 45:12-13.

[65]Clifford, 151.

will be gathered to her (v. 18). There is reciprocal
movement: in vv. 8-9 the exiles come out (ṣēʾû) from
prison and from darkness, and in vv. 17-18 conversely
Zion's destroyers go out from her (yēṣēʾû) and she can
look up to see the exiles returning. Yahweh lifts up
(yĕrûmûn) his highway to facilitate the exile's travel
(v. 11); likewise he lifts (ʾārîm) his banner and the
exiles return, ferried by rulers of the nations (v.
22). A threefold repetition of ʾēlleh denotes the
exiles as they come forth from all corners of the earth
(v. 12), and the same word is again repeated three
times as Zion in astonishment marvels at her children
(ʾēlleh) and asks from whence they have come (v. 21).[66]
The pivotal v. 7 links with two different verses in the
second half of the chapter. Like its counterpart at
the center of the second chiasm (vv. 19-21), it recalls
the present humiliation of the servant (there Zion) in
order to contrast this with his future exaltation, and
likewise it differs from its context by being cast in
1:b meter. It also parallels and repeats the vocabulary
of vv. 22-23a where kings and princesses bow down
before Zion and where, by this homage, Israel and Zion
recognize that Yahweh is faithful and has chosen them
(vv. 7b, 23b). Finally, each half of the chapter concludes with universal recognition by all nature (v. 13)
and by all flesh (v. 26b). It should be noted that the
internal chiasms within vv. 1-13 and 14-26 necessitate
only minor adjustments to the larger structural linkages between them. The parallel structure pervading
the entire chapter is diagrammed in Table 8.

---

[66]Deutero-Isaiah uses three-fold repetition of the
verb ʾmr and the particle ha- to link the sections of
the Cyrus oracle. See above, pp. 201-203.

TABLE 8: The Structure of Isa 49

chiasm	parallel	parallel	chiasm

```
  vv. 1-6      25 cola   | 9 cola      vv. 14-16
Plaint   --  I am exhausted| Has  God  forgotten  Zion?
Answer--You are my servant | Zion  is  not  forgotten

             beṭen | ben biṭnāh
Address to the nations

mē-rāḥôq                   | 7 cola      vv. 17-18
                           |        Zion lifts eyes
  Regather Israel          | Exiles gather      śĕ'û
  lĕ-hāqîm       le'ĕsop   | niqbĕṣû            Bride
  Salvation to the nations |    Zion wears exiles
  nĕtattîkā lĕ-'ôr gôyîm   |        as adornment
  yĕśûᶜātî

     v. 7       8 cola     | 14 cola     vv. 19-21
         From humiliation | From devastation
                to glory  | to prosperity
          1:b::1:b meter  | 1:b::1:b meter

                          | 11 cola     vv. 22-23
          Rulers bow down | Rulers bow down
                 mĕlākîm  | mĕlākîm
                  śārîm   | śārôtêhem
               yištaḥăwû  | yištaḥăwû
          Because Yahweh  | That Israel might
          has chosen you  | might know Yahweh

    vv. 8-13    24 cola    |         Yahweh lifts hand
                          |               'eśśā'
yĕśûᶜâ                    |         Foster father
'etteněkā li-brît ᶜam     |               Wet nurse
Restore desolate lands    |       Rulers carry exiles
lĕ-hāqîm      šōmēmôt | šōmamtîk        on shoulder
Lead out prisoners        |               nāśĕ'û
          Yahweh lifts    | Yahweh lifts
          his highway     | his banner
          yĕrûmûn         | 'ārîm

    these come from afar | From whence come these?
         'ēlleh (3x) | 'ēlleh (3x)
mē-rāḥôq

                          | 12 cola     vv. 24-26
                          | Plaint -- Can anyone rescue
                          |       prey from the strong?
                          | Answer--Prey will  be taken
Nature rejoices . . . . . | All flesh will know Yahweh
```

Our view of the chiastic and parallel structure of
chapter 49 has several exegetical implications. First
of all, the servant's exaltation is continuous with
Zion's glorification.[67] The corresponding centers of
the two chiasms are the servant's elevation from
slavery to glory before the nations (v. 7) and Zion's
restoration from an uninhabited ruin to a thriving
metropolis (vv. 19-21). Deutero-Isaiah asserted that
Israel in exile remained God's servant in spite of the
destruction of the temple, the visible manifestation of
his presence. The absence of a temple did not result
in God's abandonment of Israel. On the contrary,
Israel the servant of Yahweh was continuous with the
old temple as the recipient of Yahweh's favor in exile,
and his mission was necessarily oriented toward the
restoration of Zion as Yahweh's abode.

Second, since the restoration of Israel is primarily
envisioned as a return to its land, this mission to
Israel is no impediment to a collective interpretation
of the servant, understood as Israel in exile. The
phrase "to restore the tribes of Israel" in its context
chiastically opposite "to apportion the desolate ancestral lands" refers to the specific task of restoring
the exiles to their homelands. "Tribes" in v. 6 has the
connotation of the people's ancestral inheritances
which trace back to the period of the tribal league.
The mission of returning to the land is further specified by the parallel passages depicting the exiles'
processional return (vv. 9-12, 22-23) and by the juxta-

---

[67]This insight has been noted and then taken up into
the rather extreme hypothesis that the servant is himself Zion. See Leland E. Wilshire, "The Servant-City:
A New Interpretation of the 'Servant of the Lord' in
the Servant Songs of Deutero-Isaiah," JBL 94 (1975)
356-67.

position of the servant's mission with the repeopling
of Zion. The servant as Israel can and does have a
mission to Israel and a difficult one: to go out from
Babylon and make the hazardous journey back to the
land, thereby at once restoring the "tribes" and
repopulating Zion.

Third, the role of the nations in assisting the
return of the exiles at Yahweh's command illuminates
the interpretation of the servant's struggle in 49:4
and the expansion of his jurisdiction from Israel to
the nations in v. 6. The issue is not Israel's rejection and persecution of the servant who then goes out,
like Paul, to convert the gentiles. Rather the problem
is expressed in the lament in v. 24, "Can spoil be
taken from the mighty?" A mission to restore Israel to
its land is well-nigh impossible in exile, a situation
where foreign powers rule and Israel is of no consequence. As vv. 14-26 make clear, it is through participation by the gentile nations that God's purpose to
restore Zion can be fulfilled. The servant has run up
against the wall of Israel's impotence (v. 4), and
hence God expands the servant's jurisdiction to the
gentiles (v. 6) and gives him authority to reapportion
the land (v. 8), to order release of the prisoners
(v. 9), and to compel them to permit the exiles to
emigrate (v. 12). Not only is God's authority sufficient to suspend any countervailing claims of worldly
governments, but furthermore, God will defeat any
opposition to his will (vv. 25-26) and commands kings
to assist in Israel's restoration (vv. 22-23).

This exegesis recognizes that the primary recipient
of salvation is Israel, and that the major purpose for
the servant's international authority and exaltation as
a "light" is to bring Israel home to Zion. Neverthe-

less, we affirm that the servant's jurisdiction and
Yahweh's salvation necessarily extends to the nations.
While the first consequence of Yahweh's victory is the
liberation of Israel and the restoration of Zion, the
oppressed and exiles of all nations could also return
to their inheritances (v. 8). The nations do not come
and give homage to Zion and to Yahweh's servant for
nought. Having accepted Yahweh's lordship and assisted
in Israel's restoration, they too will know the peace,
justice and bounty of Yahweh's rule.

4. Isa 52:13-53:12: "We," the "Many," and the Nations

a. Text and Structure

We turn now to Isa 52:13-53:12, and in particular we
wish to explore the role of the nations. They appear
in discussions of the identity of the group(s) denoted
ambiguously by "we" and "the many" who had formerly
spurned the servant but who have come to honor him and
recognize that he has borne their punishment and effec-
ted their healing. The text bristles with difficulties, a full treatment of which would be a monograph in
itself. Here we only have space for a brief discussion
and justification of our translation.

52:13-15

```
Behold, my servant prospers,                                    6
    [  ]ᵃ he is lifted up and highly exalted.                   6
[  ]ᵇ Many are astonished at him,ᶜ [  ]ᵈ                        7
    [  ]ᵉ many nations are perturbedᶠ at him;                   9
    kings cover their mouths.                                   8
For what was not told them they have seen,                      8
    what they never heard they recognize.                       8
                                            1:1::1:1:1::1:1
```

53:1-3

Who can believe what we have heard?	9
to whom is the arm of Yahweh revealed?	9
He grew up like a pale shoot,[g]	7
like a root out of dry ground.	7

1:1::1:1

He had [ ][h] no stature that we should notice him,	8
no beauty that we should desire him,	8
<So marred[i] and inhuman his appearance,	7
his features unrecognizable as a man's.>[j]	7

1:1::1:1

Despised, shunned[k] by people,	7
a man in pain, visited[l] by sickness.	8
As one who hides his face from us,[m]	8
despised,[n] and we took no account of him.	8

1:1::1:1

53:4-6

Surely our sicknesses he bore,	9
and our pains[o] he carried.	9
We accounted him stricken,	9
smitten by God and afflicted.	9
But he was wounded for our transgressions,	9
crushed for our offenses.	9
The punishment that makes us whole was upon him,	8
by his stripes we are healed.	9

1:1::1:1::1:1::1:1

All we like sheep have gone astray,	8
turning each to his own way;	7
But Yahweh has laid upon him	5
the iniquity of us all.	5

1:1::b:b

53:7-9

He was oppressed and afflicted,[p] [ ][q]	6
like a lamb led to the slaughter,[r]	6
Like a ewe before the shearer,[s]	7
he was dumb[t] and opened not his mouth.	7

1:1::1:1

Arrested and convicted, he was taken away,	7
of his peers,[u] who considered it?	7
For he was cut off from the land of the living,	7
fatally[v] struck down for the sins of his people.	8

1:1::1:1

```
They madeʷ his grave with the wicked,                          8
    and with the demons his tomb;ˣ                             8
Though he had done no violence,                                6
    and there was no deceit in his mouth.                      6
                                                      1:1::1:1
```

53:10-11a

```
But Yahweh was pleased that they crushed him, [    ]ʸ          7
    that he even madeᶻ himself into a sin-offering.            7
He will see descendants, live a long life,                    7
    the will of God will prosper in his hands.                8
From his anguish he will see deliv[eran]ce,ᵃᵃ                  8
    from his [mi]sery, vindica<tion>.                          7
                                              1:1::1:1::1:1
```

53:11b-12

```
My servant stands acquittedᵇᵇ before the many;                7
    it is their offenses that he has borne.                   7
Therefore I grant him a portion with the many,                9
    with the mighty he will divide the spoil.                 9
Because he exposed himself to death,                          7
    let himself be counted among transgressors.               7
He bore the sins of the many,                                 6
    interceded for their transgressions.ᶜᶜ                    6
                                          1:1::1:1::1:1::1:1
```

TEXTUAL NOTES

[a]MT **yārûm** is lacking in G and is metrically excessive. It may be a variant of **niśśā'**.

[b]Omit **ka'ăšer** as a prosaizing particle.

[c]MT **ᶜālêkā**; emend to **ᶜālâw** with Syr, Targ.

[d]The following bicolon of MT was transposed from
53:2, where it belongs.

[e]Omit **kēn** as a prosaizing particle.

[f]MT **yazzeh**, "to sprinkle," while it agrees with the
idea of priestly absolution of the sins of the many in
53:12, would have no parallel in its bicolon. The

Vorlage of G θαυμάσονται is difficult to specify, but
the supposition of a hapax **nzh** "to leap" based upon the
Arabic is less compelling than the view of Moore,
followed by Torrey and North, of a textual corruption
of **yirgĕzû**.[68] Such a corruption is explained most
easily as a haplography of *y[rg]zw **gwym rbym**. However,
the line then appears to be metrically excessive, and
one might posit an additional dittography of **ᶜālāw**.
Alternatively, MT could also be generated by metathesis: *yrgzw **rbym** > *yz **gwy rbym** > yzh **gwym rbym**. In
any solution **rabbîm**, the catchword of the framework,
must be retained.

gWe posit **lābān** as an emendation for MT **lĕpānāw**.
Most emend to **lĕpānênû**, but we are looking for some
word describing his stunted growth parallel to "out of
dry ground" which **yônēq** by itself does not convey. On
whiteness as a mark of diseased plants, see Joel 1:7;
Lev 13. Other, inferior, suggestions include **lō' yāpeh**
(Volz) and **bĕḥārābâ** (Mowinckel).

hMT, G: **lō' tō'ar lô wĕ-lō' hādār**; 1QIsa[a]: **lō' tō'ar
lô wĕ-lō' hādār lô**; all show the conflation of two
variants **lō' tō'ar lô** and **lō' hādār lô**. Since **tō'ar** is
repeated below, **hādār** is probably original.

iMT **mišḥat** is a double reading of the hophal and
niphal participles **mošḥat** and **nišḥat**.

jWe omit the prosaizing particle **kēn** and transpose
the bicolon from 52:14b.

68G.F. Moore, "On **yzh** in Isaiah LII. 15," JBL 9
(1890) 216-222; Torrey, The Second Isaiah, 416; North,
Suffering Servant, 123.

[k]ḥǎdal should be taken in a passive sense with nibzeh, pace Thomas.[69]

[l]Where MT reads a passive participle yadûᶜ, 1QIsaᵃ, G and Syr. read an active participle wywdᶜ and 1QIsaᵇ has wydᶜ, an active verb. Thomas's extreme proposal of a second root ydᶜ meaning "to be submissive,"[70] is unwarranted, since the prosody sets yadûᶜ in parallel with ḥǎšabnûhû in the same quatrain. The passive verb indicates the sufferer's passivity, while sickness is actively visiting and "knowing" him.

[m]This colon is ambiguous; there is a question as to who is its subject. Do men hide their faces from him, or does he hide his face from us? Clifford notes the latter to be appropriate as the gesture of a leper.[71]

[n]1QIsaᵃ nibzēhû lō... "We despised him; we took no account of him" differs from MT nibzeh wě-lō' only in the word division. The consistent passive verbs favor MT.

[o]Read a feminine plural mak'ōb<ôt>ênû (cf. v. 3a) for improved meter.

[p]MT niggaś wě-hû' naᶜǎneh reads a perfect followed by a participial phrase. We emend with BHS to niggōś hû' wě-naᶜǎnâ by moving the wāw in front of the second verb, in which case the first verb should be pointed as an infinitive absolute, the second as a perfect.

---

[69]D.W. Thomas, "A Consideration of Isaiah LIII in the Light of Recent Textual and Philological Study," ETL 44 (1968) 82.

[70]Thomas, 82-83.

[71]Clifford, Fair Spoken, 174 n. 3.

qMT lō' yiptaḥ pîw is repeated at the end of v. 7. Most exegetes who see this repetition as a conflation remove the second of these, but the meter rather requires that the first be deleted, revealing a balanced quatrain. The error is simple to explain: The scribe's eye skipped ahead from naᶜănâ which he had just finished writing to the aurally similar ne'ĕlāmâ, and then he wrote lō' yiptaḥ pîw. He then realized his mistake, scratched out these words, and continued with kaś-śeh..., but his erasure was not complete. Then a later scribe working from that manuscript copied the partially erased words as part of the text.

rMT laṭ-ṭebaḥ; 1QIsaᵃ,ᵇ read the infinitive lṭbwḥ.

sOmit the suffix on MT gōzĕzêhā metri causa.

tWe read MT ne'ĕlāmâ as a masculine verb and place it in the second colon of the bicolon. This colon with its pair of verbs is parallel to the opening colon of v. 7 with its pair of verbs, with alliteration of naᶜănâ and ne'ĕlām.

uThere is dipute whether dōrô refers to "his generation" in the sense of his peers, or "his fate" or future. Those who support the latter meaning cite Akk. dûrum, "condition," and Arab daur, "time."[72] But an extrabiblical parallel supporting the first alternative is Phon. dōr meaning "family circle," "assembly" as attested on the Arslan Tash incantation text. This meaning of dōrô is appropriate as a parallel to ᶜammô (as emended) in the second half of the verse.

vFor this difficult colon, our rendering mip-pešaᶜ ᶜammô nuggaᶜ lam-māwe<t> is based upon 1QIsaᵃ mpšᶜ ᶜmw

---

[72]Thomas, 84.

nwg^c lmw and G ἤχθη εἰς θάνατον rather than MT
mip-pesa^{c c}ammî nega^c lāmô. MT ^cammî cannot be correct
since the speakers are plural. G could be paraphras-
tic, and lāmô could be the agent of the passive verb
nugga^c. However, lam-māwet is a more suitable parallel
to mē-'ereṣ ḥayyîm, and the phrase is repeated in
v. 12.

^WReading an impersonal plural yittĕnû with 1QIsa^a;
MT has yittēn.

^x1QIsa^a has w^cm ^cšyrym bwmtw with some erasures.
^cim is parallel to MT 'et. It has been suggested that
1QIsa^a bômatô may be reading a Phoenician loanword for
Heb. bāmâ, "funerary mound." MT bĕmōtāw, "in his
deaths" should in any case be emended to bĕmātô "his
tomb" with the support of both G and 1QIsa^a.

MT ^cāšîr "the rich" cannot be a correct parallel to
"the wicked" in the previous colon. Although the rich
are also often condemned as wicked in prophetic texts,
their graves were presumably well furnished tombs,
while this is a depiction of the servant's dishonorable
burial in a common grave among criminals. The emendation to śĕ^cîrîm, "goat demons," is supported by the
parallel 2 Kgs 23:8 bāmôt haš-śĕ^cārîm, "high places at
the gates." There a reasonable emendation (BHS) would
repoint to bāmôt haś-śĕ^cîrîm which hypothetically
refers to funerary mounds where a cult to appease the
spirits of the dead was practiced.[73] This requires
only a metathesis; the other common emendation to ^cōśê
ra^c is textually more difficult, and it would not
easily have been corrupted to MT.

---

[73]Thomas, 84-85.

YMT heḇĕlî is metrically excessive; 1QIsa^a reads a
piel **wyḥllhw**. Cross suggests that two piel infinitives
dakkĕ'ô and ḥallĕlô were ancient variants that have
become conflate (cf. vv. 4b-5). MT then reinterpreted
the second verb either as a substantive (consonantal
text) "with sickness" (so G, Vg) or, as pointed, a
hiphil "he made him sick." Our choice of **dakkĕ'ô** over
ḥallĕlô as original is quite arbitrary.

ZMT **'im tāśîm**, with a transitive verb and napśô as
its subject, does not fit as a parallel for the first
colon if Yahweh is the subject of **dakkĕ'ô**. But no
emendation, such as to **'ĕmet śām** "truly he [Yahweh]
made him a sin offering," or to **tūśam** "his self becomes
a sin-offering," is compelling. Such emendations flat-
ten the sense of the text, which in MT expresses the
idea of the servant's voluntary self-sacrifice, an idea
also expressed in v. 12b. Rather, we retain MT and
render the infinitive **dakkĕ'ô** of the first colon as an
impersonal passive, congruent to the meaning of the
adjective **dakkā'**, "crushed" or "contrite." Then the
two cola become consistent. Yahweh's pleasure is not
in crushing the servant, but in the servant's afflic-
tion from whatever source, which he bears without
resistance, and which God in turn is pleased to accept
as a sin-offering. The **'im** is pleonastic.

aaMT reads mē-^camal napśô yir'eh yiśbā^c bĕ-da^ctô and
is perhaps irretrievably corrupt. G, 1QIsa^a,b read **'ôr**
after **yir'eh** as its direct object, but **'ôr** could well
be a secondary formation from **yir'eh**. The image of
seeing light and being satisfied in his knowledge
hardly coheres within itself or with its context. The
following colon, which is normally rendered as beginning with the repeated **yaṣdîq ṣaddîq**, "The Righteous

One justifes," is metrically excessive. Our solution
begins by transposing these words and moving ṣaddîq
back into this bicolon as ṣĕdāqâ. Deleting the bêt
from yiśbaᶜ gives yēšaᶜ, a good parallel to ṣĕdāqâ.
bĕ-daᶜtô is perhaps a corruption of bĕ-raᶜātô by dālet/
rēš confusion; it is a suitable complement to mē-ᶜamal
napšô. The result is a balanced bicolon:

mē-ᶜamal napšô yir'eh yēš[]aᶜ
bĕ-rāᶜātô ṣĕdāq<â>

ᵇᵇThough often translated "my servant shall procure
righteousness for many," yaṣdîq as a transitive verb
"to declare just" takes a direct object, not the preposition lĕ. Hence with Mowinckel we translate as an
internal causative with ᶜabdî as the object: "my
servant stands acquitted before the many."

ᶜᶜWhere MT has pōšĕᶜîm, G and 1QIsaᵇ have pišᶜêhem
coordinate with ḥeṭ'ê rabbîm. This emendation to
pišᶜām, suggested by BHS, could generate both texts.

Most exegetes take Isa 52:13-53:12 to be a formal
unit.[74] It has a recognizable chiastic structure,
familiar in so many of Deutero-Isaiah's oracles: a
framework of divine speech in 52:13-15, 53:11b-12 and a
central report about the servant's suffering and exal-

---

[74]Except a minority who delimit the unit to chapter
53 alone. R.N. Whybray (Thanksgiving for a Liberated
Prophet: An Interpretation of Isaiah 53, JSOTS 4 [Shef-
field, JSOT, 1978] 109-134) wants to fit the oracle
into the procrustean bed of a particular genre, the
psalm of thanksgiving. Orlinsky ("The So-called
'Servant,'" 17-23) sees the portrayal of kings and
nations astonished before the servant of 52:13-15 as
depicting the servant-Israel which conflicts with his
individual interpretation of the servant in chapter 53.

tation in 53:1-11a.[75] The two halves of the framework
are balanced with 7 and 8 cola respectively and are
linked by rhetorical features. There is the typical
three-fold repetition,[76] here of terms for the nations:
rabbîm, (gôyîm) rabbîm, and mĕlākîm in 52:13-15;
rabbîm, rabbîm, and ᶜăṣûmîm in 53:11b-12. The two
halves each open with similar phrases where Yahweh
announces his servant's vindication with direct
address: hinnēh yaśkîl ᶜabdî (52:13) and yaṣdîq ᶜabdî
(53:11b), and then describe the servant's new high
stature among the nations: they are astonished (52:13),
and the servant may divide spoil among them (53:12).
However, the concluding stanza of the central section
beginning in v. 10 merges almost imperceptibly into the
second half of the framework, and we must concede that
the division at v. 11b is not entirely certain.[77]
Verses 11b-12 resume the divine speech of 52:13-15 (in
vv. 10-11a the speaker is the prophet) and contain all
the rhetorical features forming an inclusio with the
opening stanzas. Yet the motif of God exalting the
servant after he had fulfilled his role in the divine
plan as a sin-offering continues throughout vv. 10-13,
as does the thrice-repeated key word napšô.

---

[75]Westermann, 255-58; Begrich, Studien, 62-65.

[76]See above, pp. 201-203.

[77]Thus Begrich and Westermann begin the conclusion
of the framework at v. 11b; Muilenberg (IB 5, 614),
Torrey (The Second Isaiah, 412) and BHS at v. 10; North
(The Second Isaiah, 234) and Bonnard (Le Second Isaȉe,
269) at v. 11; Kaiser (Der Königliche Knecht, 87) and
Mettinger (A Farewell to the Servant Songs, 38) at v. 7
on the basis of the first person singular suffix on
ᶜammî in v. 8.

The central portion, 53:1-11a, is generally derived
from the genre of the psalm of thanksgiving.[78] It has
a balanced structure of four distinct stanzas: the
first three each of 12 cola and a concluding short
stanza of 6 cola.[79] The stanzas each have rhetorical
features emphasizing its distinct theme. Their opening
bicola (vv. 1, 4 and 7) contain pronouns designating
the principal characters and stating the theme of what
follows.

In v. 1 **mî** (bis) poses the question "who can
believe" and introduces an account of the servant's
humiliation. The lack of recognition by "we," the
speakers in this stanza, is emphasized by the inclusio
formed by the opening rhetorical question "Who can
believe what we have heard?" (v. 1) which assumes a
negative response, and the closing reply "we took no
account of him" (v. 3b). The spurning of the servant
is highlighted by repetition of the verb **nibzeh,** of
words denoting human appearance, and of words for
humanity and human society with the preposition **min**

---

[78]Westermann, 255-58; Begrich, 62-65; Cf. Whybray,
110-115. Form critics recognize that psalms of this
genre contain descriptions of the worshipper's former
distress which have many points of contact with the
individual psalm of lamentation, another genre which is
also relevant for the interpretation of Isa 53. Others
including Elliger (Deuterojesaja in seinem Verhältnis
zu Tritojesaja, 19), Fohrer (Das Buch Jesaja, 160), von
Rad (Old Testament Theology, II, 255f), etc. have
defined the chapter as a "prophetic liturgy." Baltzer,
("Zur formgeschichtlichen Bestimmung," 40-41) who views
all the servant songs together as an extended
biography, sees the fourth song as the narrative of a
heavenly trial at which the servant, having died, is
rehabilitated.

[79]The short concluding stanza is a typical Deutero-
Isaianic feature. Cf. Isa 46; 55; 51:1-8.

used in a separative sense. The language of disfigure-
ment suggests a depiction of leprosy, although, as in
psalms of lament, all these images of suffering should
be taken only figuratively.

The second stanza opens with the characteristic
particle of confession 'ākēn (v. 4), a rejoinder to the
rhetorical interrogative mî in the first stanza; repetition of ḥăšabnûhû further reinforces the continuity
between them. In v. 4 hû' and the first person plural
pronominal suffix (alternating with 'ănaḥnû and the
third person singular suffix) are subject and object of
the confession "Surely he has borne our sicknesses"
which sets the theme for what follows. In this confession the element of recognition is highlighted by
repetition of kullānû and five first person plural
pronominal suffixes on nouns denoting "our" punishment
or sin. "We" are culpable, and "we" recognize that the
servant has suffered in our stead. Furthermore, "we"
make a remarkable admission, that his suffering has
become the cause of our healing.

The third stanza opens in v. 7 with hû', the
expressed subject of an extended description of the
servant's suffering in the third person. Continuing
the metaphor of sheep which began in v. 6, it points to
the servant's solidarity with "we," the speakers of the
previous stanza: "we like sheep have gone astray..."
becomes "he... like a lamb led to the slaughter." This
report depicts the servant's oppression in terms of a
legal proceedings: arrest, trial, imprisonment, execu-
tion, and burial. It emphasizes his humble and passive
acceptance of his fate by the repeated mention of his
silence ("he opened not his mouth," "there was no
deceit in his mouth") and by a string of seven passive

verbs.[80]

In the concluding short stanza Yahweh is identified
as the subject (v. 10). Here is a prophetic word
giving God's judgment upon the servant, in whose
travail God takes pleasure (ḥāpēṣ), and consequently
God will give him a successful future. While the
servant had been condemned by a wordly court, God
declares him innocent (yaṣdîq); he has suffered for the
crimes of others. Furthermore, by wordplay on **yhwh
ḥāpēṣ** and **ḥēpeṣ yhwh** the prophet inverts the image and
gives the servant's suffering significance for the
success of God's own purposes.

We have shown that the structure of the fourth
servant song follows the artistic canons typical of
Deutero-Isaiah. Its envelope construction is similar
to the Cyrus oracle, Isa 44:6-23 and 45:14-25, and its
stanzaic structure in the central section is consistent
with the stanzaic form of chapters 46 and 55. In
Deutero-Isaiah's other oracles with an envelope construction, we have seen that the framework and the
central section are interdependent, and the framework
often provides a setting[81] or specification[82] for the
central oracle. Similarly, we will argue that mention
of "nations" and "kings" in the framework of the fourth

---

[80]Eight if **yittěnû** (**way-yittēn** in MT) is rendered
yuttan; it describes the actions of unnamed persons
upon the servant and hence has a passive sense.

[81]E.g., 44:6-8,21-22 sets the satire against idolatry in a trial of the nations; 45:14-17,23-25 sets a
trial speech within an anticipated universal confession
of the nations at Zion.

[82]The framework of the Cyrus oracle specifies the
central act of Cyrus which is only hinted at by the
central section, namely the rebuilding of Zion.

servant song gives specificity to "we," the chorus in
the central section. The framework also repeats the
central section's notices of the servant's vindication
and his bearing the sins of others. From this description of the structure of the song, we turn to two
problems involving the servant's relationship to the
nations, namely the notices that he has borne their
sins (53:12) and the connection between the nations and
the chorus who confesses its indebtedness to the
servant in 53:1-6.

b. The Servant's Intercession for the Many
      There is little dispute that in the framework
(52:13-15; 53:11b-12), the "many,"[83] paralleled by
"many nations," "kings" and "the mighty," are the
nations.[84] They are astonished at the servant's sudden

---

[83]Elsewhere in the OT the term **rabbîm** is often
coupled with **Cammim** or **gôyîm** and denotes the nations;
cf. Isa 2:2-4/Mic 4:1-5; Deut 7:1,17; 15:6; 28:12; Pss
89:51; 135:10; Jer 22:8; 25:14; 27:7; Ezek 3:6; 26:3;
31:6; 32:3; 38:22; 39:27; Mic 4:11,13; 5:6,7; Hab
2:8,10; Zech 2:15; 8:22; etc. **rabbîm** by itself often
indicates an unspecified group of enemies: Jer 20:10;
Pss 3:2-3; 31:14; 55:19; 56:3. An **Cam rab** denotes an
enemy army: Isa 13:4; Ezek 15:9,15,17; 26:7; etc. See
H. W. Hertzberg, "Die 'Abtrünnigen' und die 'Veilen:'
ein Beitrag zu Jesaja 53," Verbannung und Heimkehr:
Beiträge zur Geschichte und Theologie Israels im 6. und
5. Jahrhundert v. Chr., Festschrift Wilhelm Rudolph,
ed. A. Kuschke (Tübingen: JCB Mohr, 1961) 102-03.

[84]So Muilenberg, 617; Blank, 87; Bonnard, 268-69;
Torrey, 416; North, Suffering Servant, 151; Clifford,
Fair Spoken, 176-77; Whybray, Isaiah 40-66, 169;
DeBoer, OTS 11, 112-13. On the other side, Westermann
(p. 259) sees the language of kings and nations as
figurative: "Deutero-Isaiah is thinking of the widespread publicity to be given to the work, but not of
heathen spheres outside Israel." McKenzie (Second

success and recognize in him something they had never heard nor seen. They are also beneficiaries of the servant, who bears their sins and intercedes for their transgressions. The framework by itself gives the servant a universal significance; he bears the sins of the nations and reveals to them the purposes of God which they had not heretofore understood.

What could be the meaning of the servant bearing the sins of the many? In priestly legislation and Ezekiel the term **naśa' cawōn** and its variations often refers to the imputation of guilt or the consequent penalty either for personal sins[85] or for the sins of others, especially for the sins of the fathers.[86] In addition, **naśa' cawōn** refers to the special function of the priest to atone for the sins of the congregation by ritual actions. The priest (and Levite) alone could minister in the sacred precincts of the sanctuary, where common people could not enter under penalty of death, hence by their ministrations they "bear the iniquity" of the congregation by representing them before Yahweh (Num 18:1,23). The "iniquity" of the congregation was represented in a ritual object which the priest wore on his person and carried into the holy place (Exod 28:28). In the performance of the sin offering the priest "bears the iniquity of the congregation" in the sense of making atonement for them, as

---

Isaiah, 132-34) considers "the many" of 52:14 and 53:11,12 to be Israelites and "the many" of 52:15 to be the gentiles; hence the servant only suffers for Israel. His position unacceptably violates the canons of prosody.

[85]Exod 28:43; Lev 5:1,17; 7:18; 17:16; 19:8,17; 20:17,19,20; 22:9,16; 24:15; Num 5:31; 9:13; 18:22,32; 30:16; Ezek 14:10; 23:49; 44:10,12.

[86]Num 14:33-34; Ezek 18:19-20.

in Lev 10:17 where these two phrases are in parallel.
Finally, in the Yom Kippur ritual of the scapegoat (Lev
16:22) the priest transfers the sins of the congregation onto the goat, who is then sent away, removing the
sins into the wilderness.[87]

Deutero-Isaiah has conflated the two older priestly
uses of the term nāśā' ᶜāwōn into a novel notion of
vicarious suffering:[88] on the one hand, to bear iniquity was to be punished for one's sins; on the other
hand, the priest bore the iniquity of others by perfor-
ming ritual actions. The servant suffers undeserved
punishment for crimes he did not commit; therefore if
he is bearing guilt, it is for sins not his own. Enter
the second notion of the priest who bears the iniquity
of the congregation, not by suffering, but nevertheless
by actions labeled by the same term nāśā' ᶜāwōn.
Hence, the servant-Israel's suffering is resignified as
a priestly atonement for the sins of the nations.

On the other hand, von Rad has argued for the
vicarious atonement of the fourth servant song as a
development out of prophecy. The exilic prophets had
come to emphasize the intercessory character of the
prophetic office and the degree to which it entailed
personal suffering.[89] In the confessions of Jeremiah

---

[87]For two valuable word studies, see W. Zimmerli,
"Die Eigenart der prophetischen Rede des Ezechiel," ZAW
66 (1954), 9-12; Whybray Thanksgiving, 31-57.

[88]We do not find any cogency in Whybray's assertion
that vicarious atonement is entirely a Christian imputation foreign to Deutero-Isaiah. He is only correct
insofar as he demonstrates that the notion is without
parallel in the Hebrew Bible. Yet there are several
lines of development which can be traced from earlier
notions of priestly atonement and prophetic intercession to Deutero-Isaiah's notion of vicarious suffering.

[89]von Rad, Old Testament Theology, II, 274-77.

and the symbolic acts of Ezekiel, the prophets' own
suffering was understood to be in solidarity with the
travail of their people. The Deuteronomistic historian
depicted Moses as one who, through prayer, fasting, and
ultimately by his own untimely death outside of the
promised land, took God's wrath against Israel upon
himself. Ezek 4:4-6 specifically uses the term nāśā'
ᶜāwon to refer to Ezekiel's symbolic action of lying on
his right side and then on his left side to represent
the years of suffering of Israel and Judah--a contor-
tion that no doubt entailed considerable pain. His
suffering, while not vicarious atonement, typified the
degree to which the prophetic mission had come to
exemplify the travail of his people.[90]

Yet Isa 53, while perhaps influenced by these
prophetic reflections, is full of the terminology of
its antecedent priestly traditions. It was within the
traditional jurisdiction of prophets to give God's
judgment on the acceptability of priestly rites. Using
the verb ḥpṣ (53:10) the prophets expressed God's
rejection of the sacrifices of the Israelite cult (Hos
6:6; Isa 1:11; Mal 1:10). Conversely, Deutero-Isaiah
proclaims the servant's suffering as a sin-offering
('āšām) that is acceptable to Yahweh (yhwh ḥāpēṣ) as he
bears the iniquity (nāśā' ᶜāwon) of others.[91] Here is
a traditional prophetic ruling on the acceptability of
the community's priestly sacrifice, but now the community, personified as the servant, becomes itself the
sin-offering that brings healing and divine blessing.

---

[90]Cf. Ezek 12:1-6; 24:16-27.

[91]See Paul Hanson, The People Called: The Growth of
Community in the Bible (New York: Harper & Row, in
press) chapter 7.

By a prophetic word, Deutero-Isaiah declares the acceptability of a priestly role for the servant-Israel.

We are left with a difficulty: how can the suffering
of the servant-Israel in exile be translated into any
benefits for the nations? Prophetic intercession as
with Moses derived from his role as Israel's representative before God, but can the servant be described in
similar terms as representing the nations? The
priest's office is more serviceable, since his ritual
actions were efficacious for removing sin because of
his privileged access to God's temple. In relation to
the nations, the servant-Israel also has privileged
access to God, an access soon to be substantiated by
his return to Zion, which was portayed in Israel's
faith as the navel of the world (Ezek 38:12), source of
life-giving waters (Isa 55:1-2), and seat of God's
world government bringing peace to the nations (Isa
2:2-4). There Israel is to administer God's abundance
to the entire earth (Isa 55:1-5).[92] Although the
temple had been destroyed and Israel had gone into
exile, Deutero-Isaiah insisted that Israel was still
God's servant and his chosen people. The servant in
exile is also continuous with the future exaltation of
God's people in Zion, to which he will return. Even
without a standing temple, the servant-Israel was in a
position of intimacy with God and could mediate God's
salvation to the nations (49:7). Hence, in exile, the
servant could act as priest and offer atonement to the
nations, looking to the day when the temple would be
rebuilt, the cosmos be set aright, and healing be
brought to the nations (51:4-5). Thus the grounds for
the servant's office to bear the guilt of the nations

[92]Cf. pp. 222-28.

lie not in his suffering per se, but in the special
efficacy of that suffering by virtue of his special
relationship to God. That special relationship is
to be manifest in God's exaltation of his servant, who
is to have access to the restored temple as priest.
The servant's role as priest to the nations would
become particularly important for Deutero-Isaiah's
disciples in Isa 60-62 (61:6) who sought to implement
the vision of their teacher.93 By royal, prophetic and
priestly designations, the servant encompasses the
entire agency of Yahweh's sovereignty.

c. "We" and the Many: The Chorus in Isa 53:1-6

We now turn to the question of whether the unnamed
chorus, speaking in the first person plural, that confesses their indebtedness to the servant in 53:1ff. is
to be identified with the nations, "the many" of the
framework. Four possibilities for the identity of "we"
in this chorus have been presented. Most commonly "we"
are either the nations as a continuation of the frame-
work94 or Israelite acquaintances of the servant.95
Two recent suggestions are Baltzer's that the chorus is

93Hanson, Dawn of Apocalyptic, 63-4, 67-8, 75.

94Melugin, Formation, 167-8; Torrey, The Second
Isaiah, 416; Muilenberg, IB 5, 619; North, Suffering
Servant, 151; Bonnard, Le Second Isaïe, 269; Blank,
Prophetic Faith, 87; Wright, The Book of Isaiah, 130-
32.

95See Hertzberg, "Die 'Abtrünnigen' und die
'Veilen,'" 96-108; Clifford, Fair Spoken, 178;
McKenzie, Second Isaiah, 133f.; Whybray, Isaiah 40-66,
170-176; Mowinckel, He that Cometh, 199; de Boer, OTS
11, 115; P.-E. Dion, "L'universalisme religieux dans
les différentes couches rédactionelles d'Isaïe 40-55,"
Bib 51 (1970) 177.

constituted by members of the divine council,[96] and Cline's intriguing literary approach that makes a virtue of the poem's ambiguous language.[97]

Rhetorical features argue for the continuity of the speakers in the central section with the kings and the "many" in 52:13-15. There is a smooth transition between 52:15 where the nations recognize what they had not heard (šāmĕ'û) and 53:1 where "we" hear a report (šĕmu'ātēnû).[98] The nations' astonishment is consistent with the speakers' change in attitude from disdain to respect. Repetition of the verbs hitbônānû and ḥāšabnūhû in 52:15, 53:3,4 gives rhetorical support for this connection. Similar rhetorical connections-- repetition of the verbs nāśā', sābal and hipgî'--bind the confession that the servant bears "our" sins in vv. 4-6 with the statement in 53:12 that the servant intercedes for the sins of the many. Otherwise, if the servant bore only the sins of Israel in 53:4-6, then there would be little basis for 53:12. The servant's vicarious atonement for the nations is hardly necessary for his exaltation from contempt (cf. 49:7).

The poem's context in the Deutero-Isaianic corpus also supports an identification of "we" with the nations. In particular 52:15, "what they had not been told they have seen," and 53:1, "To whom has the arm of Yahweh been revealed?" together pick up the conclusion

_____

[96]Baltzer, "Zur formgeschichtlichen Bestimmung," 40-41.

[97]David J.A. Clines, I, He, We and They: A Literary Approach to Isaiah 53, JSOTS 1 (Sheffield: JSOT, 1976).

[98]See North, Suffering Servant, 151. For Westermann (Isaiah 40-66, 260), who recognizes the continuity with the framework, "we" and "the many" are both audiences of Israelites scattered throughout the earth.

of a preceding hymnic passage 52:10, "Yahweh has bared
his holy arm in the sight of all the nations; all the
ends of the earth will see the salvation of our God."
In fact, Melugin identifies the entire song as an
expansion upon 49:7 where kings will see and bow down
before the despised one.[99]

Several arguments have been put forward for identifying the chorus with Israelite compatriots of the
servant, some more compelling than others. As a modified psalm of thanksgiving, it does partake of a genre
which Israelites would sing to celebrate the vindication of one of their own; yet on other occasions
Deutero-Isaiah puts Israelite forms into the mouths of
nations, most notably the confession of faith in Yahweh
in 45:15-17,23-25. The remark that the servant grew up
"before us" (v. 2) would suggest an intimacy with the
speakers, but that reading is itself a questionable
emendation.[100] The notice in v. 8 that he was stricken
for the "sins of his people,"[101] that is the sins of
Israel, suggests that Israel is confessing that "he has
borne our sicknesses..." in vv. 4-6. The confession
"we like sheep have lost our way" appears more appropriate to Israel than to the nations, since only Israel
had known Yahweh in the past. Yet in the trial
speeches all nations are held responsible for recognizing that true allegience is to Yahweh (41:24).

Hertzberg distinguishes two groups, the transgressors (pōšĕᶜîm) and the many (rabbîm). He adduces biblical parallels for identifying the "many," in the

[99]Melugin, Formation, 168.

[100]See above, p. 291 textual note #g.

[101]The argument is much the same if we read with MT
"my people," but see above, pp. 293-4 textual note #v.

framework with the nations,[102] and he relates the term
pešaᶜ in Isa 53:5,8 to the Israelites' own sin on the
basis of usage elsewhere in Deutero-Isaiah.[103]
However, his case is weakened by 53:12 where pôšĕᶜîm
(emended to pišᶜām) and hēṭ' rabbîm are in parallel.
If the text of MT is retained, the two hypothetical
groups pôšĕᶜîm and rabbîm are equated by the prosody.
If emended to pišᶜām, the verse has the root pšᶜ specifically applied to the many, contradicting Hertzberg's
hypothesis. This verse shows rather the standard
parallel usage of ḥaṭṭā't and pešaᶜ, the same parallel
usage as found in 43:27 where they both refer to
Israel's sins. Indeed, the two attestations of ḥāṭā'
outside of the fourth song also refer to Israel and
could hypothetically be the marker of that group if it
were not for 53:12.

The supposition that Isa 52:13-53:12 is a scene in
the divine council is a more fruitful approach. The
divine council, composed of representatives of the
nations, is the setting of the servant passages 42:1-
4,5-9 and 49:1-6,7,8-13. Baltzer points to the lack of
concrete imagery and the fact that in 52:13-15 God is
speaking and giving a report praising the servant
directly to an audience, with any notice of prophetic
mediation suppressed.[104] If this is the narration of a
legal process, then the verdict of acquittal in v. 11b

---

[102]Hertzberg, "Die 'Abtrünnigen' und die 'Vielen',"
98-102. See above, p. 301 n. 83.

[103]The participle pôšēᶜ refers to Israel in Isa 46:8
and 48:8. The root pšᶜ, also attested at 43:25,27,
44:22 and 50:1, in each case refers to the sins of
Israel.

[104]Baltzer, "Zur formgeschichtlichen Bestimmung," 40-41.

is announced by Yahweh after others in the council have
reported on the servant's persecution and death and
have confessed that he had wrongly suffered for the
crimes of others. The address by a chorus in the first
person plural is also typical of scenes in the divine
council.[105]

In this regard, our previous remarks on the setting
of the trial speeches where the prophet has utilized
the divine council as a literary motif become relevant
for Isa 53. In discussing the trial speeches of Isa
41-42, it was noted that the audience for the trial in
the heavenly council, speaking as "we," was a vehicle
to involve Deutero-Isaiah's audience whom the prophet
exhorts against idolatry: "an abomination is he who
chooses you [the pagan gods]" (41:24). The nations and
their gods serve as a virtual audience in order to
convince an actual Israelite audience of claims for
Yahweh's divinity.[106] Then in the trial scene 43:8-13,
Israel is brought forward before the assembled nations
in the divine council and is addressed as the principal
character of the scene. Two levels of meaning were
recognized for these trials before the divine council:
a literal judgment upon the foreign gods and a setting
for the prophet's arguments with those Israelites
attracted to pagan cults.

Similarly, the divine council of the nations as the
literary setting of Isa 52:13-53:12 is meant to be a
vehicle to involve the prophet's audience. The chorus
which confesses the servant's innocence and his having
suffered on their behalf is ostensibly the nations who

---

[105]See above, p. 115 n. 135.

[106]See above, pp. 116, 117-19.

are members of the council. However, Deutero-Isaiah's
actual audience was his fellow Israelites, who would
naturally identify themselves with one of the per-
sonages in the poem, either as "we" in the chorus or as
the servant.107

For Israel which identified itself as the servant,
Isa 53 is a modified thanksgiving psalm celebrating
Israel's imminent release from captivity and repatriation. The confession of the nations becomes, like the
confessions in Isa 45:14-25, an expression of Yahweh's
sovereignty by which he vindicates his wronged and
oppressed people. The nations of the divine council
testify to Israel's innocence and recognize that Israel
as God's servant has suffered on their account and for
their salvation. For Israel the servant of God, this
poem validates her suffering as part of God's plan[108]
and bestows upon her priestly status as the nation who
will give expiation to the multitudes.

However, those Israelites in Deutero-Isaiah's audience who might not recognize themselves in the servant,
for whom the servant was an unreasonable ideal, might
identify themselves as "we." On their account the

---

[107]Clines (I, He, We and They, 59-65) rightly recognizes the ambiguity of "we" and of "he" (the servant)
in the text as the occasion of such a "language event,"
when the world of the poem draws the reader to identify
himself with its personae. However, our analysis is
not broadly hermeneutical, seeking to interpret an
ancient text from the vantage point of the present.
Here we seek only to understand the event of interpretation in its original historical matrix. Deutero-
Isaiah wrote with a purpose for his own people which he
expressed through conscious literary design.

[108]This is Deutero-Isaiah's final answer to the
problem of the righteous sufferer, a different one from
that of Job.

servant is a collective that is less than all Israel--
either a prophetic minority or an "ideal" Israel. The
prophet may have had in mind those apostate Israelites
who had acculturated to Babylonian society, and he
wrote their confession even as he placed it in the
mouths of the nations assembled at the divine council.
The nations function as a foil to challenge this group
among the prophet's Israelite audience; they can recognize themselves as among the nations, "the many," who
have sinned against the servant. As was discussed in
considering the trial speeches, the exiles' Babylonian
context made them sensitive to the opinions of their
gentile neighbors and required Deutero-Isaiah to phrase
his disputes in a universal setting.[109] The same role
for the nations as a virtual audience in order to
convince the acculturated exiles may apply in Isa 53.
If even kings and great nations will recognize and
honor the servant, surely the apostate exiles can do
the same!

The anonymous language used of the servant and of
those making confession in this poem suggests that
Deutero-Isaiah left it to his audience to identify with
either of these roles, depending upon whether they had
held fast to Yahweh and believed in his promised restoration or had assimilated and come to see themselves
as citizens of Babylon. The evident division in the
third song between those who "fear Yahweh" and those
who "set brands alight" (50:10-11) speaks of a time
when Israel could no longer be addressed as a single
entity. Deutero-Isaiah, in the trial speeches and
polemics against idolatry, simiarly addressed an
audience which had partly assimilated to Babylonian

---

[109]See above, pp. 121-22.

culture. Then, his servant, an appellation for Israel
as a whole, was characterized as blind (42:18-20; 43:8)
as the prophet sought to persuade Israel to live up to
her vocation (42:18-43:7; 43:8-44:5; 44:6-23; ch. 46).
Now, as the servant is lifted up to fulfill his vocation, he is idealized to represent the faithful in
Israel, leaving some acculturated Israelites to behold
the servant from a distance.

There was one historical event which would in fact
consolidate such divisions within the exilic community,
forcing the exiles to make a decision for or against
Yahweh's purpose as understood by Deutero-Isaiah. That
event is the immediate literary context of the fourth
servant song (52:11-12), namely the call to return to
Jerusalem following Cyrus's conquest of Babylon.110
The focus of the servant's mission in Isa 49 is to
reconstitute Israel at Zion, and the locus of Israel's
government in 55:1-5 is also Zion. It is to Zion that
nations and kings come to honor the servant in 49:7,
and to Jerusalem they come bearing tribute and making

110Bonnard (Le Second Isaïe) and Stuhlmueller
("Major Transitions") both see such a shift in the
prophet's career between chapters 41-48 and 49-55.
They consider the decisive historical event separating
these chapters to be the fall of Babylon and the consequent opportunity to return to Jerusalem, and they
attribute 49-55 to a period after the return when the
prophet had become discouraged with the lack of response to the initial call to return. While agreeing
that the fall of Babylon was the likely occasion of at
least some of these later chapters, we doubt whether
Deutero-Isaiah remained in Babylon, living in discour-
agement, for long after its fall. The intense and
early activity of Deutero-Isaiah's disciples in Jerusalem, and the probable Deutero-Isaianic authorship of
ch. 34-35, whose bitterness towards Edom is evidence
they were written in Jerusalem, suggests that the prophet, true to his own words, took an early opportunity
to return to Zion.

confession in 45:14; 49:22-23. That the restoration of
the servant results in his repossessing the land is
hinted at by the verbs 'ăḥalleq and yĕḥalleq in v. 12--
God will restore his inheritance among the nations.[111]
Deutero-Isaiah can proclaim the glorification of the
servant because the time was propitious for Israel to
repopulate Zion and minister at the restored temple.

Since the chorus which confesses the servant's
righteousness is ostensibly the nations, those Israelites who would identify themselves with the chorus are
implicitly equated with them. Insensible of the coming
redemption of the servant-Israel in spite of Deutero-
Isaiah's insistent prophecy, they, like the nations in
49:7, will suddenly see and marvel at the servant's
glorification (52:15). This equation in Isa 53 of a
portion of the Israelite audience with the chorus of
the nations reveals a blurring of the distinction
between Israelites and gentiles, a move already anticipated in the trial speeches. Hanson has noted in early
apocalyptic a shift in the axis of moral judgment from
Israel vs. the nations to a moral dualism of the
righteous servant(s) vs. sinners within the Israelite
community.[112] Moral dualism was born of intra-community
conflicts, and it grew more significant than Israelite
nationalism in proportion to the estrangement of the
apocalyptic writers from the power structure of post-
exilic Israel. The dissolution of a nationalistic
concept of salvation in favor of a moral dualism would
also encourage in apocalyptic a universal perspective.

---

[111]See Clifford, Fair Spoken, 181, who has an
admirable sense for place. Cf. Spykerboer, Structure,
176-78.

[112]Hanson, Dawn of Apocalyptic, 150f., 396.

Perhaps this development is presaged by the purposeful
ambiguity of the fourth servant song, also born in a
situation of social conflict.

5. Conclusion: The Servant, Israel, and the Nations

We have chosen to discuss the first, second, and
fourth servant songs because they depict in various
ways the relationship of the servant to the nations.
The first and second songs are not independent oracles
separable from their contexts, but should be viewed as
continuous with the compositional units of which they
are constituent subunits. The first song, part of the
unit 41:1-42:17, is juxtaposed with a parallel passage
reassuring the servant-Israel (41:8-13), thereby supporting the collective identity for the servant. The
servant's universal scope and běrît ʿam is related to
the democratized Davidic covenant of Isa 55:3-5, especially since the first song's structure and place in
its compositional unit corresponds to the anointing of
the Davidic king in antecedent texts from the royal
cult (cf. Pss 2, 89). Similarly, Isa 49:1-6 occurs
within the compositional unit 49:1-26. There the grant
of international authority to the servant and his use
of that authority to liberate the prisoners and restore
the lands which had been devastated by Babylon form a
chiasm around v. 7, which depicts the resultant exaltation of the servant-Israel. The second half of chapter
49 parallels the first, and the juxtaposition of the
servant-Israel's exaltation in v. 7 with Zion's exaltation in vv. 19-21 intentionally underlines the continuity between the servant-Israel in exile and Zion of
the future. The servant's exaltation from poverty in

49:7 is identical with the perspective of the framework
of the fourth song.   There the servant, again understood as Israel, performs priestly atonement for the
nations both through her silent suffering in exile and
through her revelation to the nations when she is
glorified.

In keeping with the interdependence of the servant
passages with their contexts, they portray a place for
the nations that is on the whole continuous with other
texts in the corpus of Deutero-Isaiah.   There is no
great jump from nationalism to universalism, from a
concern with Israel to a concern with the nations.   The
prophet's vision of God's universal sovereignty, with
Israel as his royal representative and the nations as
faithful vassals, is expressed in Isa 45:14-25; 51:4-5
and 55:1-5 and is implicit throughout the rest of the
book of consolation. This is identical to the prophet's
conception of God's world government by the servant,
understood to be Israel.   The servant in Isa 42 is
given jurisdiction over the nations, he will bring
forth God's **mišpaṭ** and **tôrâ**, and he is given a **běrît**
cām, a covenant with international scope.   Israel is
the primary but not the sole beneficiary of God's
sovereignty throughout Isa 40-55; likewise the
servant's universal authority in Isa 49 will first
effect the restoration of Zion, but then it will also
extend salvation to the coastlands.   Similarly, in the
fourth song, God vindicates the servant in the face of
oppression, but in addition, the servant's suffering
brings healing to the nations as he serves as their
priest and mediator before Yahweh.   The servant songs
thus develop and expand upon Deutero-Isaiah's consistently universal vision of God's sovereignty.   Their
"universalism" keeps Israel at the center: Israel as

God's servant is exalted over the nations in its role
as royal representative of God's imperial rule.

If there is any truly new dimension to the servant's
relation to the nations, it comes from a shift in the
prophet's view of Israel, not of the nations. The
servant's anonymity in all the songs, and the prophet's
intention in the fourth song that a faction of his
Israelite audience identify with the chorus of the
nations who confess the probity of the servant, suggest
that intra-Israelite conflict had led to a blurring of
the distinction between Israel and the nations in favor
of a standard of judgment contrasting the servant--the
ideal Israel--and the many--those of Israel and the
nations who had ignored or spurned God's will. For
Deutero-Isaiah, Yahweh's international sovereignty is a
constant. It creates the theological context within
which is played out the changing relationship between
Yahweh and the Israelites of the prophet's audience,
who are repeatedly called to live up to the vocation of
Yahweh's servant.

1. Concluding Observations on Compositional Analysis as a Method

This study of Deutero-Isaiah delimits large compositional units, each containing multiple formal units as defined by form critics. The method of "compositional analysis" employed here is an attempt to do justice to both the rhetorical features of Deutero-Isaiah's compositions and to the forms and traditions which he employed.

Compositional analysis determines the compositional units by rhetorical features and other clues from the text. We find large-scale parallelism and chiasm in units throughout the Book of Consolation. These large-scale structures are not the secondary creations of a redactor, since they partially determine the structures of the smaller subunits that are often distinguished as separate units. Several passages which have troubled form critics, notably Isa 45:9-13 and 49:7-13, can be better understood in the context of the larger compositions of which they are subunits; the need for drastic emendations as suggested by some form critics disappears when the peculiar form of these passages in seen as arising out of its role in a larger structure. Furthermore, delineation of larger structural patterns can serve as a control for hypotheses that would omit certain passages as redactional additions. We noted

that the idol passages in particular, which are often
considered to be secondary, are integral to their compositional units and could be removed only with great
violence to their units' large-scale structure.   The
first and second servant songs are similarly integrated
into their compositional units.

Compositional analysis is also concerned to investi-
gate the forms and antecedent traditions employed by
the prophet.   In order to control for the prophet's
unique style, we prefer to define forms by their use in
texts other than Deutero-Isaiah, rather than simply to
classify the prophet's writing, chopped up into small
pieces, into similar oracle types.   Thereby we avoid
the problem faced by much form criticism of Deutero-
Isaiah, namely that this prophet's specific genre
types--salvation oracles, trial speeches, and disputa-
tions--are poorly related to preexilic antecedents.   In
the compositional units studied here we have identified
a call narrative (Isa 49:1-6), a psalm of thanksgiving
(53:1-10), confessions of penitents (45:14d-17, 24-25),
royal oracles (42:1-4; 45:1-7), a taunt against a
defeated enemy (46:1-2), an invitation to a cultic
feast (55:1-3a), and several hymns (42:10-13; 44:23;
45:8).   The satire against idolaty is an exilic genre,
perhaps created by Deutero-Isaiah himself.   While on
other occasions these forms may have defined independent oracle types, in Deutero-Isaiah they function as
subunits within his larger compositional units.

However, for several of the compositional units,
conformation to a preexisting form or traditional pattern is their major structuring device.   Forms which
themselves define their compositional units include:
(1) the prophetic lawsuit, which stands behind 43:8-

44:5 and 42:18-43:7;[1] (2) the ritual pattern of the battle/judgment of the divine warrior and his subsequent victory procession as celebrated in the royal cult, which stands behind each half of 41:1-20, 21-42:17, the first half of 43:8-44:5 and the framework of 44:6-23;[2] and (3) the song cycle, a form which structures 51:1-8.[3] Thus, forms and rhetorical features are equally important for delimiting the prophet's compositional units.

Note that this list of forms includes preexilic traditions which are commonly considered under the method of history of traditions rather than form criticism. However, such a distinction is artificial in this period, where the prophet is heir to diverse traditions, both oral and written, from the long epic accounts of Israel's history to the short sayings of ecstatic prophets. For example, the ritual pattern of the conflict and victory of the divine warrior is a tradition with roots at least as ancient as Canaanite culture, and it continued to exist as a distinct pattern in a living cultic setting up to the destruction of the temple. We consider this ritual pattern itself to structure texts on a large scale in the same manner as other forms are determinate of regular features of texts in the small. Similarly, the prophetic lawsuit form had a long history prior to Deutero-Isaiah, during which it had attained a complex and extended structure suitable to its use by the prophets for instructional and penitential purposes.

---

[1]See above, pp. 73-77, 81-83; 110 n. 128.

[2]See above, pp. 48-52, 58-62, 71-72, 177-78.

[3]See above, pp. 257-58 n. 21.

Our method pays dividends for form criticism by better attending to preexilic antecedents of Deutero-Isaiah's forms. We discussed above[4] the difficulties encountered by earlier form critics when they tried to trace the antecedents to the trial speeches; these problems can be largely resolved when the trial speech is recognized as a subunit of a larger formal or traditional pattern. Thus the apparent discontinuity between the purpose of actual legal proceedings--to render a verdict--and the prophet's use of legal language for a disputational purpose in the trial speeches has often been attributed to Deutero-Isaiah's creativity. However, once the trial speeches are recognized as components of larger formal units, e.g. the prophetic lawsuit which had a disputational purpose in preexilic prophecy, we obviate the need to lay such a heavy burden on the prophet's creativity--a wild card term in any form-critical analysis.

A similar clarification could no doubt be made of the antecedents for the "salvation oracle" and the "proclamation of salvation." As independent forms, these oracles have few antecedents among the preexilic prophets,[5] and hence Begrich suggested they imitated a hypothetical oracle given in a liturgical setting.[6] But such oracles by priests or cult prophets can only be divined with difficulty in the stanzas of certain

---

[4]See above, pp. 107-113.

[5]We would also allow the possibility of Babylonian influence; see the parallels in Assyrian oracles discussed by Westerman, Isaiah 40-66, 72; P. B. Harner, "The Salvation Oracle in Deutero-Isaiah," JBL 88 (1969) 418-34.

[6]Begrich, Studien, 97; Schoors, I am God your Savior, 32-45; Melugin, Formation, 13-27.

psalms of lament.[7] They never stand on their own, nor are they a feature of preexilic prophecy.[8] However, if the attempt to dissect out short formal units is abandoned, and instead one accepts that these salvation oracles are subunits of larger forms, then their possible antecedents multiply. Words of promise and war oracles exhorting Israel not to fear were carried as subunits not only in psalms of lament, but also in prophetic lawsuits (i.e. Deut 32) and in texts of the royal cult with the pattern of the conflict and victory of the divine warrior.[9] The profusion of words of promise in Deutero-Isaiah can be explained by his inheritance of these well-attested preexilic forms without having to posit a hypothetical preexilic oracle type.

This method of compositional analysis has major exegetical implications, especially when interpretation has largely focused on short passages taken in isolation. The idol polemics, for example, have often been interpreted out of context as a redactional stratum, but there is much to be gained by understanding the prophet's idol polemics as the theological counterpoint to his universal monotheism. Each idol passage fulfills a specific role in its compositional unit, most often

---

[7]E.g. Pss 12:6; 35:1-4; 60:8-10; 108:8-10; Lam 3:57. Many of these are recollections of prior oracles, and some are priestly oracles (Ps 115:12-16) which bear little resemblance to the salvation oracle as it is usually construed.

[8]Von Waldow's attempt to posit a text as late as 2 Chr 20 as the premier example of a prophetic salvation oracle ("Anlass und Hintergrund," 73-90) points up the poverty of this approach.

[9]I.e. the royal oracles in Pss 89:20-38; 132:11-18. Cf. Cross, Canaanite Myth, 99-111, 228-29.

to set up a contrast with the power of Yahweh the one
true God.   The trial speeches also play off their
contexts to enrich the prophet's message.   Thus the
unit 43:8-44:5 has a trial speech against the nations
creating the setting for a **rîb** against Israel, thereby
investing that second trial speech with a universal
significance; Israel will become Yahweh's faithful
servant in order to be a witness before the nations.
In the unit 45:14-25 the trial speech and its oath
serve to substantiate the initial eschatological vision
of the nations bringing tribute to Jerusalem; they come
because Yahweh has given his irrevocable oath that all
nations will bend the knee and acknowledge his sovereignty.   These are only several of the many instances
where compositional analysis enriches exegesis by
bringing out relationships between passages that have
often been studied in isolation.

The servant passages, too, have often been studied
out of context, leading to a plethora of interpretations with few criteria for choosing among them.   However, when the first and second songs are recognized to
be subsections of larger compositional units, then a
collective interpretation of the servant appears
certain, as the servant is correlated first with Israel
and then with Zion.   The announcement of Yahweh's
servant in Isa 42:1-9, corresponding to the reassurance
of Israel the servant in 41:8-13, comes as the second
movement of the ritual pattern which began with the
trial speechs' judgment upon the nations and their
gods.   Israel and then the servant are each justified
where the gods of the nations have been condemned, and
as Yahweh's chosen agent, each either receives or
brings vindication in a world where the pagan gods had
brought only oppression.   When Isa 49 is read as a

double chiasm, the servant's authority over the nations
is bound up with the mission to enable the return of
Israel to her land and the restoration of Zion.   There
is a close relationship between the servant and Zion in
their common distress and their future common exaltation.   This suggests that the servant, as Israel in
exile, continued in the divine grace that had formerly
been bestowed upon Zion, and that the Israel's future
as God's servant would be connected with God's renewed
dwelling at Zion.   The paradox that the servant-Israel
has a mission to Israel is resolved when that mission
is specified as to restore the exiles to their ancestral lands.

2. The Nations and God's Universal Sovereignty

We have studied the place of the nations in Deutero-
Isaiah from four perspectives: as parties to and audience at the trial speeches, as the objects of polemics
against idolatry, envisioned as serving Yahweh and
Israel at the restored Zion, and in relation to the
servant.   These four perspectives yield a consistent
view of the nations as subject to God's sovereignty.
The nations are meant to recognize Yahweh as God, to
reject idolatry, to serve Yahweh's purpose to restore
and glorify his temple at Zion, and to come under the
administration of Israel as Yahweh's servant and mediator of a covenant to the peoples.   Yet the fate of the
nations is always used to underscore and give weight to
the prophet's message to Israel.   Deutero-Isaiah's
central concern was to give his Israelite audience hope
and purpose in the midst of exile where she was dwarfed

by powerful nations. Hence, his message that the nations would come to serve Yahweh was meant to reinforce Israel's sense of importance and sense of vocation as Yahweh's servant. The nations will acknowledge and bow before Yahweh not because Deutero-Isaiah was so concerned for their welfare, but because their recognition and worship of Yahweh would give additional glory to Israel and meaning to her vocation.

Thus the trial speeches, set in the divine council, ostensibly refute the claims of the pagan gods before a universal audience consisting of both Israel and the assembled nations. Yet these speeches are designed for the prophet's actual Israelite audience. They address two pressing issues of the exile: doubt as to whether Yahweh was God, and the apparent splendor of the pagan culture in which the exiles found themselves. Israel in exile was much attracted to Babylonian culture, and the opinions of their gentile neighbors became a concern as many acculturated to local customs. Much as his contemporary Ezekiel, Deutero-Isaiah argues for Yahweh's sole divinity and further declares that all those assembled at the trial will assent to his claims. The trial speech is a setting for the prophet to argue for Yahweh's divinity as a universal claim. While his audience is primarily Israel, his message, even to be convincing to Israel, is necessarily phrased in a way that would appeal to all. When, in the last trial speech in Isa 45:14-25, Yahweh gives his verdict, it is in the form of an oath that all nations will bend the knee and swear allegiance to Yahweh as God. With all nations confessing fealty to Yahweh, Israel should certainly have confidence in her Redeemer.

The polemics against idolatry similarly universalize what had been an article of faith for only Israel. In preexilic Israel, polemics against worship of images as human creations were tied to Israel's exclusive covenant with Yahweh, so that idolatry was termed fornication and associated with foreign alliances and foreign gods. However, Deutero-Isaiah lifts up Israel's aniconic tradition--the understanding of idols as without any divinity--as the sole basis for their ridicule. Thereby he can make a universal argument, one that is "self-evident" to all who have eyes to see, although in fact only Israel, which possessed such an aniconic tradition, would find his arguments persuasive. As in the trial speeches where Yahweh's divinity is argued before the inherently universal setting of the divine council, so in the idol polemics Deutero-Isaiah sets forth universal claims binding upon everyone. When in Isa 45:14-25 the nations confess allegiance to Yahweh, they also repudiate idolatry.

Deutero-Isaiah's eschatology gives Israel international prominence and portrays Zion as the locus of world pilgrimage. Yahweh's universal sovereignty derives from the traditions of the royal cult, where the creation of the cosmos is founded upon God's conquests, and where a subsequent procession to Zion is the occasion for God's gift of abundant rains and fertility to the earth. Deutero-Isaiah assigns the task of prosecuting Yahweh's war to Cyrus, who then is to consummate his assigned task by rebuilding the temple. This is royal theology, not <u>realpolitik</u>, since any thought to Zion would be totally incidental to Cyrus's own plans. Yet Zion's rebuilding is to initiate the eschaton, when the desert will bloom and God's righteous sovereignty will commence (45:8). Isa 55 depicts a messianic ban-

quet at the new Zion, and Israel, like David of old, is
to command the nations to come running to serve her.
Passages which envision the day when all nations would
come to Zion bearing tribute and bringing the exiles
home draw upon memories of the age of Solomon when such
processions of the nations were a regular occurence.
The nations become Yahweh's vassals, and hence are
subservient to his servant Israel. As vassals, the
nations will be punished should they rebel; but with
loyal service they will receive benefits from their
divine suzerain.

Just as the servant passages are continuous with the
body of Deutero-Isaiah's prophecies, so their conception of the nations is congruent with that just
described for Deutero-Isaiah as a whole. Like Israel
in Isa 55, the servant receives a covenant which gives
him authority over the nations, to bring forth Yahweh's
mišpaṭ and tôrâ. The servant in Isa 49 is to mediate
Yahweh's salvation to the ends of the earth, and once
granted this universal authority, his task is to
restore Israel and all nations to the lands from which
they had been dispossessed and especially to restore
Zion. The fourth servant song moves a step further; it
gives Israel the servant a role as priest to the
nations whose suffering in exile opens the way for the
nations to be healed of their sin. We discussed the
ambiguity in the identification of the chorus, the "we"
of this song, which is ostensibly the nations who come
to recognize the servant's innocence and his suffering
on their behalf. As in the trial speeches, here the
prophet appeals to a segment of his Israelite audience
which had acculturated to Babylonian society by placing
the confession of the servant's probity in the mouths
of the nations.

3. Postscript: Deutero-Isaiah, Trito-Isaiah, and the Origins of Mission

It is inappropriate to speak of a theology of mission in Deutero-Isaiah, and he did not envision proselytes.[10] The prophet makes no mention of Sabbath, circumcision, or any normative requirements which within one or two generations would become obligatory for the school of Trito-Isaiah (56:3-7). The formal category of "proselyte" was to come even further in the future. Rather, Deutero-Isaiah addresses the nations as corporate entities. He expected the nations to demonstrate their new religious loyalty by acts of service to his people, restoring the exiles to the land, and rebuilding the ruins of Jerusalem. As Yahweh's vassals, the nations were to honor the customary political and religious obligations that would be placed upon the princes of any vassal state, as they were placed upon the vassals of Israel and Yahweh in the old Davidic empire: to show deference by bowing down before its king, to contribute their treasures to support its cult, and to furnish laborers to build its cities.

But in addition, Deutero-Isaiah adds to these obligations the covenantal demands of sole allegiance to Yahweh and repudiation of idolatry as set forth in the confessions in Isa 45:14-25. The nations could not simply worship Yahweh as an imperial deity alongside their local gods, as was the ancient Near Eastern custom. Deutero-Isaiah universalized the Mosaic covenant to the nations, and in this limited sense, he demanded of them a conversion.

---

[10]Cf. above, p. 84.

Briefly, we can further trace a trajectory from an incipient demand for conversion of the nations in Deutero-Isaiah's eschatology to the beginnings of an actual missionary impulse among his disciples. Hanson has demonstrated that Deutero-Isaiah's disciples transformed the expected pilgrimage of the nations into a social program.[11] These disciples wrote Isa 60-62 with studied references to the prophecies of their master, joined in catena fashion. They saw themselves as fulfilling the vocation of the servant (61:1-3)[12] and stood as "watchmen," waiting in expectation for the imminent glorification of Zion (62:6). Once the nations would arrive with their offerings to rebuild the temple and glorify the new Zion (60:3-16; 61:5-6), they expected all Israel to become a nation of priests (61:6), to minister to the nations and be supported by their wealth. Hanson contrasts this social program with the competing program of the hierocracy as described in Ezek 40-48, a pragmatic program in which Israel rebuilds the temple but its access is limited to a restricted class of priests. Note that success of the Trito-Isaianic social program depended upon the fulfillment of Deutero-Isaiah's expectation that the nations come and glorify Zion, thereby supplying the wealth and the large population which could support an expanded priesthood extending to the whole nation of Israel. If Israel had to rebuild the temple on its own, its meager resources would only be able to support a much restricted priesthood, thus playing into the hands of those who could demonstrate their Zadokite lineage.

---

[11]Hanson, Dawn of Apocalyptic, 64-75.

[12]Cf. Isa 63:17; 65:8-9,13-15; 66:14.

The delay of the expected general pilgrimage of the nations must have been a serious threat to the community ideal of Trito-Isaiah.[13] Hence this group seized upon those few individual foreigners who wished to join the congregation of Yahweh as a sign that the eschaton was still imminent. Yet this openness to foreigners was precisely the point which the hierocrats who wrote Ezek 44 found most objectionable about the program of Trito-Isaiah. They attacked the Levites--which Hanson identifies as the party of Trito-Isaiah--for profaning the sanctuary by allowing foreigners entrance to the altar (Ezek 44:6-9). Isa 56:3-8 and 66:18-24, the redactional framework of Trito-Isaiah which Hanson dates from the mid-fifth century, exhibits such a universalism in polemical opposition to the restricted nationalism of the ruling hierocratic party.[14] Isa 56:3-8 praises the gentile converts who had been excluded by temple officials, and Isa 66:18-24 flaunts the priestly ideology of national purity by proclaiming that outstanding foreigners would become priests and Levites. Note that in both of these passages we have moved from the nations as corporate entities to individual converts, reflecting the realistic situation of the period.

To summarize, while Deutero-Isaiah may have argued universal claims in a gentile context, and while his polemics against idolatry may have become useful to later missionaries, he himself lacked any motivation

---

[13]On strategies for dealing with the cognitive dissonance created by the delay of prophecy, see Robert P. Carroll, *When Prophecy Failed: Reactions and Responses to Failure in the Old Testament Prophetic Traditions* (London: SCM, 1979).

[14]Hanson, 385-86, 388-89.

for missionary work. However, there is a trajectory
from Deutero-Isaiah's eschatology to the beginnings of
Jewish proselytism. His vision of the nations making
pilgrimage to Zion was transformed, in the hands of his
disciples in the early days of the restoration, into an
attitude welcoming converts to Judaism. These disciples made Deutero-Isaiah's eschatology of a pilgrimage
of the nations to Zion the basis for a particular
social vision that included a place for the nations,
and they welcomed individual gentile as a sign of the
continuing validity of that vision. In spite of opposition from official priestly circles, the missionary
impulse, with its high view of gentile converts or
"god-fearers," took root in post-exilic Judaism as
evidenced by such texts as Isa 19:18-25, Zech 14:16,
Pss 115:9-11, 118:2-4, 135:19-20 and the books of Ruth
and Jonah.

INDEX OF BIBLICAL CITATIONS

Pages in **boldface** indicate where the text of a passage is treated in detail.

INDEX OF HEBREW AND SEMITIC TERMS

INDEX OF AUTHORS

GENERAL INDEX

Also Published by the Edwin Mellen Press:

STUDIES IN THE BIBLE AND EARLY CHRISTIANITY

1. Hugh M. Humphrey, **A Bibliography for the Gospel of Mark, 1954-1980**

2. Rolland Wolfe, **The Twelve Religions of the Bible**

3. Jean LaPorte, *Eucharistia* **in Philo**

4. Peter Gorday, **Principles of Patristic Exegesis: Romans 9-11 in Origen, John Chrysostom, and Augustine**

5. Marcus J. Borg, **Conflict, Holiness & Politics in the Teachings of Jesus**

6. Watson E. Mills, **Glossolalia: A Bibliography**

7. Matthew Baasten, **Pride According to Gregory the Great: A Study of the Moralia**

8. Douglas E. Oakman, **Jesus and the Economic Questions of His Day**